D1562315

BRITISH LOCOMOTIVES

FRONTISPIECE No. 1.

London and North-Western Railway 8-wheeled compound express passenger engine, designed by Mr. F. W. WEBB, and built at the Company's works, Crewe, in 1893. Exhibited at the Chicago Exhibition, 1893.

PRINCIPAL DETAILS OF ENGINE.

Diameter of driving-wheels, 7 ft. 1 in.
Diameter of leading and trailing-wheels, 4 ft. 1⅛ inches.
Diameter of high-pressure cylinders, 15 inches × 24 inches stroke.
Diameter of low-pressure cylinders, 30 inches × 24 inches stroke.
Heating surface : 1206 sq. ft.
    Fire-box   ..   ..   120·6 sq. ft.
    Combustion-chamber   391   "
    Tubes, front   ..   853   "
    Tubes, back   ..   493   "
           Total .. 1595·7   "

WEIGHT

	T.	C.
Leading-wheels	12	16
Low-pressure driving-wheels	15	10
High-pressure driving-wheels	15	10
Trailing-wheels	8	6
Total weight of engine in working order	52	2
Total weight of tender in working order	25	0
Total engine and tender	77	2

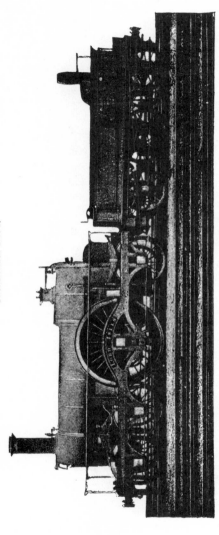

Great Western Railway broad-gauge express locomotive, designed by the late Sir DANIEL GOOCH, and built at the Company's works, Swindon, in 1851. Exhibited at the Chicago Exhibition, 1893.

PRINCIPAL DIMENSIONS.

Cylinders, 18 inches diameter by 24 inches stroke.
Driving-wheels, 8 ft. diameter.
Leading and trailing-wheels, 4 ft. 6 inches diameter.
Heating surface : Tubes .. .. 1611 sq. ft.
Fire-box .. 156 "
Total .. 1767 "
Total grate area .. 25·46 "

WEIGHT IN WORKING ORDER.

					T.	C.
Leading-axles	..	..	..	..	15	0
Driving-axles	..	..	..	..	14	0
Trailing-axles	..	..	..	..	9	4
				Total ..	38	4
Weight of tender in working order	..		..	24	0
				Total ..	62	4

Working-pressure 120 lbs. per sq. in.

The hood at the end of the tender protects a seat in which a look-out man facing the train used to sit, thereby affording a means of communication between the passengers and engine-driver—a practice now discontinued except with Royal trains.

Published by
GRESHAM BOOKS
Unwin Brothers Limited
The Gresham Press
Old Woking
Surrey

in association with
TECHNICAL INDEXES LIMITED
Easthampstead Road, Bracknell, Berks.

© Gresham Books, 1979
Introduction © Andrew Smith, 1979
First published 1893 and 1894
This facsimile edition published 1979

ISBN 0 905418 72 7

Printed by Unwin Brothers Limited, The Gresham Press, Old Woking, Surrey

BRITISH LOCOMOTIVES

THEIR HISTORY, CONSTRUCTION, AND MODERN DEVELOPMENT.

BY

C. J. BOWEN COOKE,

OUTDOOR ASSISTANT LONDON AND NORTH-WESTERN RAILWAY LOCOMOTIVE
DEPARTMENT.

WITH NUMEROUS ILLUSTRATIONS FROM SKETCHES AND DIAGRAMS
BY C. E. JONES AND R. A. McLELLAN,
AND REPRODUCTIONS OF OFFICIAL DRAWINGS AND PHOTOGRAPHS.

Gresham Books
in association with
TECHNICAL INDEXES LIMITED

INTRODUCTION TO
THIS EDITION

by Andrew Smith, C. Eng

Before the turn of the century when this book was first published, the design and manufacture of railway steam locomotives was in the mainstream of engineering development. By the time the book's author died in 1920, the peak had virtually been reached and although the succeeding years saw some new innovations, there was never again the same thrust and excitment as had existed during that earlier period.

At the end of the 19th century, the mobility of almost everyone in the land depended on the railways. People who could rarely have ventured further than walking distance from their homes, were now using the railway system to travel far and wide. Resorts developed at seaside fishing villages which were lucky enough to be served by the railway and 'annual holiday' and 'day outing' travel was provided by an ever increasing mileage of track and frequency of trains.

It was only natural that these travellers, still largely horse orientated, should take a keen interest in the running of this amazingly efficient transport system and especially in the motive power that made it possible. When it appeared, this book was one which every devotee of the steam locomotive regarded as a necessary part of his literature on the subject; even today details from *British Locomotives* are still quoted in other books.

The book traces the development of the steam locomotive from the trundling three-wheeler of Cugnot in 1769 to the modern developments taking place within the locomotive departments of the British companies at the time the book was written in 1893-94. And all this is seen, not by an enthusiastic amateur, but by a professional who had spent the whole of his working life concerned with the locomotives of the London and North Western Railway; the 'Premier Line', of which he was subsequently to become Chief Mechanical Engineer.

It is also an interesting feature of this reprinting, that it should appear on the 150th anniversary of the famous railway 'Rainhill Trials', which Bowen Cooke deals with at some length in the early part of his book.

These Trials, which to the layman, appeared to herald the beginning of the railway system as we know it, were, in fact, a last desperate attempt by the Directors of the Liverpool and Manchester Railway to resolve the problem of using locomotives, stationary engines with ropes, or horses as the motive power.

George Stephenson who had been appointed as engineer to the railway, reported to the Board of Directors in January 1828 that he had perfected a locomotive engine and boiler of new construction, which he was prepared to recommend for adoption as the motive power for the railway. The directors thereupon authorised him to build this engine to draw 20 tons of goods and 50 passengers, to weigh about 6 tons, and to cost £550.

However in 1829, as is now a matter of history, the directors still unable to come to a definite decision, eventually offered a prize of £500 for a locomotive which could fulfill a number of stipulated conditions. The contest resulted in the success of Stephenson's engine the 'Rocket'.

Finally the author, Charles John Bowen Cooke was born near Peterborough in January 1859, the son of a parish Rector. He was always interested in railway locomotives and in 1875 started an apprenticeship with the London and North Western Railway. He wrote this book while still in his early thirties and an assistant to the then Chief Mechanical Engineer, Francis W. Webb.

He had an enthusiastic interest in all matters relating to locomotive design and practice, especially that taking place overseas. When F. W. Webb was succeeded in 1899 by George Whale, Bowen Cooke became his chief assistant. Bowen Cooke was Chief Mechanical Engineer by 1909.

His keen interest had led him to a careful study of the effects of superheating the steam, especially the experiments of Dr Schmidt on the Continent. As soon as he took charge therefore, he inaugurated the design and manufacture of the 'George the Fifth' Class of 4-4-0 locomotives fitted with superheaters. At the same time and as a comparison, a similar locomotive bearing the name 'Queen Mary' was built, but without superheaters.

An amusing incident at this time was reported at the International Railway Congress in Switzerland when the British representatives threatened to walk out because transactions were in French and German only. This did not worry Mr Bowen Cooke who was fluent in German having had his early technical education in that country!

With the outbreak of World War I, Bowen Cooke redoubled his engineering efforts at Crewe, not only keeping the L.N.W.R. locomotive numbers up to strength, but also providing large quantities of equipment for the war effort. For his work he was awarded the C.B.E., but regretfully the strain of his wartime commitments had left him in poor health and he died in Cornwall in the autumn of 1920 aged 62.

Charles John Bowen Cooke was a big man both in stature and character. His memorial at the church of St. Just-in-Roseland where he is buried says, "His life was gentle, and the elements so mix'd in him that nature might stand up and say to all the world, This was a man."

PREFACE.

So many books have already been written about loco-motives that an additional work on the subject demands some apology for its appearance.

It is an indisputable fact that, besides persons connected with this particular branch of engineering, there are a great many people in the world who take an intelligent interest in railway working and locomotives; it is to such persons that this book is more particularly addressed, although at the same time the author ventures to hope that even practical railway mechanics may find some useful information in its pages. If he is so fortunate as to number among his readers any of the latter class, he prays for their leniency and forbearance.

The books which have hitherto been published on the locomotive appear to be either altogether technical and scientific in their character, or else to deal with the subject entirely from a non-professional point of view. The former can only be understood by experts, and the latter do not give much idea of the principles of working or of construction.

The author has himself felt, and heard it expressed by others, that there is a want of some work striking a mean between these two extremes; and it is in the hope of supplying that want that he places this book before the public. It has been his endeavour by simple wording and plain diagrams to give some general information regarding the details of construction of modern locomotives; and in order to make the different points as clear as possible, the working drawings and sections are of the simplest description, and should, by comparison with the text, be easily understood without any previous technical training. These diagrams will, he trusts, enable the reader to gain some general mechanical knowledge without having to master the contents of a text book or scientific work.

Again, there may be other people who would like to know more about locomotives without caring to go minutely into details of construction. The author hopes that to such persons the historical chapters, and those on modern engines, may prove interesting. In them the reader— assisted by illustrations entirely of a pictorial character— will be able to trace the history of the locomotive from the commencement of its career down to the latest creations of the most celebrated engineers of the present day.

In his connection with the outdoor working of the locomotive department of the London and North-Western Railway, the writer is brought into close contact with the officials of other departments, and he has invariably found that railway men, in whatever branch of the service they are engaged, take an interest in everything appertaining to the working of locomotives. It is therefore to his fellow railway men of all departments and grades that he would venture to dedicate this work.

There are two very interesting engines now in the great Exhibition at Chicago, which are thoroughly representative examples of the highest types of locomotives of past and present times. One is the Great Western Railway broad gauge engine, "Lord of the Isles," built by Sir Daniel Gooch in 1851; and the other is Mr. Webb's 7 ft. compound engine, "Queen Empress," built at Crewe Works during the present year. The author is indebted to the locomotive superintendents of the Great Western and London and North-Western Railways for enabling him to give the illustrations of these engines, which form the frontispiece to this work.

The endeavour has been made to avoid all controversial matter in these pages, but before concluding these few remarks one word may be said on the subject of railway speeds. It has been contended by some authorities that a greater speed than seventy-five miles an hour is practically never maintained. But the following are two or three instances of high speeds which have come under the author's own personal knowledge, and for the accuracy of which he can vouch.

On February 7, 1893, the 7 ft. compound engine, No. 1309, when working the 3.30 p.m. up Scotch express from Crewe to London, ran from Standon Bridge to Norton Bridge, a distance of 4⅜ miles, in three minutes. Speed, 87 miles per hour; approximate weight of train and engine, 240 tons; gradient, 1 in 650 and 1 in 505 down.

On April 17, 1893, 7 ft. compound engine, No. 1307, when working the 8 p.m. Scotch express from Euston, ran from Nuneaton to Tamworth, a distance of 12¾ miles, on a practically level road, in 10½ minutes. Speed, 73 miles an hour; weight of train, 11 vehicles (equal to 14½, counting each 8-wheeled vehicle as 1½). The total moving weight was 271 tons, exclusive of passengers and luggage. It is a very creditable performance to drag a dead weight of over 200 tons, exclusive of engine and tender, for 12¾ miles over a level road at such a speed. At the time of making this trip, the engine had run over 85,000 miles since last in the shop for repairs.

As a further example of an exceptionally high speed, a run made over the same ground by one of Mr. Webb's 6 ft. 6 in. coupled engines, No. 1484, may be quoted. On April 20,

1893, this engine when working the 12 noon express Euston to Manchester, passed Nuneaton at 2.12, and Tamworth at 2.21½ p.m., thus covering the 12¾ miles in 9½ minutes, being an average speed of 80½ miles per hour. On this occasion the train consisted of nine main line vehicles.

It should, however, be borne in mind by those persons entrusted with the timing of passenger trains, that such speeds as these must not be quoted as precedents for ordinary working. Under favourable circumstances they may be attained by engines in a high state of efficiency; but locomotives, like human beings, while able, when put on their mettle, to exhibit extraordinary powers, are also like them subservient to natural laws, and therefore give better satisfaction when their powers are normally exerted within reasonable limits only. It is far more satisfactory to the public generally, and to the Railway Companies themselves, when trains are timed at such a speed as will enable them to be worked punctually under all circumstances.

Heavier trains due to heavier traffic, difficulties in working due to climatic influences, which are of a very varied character in these isles, all affect the capabilities of a locomotive, and it is better for these different elements to be taken into consideration. Let but our engines have a fair chance, and they will not disgrace themselves in the eyes of the many millions of people who regulate their actions in accordance with the programme so clearly set forth in Bradshaw, and whose execution depends so much upon " British Locomotives."

The author's best thanks are first of all due to Mr. F. W. Webb, the Locomotive Superintendent of the London and North-Western Railway, for the valuable information which he has placed at his disposal and allowed to be published.

It is through his kindness that the sectional drawing of the 7 ft. compound engine, and the many illustrations of the different types of the London and North-Western engines, are reproduced. His best thanks are also due to his immediate chief, Mr. A. L. Mumford (Assistant Locomotive Superintendent, London and North-Western Railway), for the benefit he has derived from that gentleman's long experience in the working and management of locomotives ; to Mr. E. R. Calthrop (late of the G. I. P. Railway, India) for many valuable hints, and to the following Superintendents for kindly supplying information concerning the engines of their respective companies and photographs from which the illustrations are reproduced :— Messrs. J. A. F. Aspinall, W. Adams, R. J. Billinton, W. Dean, J. Holden, S. W. Johnson, W. Kirtley, T. Parker, J. Pryce, P. Stirling, J. Stirling, and W. Worsdell, on the English Railways ; J. Lambie, and M. Holmes, Scotch Railways ; and H. A. Ivatt, of the Great Southern and Western Railway, Ireland.

The sketches of the historical engines have been well and carefully done by Mr. C. E. Jones (of the Locomotive Drawing Office, Crewe), and the constructive drawings and diagrams are, with one or two exceptions only, by Mr. R. A. McLellan, who has taken great pains with them, besides materially assisting the author in collecting the information on the valve-gear contained in Chapter IV.

In conclusion, the writer wishes to acknowledge his gratitude to his friend, Mr. H. V. Weisse (Head-master of the Rugby Lower School), who has most patiently and carefully revised the text of this book.

Rugby, June 1893.

CONTENTS.

LIST OF ILLUSTRATIONS.

BRITISH LOCOMOTIVES.

CHAPTER I.

EARLY HISTORY.

THE first self-moving locomotive engine of which there is any authenticated record was made by a Frenchman, named Nicholas Joseph Cugnot, in the year **1769**. It was termed a "land-carriage," and was designed to run on ordinary roads. There are no particulars extant of this,

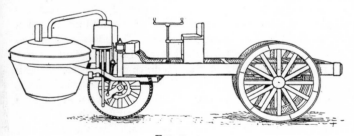

FIG. 1.

the very first locomotive, but in **1771** a larger engine was constructed from Cugnot's designs, which is still preserved in the Conservatoire des Arts et Métiers at Paris.

This engine, of which Fig. 1 is an illustration, was driven by two single-acting vertical cylinders, 13 in. in diameter.

The steam was admitted to the cylinder by a four-way cock; and the pistons worked downwards, acting upon a ratchet-wheel on the driving-axle. Each stroke of one piston gave a quarter of a revolution to the driving-wheel. The boiler was of copper, with a fire-grate, and two rectangular flues serving as chimneys. It could only maintain steam for a quarter of an hour, and the maximum speed attained was $2\frac{1}{4}$ miles per hour on a level road. The machine was fitted with a simple form of steering-gear. The French Government took some interest in this notion of a steam land-carriage, and voted a sum of money towards its construction, with the idea that such a machine might prove useful for military purposes. After the engine had been tried two or three times it overturned in the streets of Paris, and was then locked up in the arsenal, and thus ended its brief career.

In **1784** Watt took out a patent for a steam-carriage. In a letter to Mr. Boulton he mentions the following details of its proposed structure. "The boiler to be of wood or thin metal, to be secured by hoops or otherwise, to prevent its bursting from the pressure of steam"! An internal fire-box was described, and the idea of a multitubular boiler hinted at. It is thought, however, that this engine was invented and constructed by Mr. Murdoch, Watt's assistant, and that he made it at Redruth in Cornwall, where it is supposed to have run on ordinary Cornish roads in the years 1785-86. The engine had a single vertical cylinder connected to one end of a beam, pivoted at the other end. A connecting-rod was fixed to the beam near the piston-rod, and turned a crank axle on a pair of driving-wheels. The cylinder was partly immersed in the boiler, which was heated by a furnace underneath. At the front of the engine was a third wheel working in a socket by which the engine was steered. A doubt exists as to whether this engine was ever actually built as intended, or whether the idea got no further than the model illustrated in Fig. 2, which was undoubtedly made by Murdoch, and is now preserved in the possession of Messrs. Tangye Bros., Birmingham. Watt himself had no faith in the proposal to adapt steam to locomotive carriages, and did not personally follow up the idea ; indeed, Murdoch got into trouble with his employers for having given so much of his time

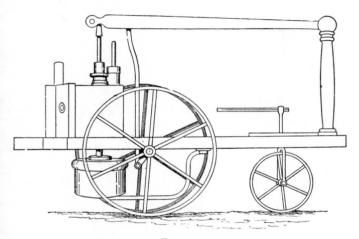

Fig. 2.

to this subject, instead of devoting himself entirely to the Soho engineering business.

In **1786** William Symington, a Scotchman, constructed a model of a steam-carriage, but nothing was done to turn his ideas to any practical account.

In **1802** we first hear of Richard Trevithick as a pioneer of locomotive engineering. In that year, with his cousin Vivian, he took out a patent for a high-pressure engine and its application to steam-carriages, and in the same year he made a model of a steam-carriage (Fig. 3), the original of which is now in the South Kensington Museum.

In **1803** Trevithick constructed an engine (illustrated in Fig. 4) which worked on a cast-iron tram-road at Merthyr Tydvil. This was probably the first locomotive of which any practical use was made. It had 8 in. horizontal cylinders and

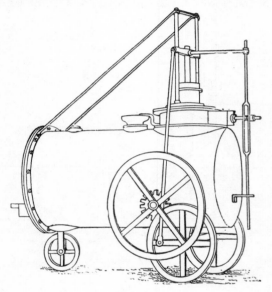

FIG. 3.

a stroke of 4 ft. 6 in. The piston, to which a connecting-rod was attached, acted upon an arrangement of geared spur-wheels. As there was only one cylinder, the engine was fitted with a fly-wheel, to assist it over the dead points. The driving-wheels worked simply by adhesion to a smooth tram-way. The engine is said to have done useful service

at Pen-y-darren Works, and was capable of drawing ten
tons of bar-iron, besides the carriages, at a speed of
nine miles an hour. It is stated on good authority that
the exhaust steam from the cylinders was turned into the
chimney, and that Trevithick therefore was the original inventor of the blast, one of the most indispensable elements
in the working of modern locomotives.

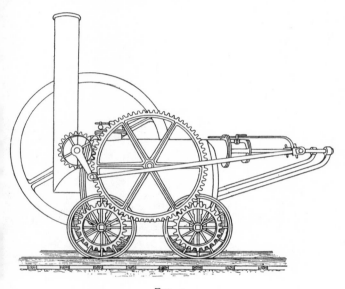

FIG. 4.

Trevithick himself took out no patent for the blast,
probably not realizing the vast importance of an arrangement
which he perhaps adopted merely as the most convenient way
of getting rid of the waste steam from the cylinders. The
machine was considered to be a commercial failure, and
little or nothing was heard of it after the year **1804**.

Trevithick also made a model of a steam-coach, which he exhibited about **1804-5** in London, on the site of the present London and North-Western Railway terminus at Euston. Wearied, however, with the apathy of those whom he

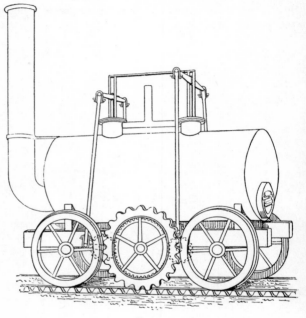

FIG. 5.

expected to take an interest in the furtherance of his projects, he took his machine away, and nothing more was heard of it. Trevithick made another engine in **1809** for the Wylam Railway, but this does not appear to have ever been used.

In **1811** Matthew Murray, of Leeds, constructed a locomotive (illustrated in Fig. 5) for Mr. John Blenkinsop (of the Middleton Colliery, near Leeds), which was put to work in August **1812**. Blenkinsop took out a patent for increasing the tractive force by means of a pinion working in a rack-rail. The boiler was cylindrical, with convex ends; there were two vertical double-acting cylinders, 8 in. in diameter with a stroke of 20 in., with pistons acting on cranks working at right angles to each other, which remain the arrangement adopted universally at the present day. Several of these engines were built and proved capable of drawing 94 tons on a level road at $3\frac{1}{2}$ miles an hour, the maximum speed attained with a light load being ten miles an hour. They were inspected in 1816 by the Grand Duke Nicholas, afterwards Emperor of Russia, and there is evidence of their being still at work in **1831**. Murray's engines may therefore lay claim to be the first engines permanently applied to railways on a commercial basis.

In the meantime, other brains had been at work on the locomotive. Mr. Blackett, the proprietor of Wylam Colliery near Newcastle-on-Tyne, wrote to Trevithick on the subject; and in **1811** one of the latter's engines was sent from Cornwall to Newcastle. It was, however, never used as a locomotive, but was subsequently employed as a stationary engine. A very primitive machine it must have been, as George Stephenson, who had never before seen a locomotive, upon inspecting it declared he could make a better one himself. William Hedley, Mr. Blackett's colliery inspector, set to work to construct a locomotive, having before him Trevithick's engines, and one of Blenkinsop's, which had been sent to work on the Coxlodge Colliery railway near Newcastle. To lay down a rack-rail—on Blenkinsop's system—on the five miles of the Wylam Railway would have cost about £8000, in addition to the expenses involved by adopting his patent. Hedley seems to have understood the insufficiency of adhesion between the rails and the driving-wheels of light engines ; yet he determined to adopt the system of direct acting driving-wheels, and to find means to overcome the difficulty. The result of his labours was that in **1813** he produced an engine which worked by the friction of its driving-wheels on smooth rails.

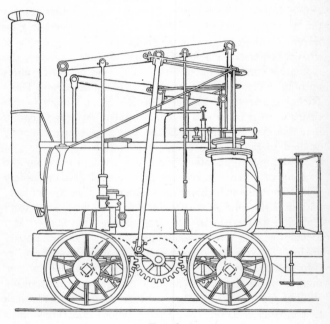

FIG. 6.

The engine had a cast-iron boiler, with a single internal flue and one cylinder. Its performance was not altogether satisfactory, but was sufficient to encourage Mr. Blackett to commission Hedley to make another and better engine.

Benefiting by previous experience, Hedley constructed

a second engine (Fig. 6), in which he embodied many improvements upon his previous venture. It had a wrought-iron boiler with a return flue, the chimney being at the same end as the fire-hole door. There were two vertical cylinders working on two large beams over the top of the boiler. The beams were connected to a crank underneath the boiler, which communicated the motion by toothed-gearing to four wheels of equal diameter working by adhesion to the rails. This engine was the famous " Puffing Billy," which is now preserved in the South Kensington Museum.

In **1815** Hedley constructed more powerful engines on the same principle, with eight wheels all geared together, in which, as well as in the engines constructed by Trevithick and Murray, the steam-pressure was 50 lbs. to the square inch.

Next in order among the great pioneers of locomotive development comes George Stephenson. He was at this time employed at the Killingworth Colliery, and had carefully watched the working of Hedley's engines since their first introduction on the Wylam Railway.

In **1814** a locomotive built under Stephenson's supervision was turned out of Killingworth Works. It was made on the lines adopted by Hedley, and had vertical cylinders and toothed-gearing communicating the motion to the driving-wheels. The engine was capable of drawing eight loaded waggons weighing 30 tons up an incline of 1 in 450 at the rate of four miles an hour ; its average speed was, however, only three miles an hour. After a year's trial the locomotive was found to compare unfavourably with horse-power in point of economy, and altogether the results of its working are said not to have been so good as those of Hedley's or Murray's engines.

In **1815** Stephenson constructed another engine (illustrated in Fig. 7). It also had vertical cylinders ; these were immersed in the boiler, one at each end. Each piston-

rod was connected to the centre of a long cross-head or arm,
stretching right across the whole width of the engine, and
connected by rods to cranks fixed to each wheel.   It was
intended to employ coupling-rods working on crank axles,

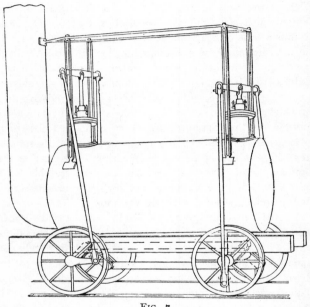

FIG. 7.

but this idea was abandoned, and the wheels were coupled
by an endless chain.

Some years after, the Killingworth engines were improved and simplified in several details. They were mounted
on springs, and the wheels coupled by outside connecting-
rods.

During the ten years succeeding **1815**, no great strides

were made in the development of the locomotive, but its
practical application was an accomplished fact, for steam
locomotive engines were actually working in lieu of horses
on various colliery lines. They were, however, of such clumsy
construction, and had so many defects, that their superiority
to horse-power, either as regards utility or economy, was by
no means established.

Nevertheless, during this period the locomotive question
was exercising the minds of many engineers, and a variety
of designs were brought out. These appear to have
chiefly related to proposals for constructing steam land-
carriages, as they were called, for working on ordinary
roads. Several of these proposals were carried into effect
with more or less success, but the final result of all experiments was to show that locomotives that ran on railway lines
were the only kind likely to prove of any practical value.

Still, some of these land-carriages display great ingenuity
on the part of their inventors, and although perhaps they
had not much to do with the subsequent development of
the locomotive, they may be touched upon as interesting,
because they show the ideas people had on this question at
the time.

In **1821** Julius Griffiths, of Brompton, Middlesex, constructed a steam-coach. The body of the carriage, which
was guided by a lever acting on the fore-wheels, was to carry
passengers and goods; whilst the active machinery—consisting of two vertical cylinders, a boiler with metal pipes,
furnace, condenser, and other appendages—was situated in
the rear of the conveyance. The power was communicated
by rods connected with toothed-wheels geared to the hind-
wheels. It is a question whether this engine was ever brought
to a sufficient stage of completion to make a run at all.

Messrs. Burstall & Hill, of London, constructed a steam-
coach (Fig. 8), which was made the subject of various

experimental trials. The greatest speed attained was from
three to four miles an hour, and there were repeated failures
through defects in the boiler. The general arrangement of
the machinery of this engine was the same as that of the
" Perseverance," which was entered by Mr. Burstall for the
Rainhill contest in 1829. The following description appears
in an old number of the *Edinburgh Journal of Science*—

FIG. 8.

"A represents the boiler, which is formed of a stout
cast-iron or other suitable metal flue, enclosed in a
wrought-iron or copper case, as seen in section, where
A is the place for fuel, and *a a a* are parts of the flue,
the top being formed into a number of shallow trays or
receptacles for containing a small quantity of water in a
state of being converted into steam, which is admitted from
the reservoir by a small pipe. B is the chimney, arising
from the centre flue; at D are the two cylinders, one
behind the other, which are fitted up with pistons and

valves, or cocks, in the usual way for the alternate action of steam above and below the pistons.

"The boiler being suspended on springs, the steam is conveyed from it to the engines through the helical pipe *c*, which has that form given to it to allow the vibration of the boiler without injury to the steam joints. E is the cistern containing water for one stage, say fifty to eighty gallons, and is made of strong copper, and air-tight, to sustain a pressure of about 60 pounds to the square inch. At *e* is one or more air-pumps, which are worked by the beams (F F) of the engines, and are used to force air into the water vessel, that its pressure may drive out, by a convenient pipe, the water into the boiler at such times and in such quantities as may be wanted. The two beams are connected at one end by the piston-rods, and at the other with rocking standards (HH). At about quarter of the length of the beams from the piston-rods are the two connecting-rods, *gg*, their lower ends being attached to two cranks formed at angles 90 degrees from each other on the hind axle, giving, by the action of the steam, a continued rotary motion to the wheels, without the necessity of a fly-wheel. The four coach-wheels are attached to the axles nearly as in common coaches, except that there is a ratchet-wheel formed upon the back part of the nave with a box wedged into the axle containing a dog or pall, with a spring on the back of it, for the purpose of causing the wheels to be impelled when the axle revolves, and at the same time allowing the outer wheel, when the carriage describes a curve, to travel faster than the inner one, and still be ready to receive the impulse of the engine as soon as it comes to a straight course.

"The patentees have another method of performing the same operation, with the further advantage of backing the coach when the engines are backed. In this plan the naves are cast with a recess in the middle, in which is a double bevel clutch, the inside of the nave being formed to correspond. The clutches are simultaneously acted upon by connecting levers and springs, which, according as they are forced to the right or left, will enable the carriage to be moved forward or backward.

"To the fore naves are fixed two cylindrical metal rings, round which are two friction bands, to be tightened by a lever convenient for the foot of the conductor, and which will readily retard or stop the coach when descending hills. K is the seat of the conductor, with the steering-wheel (L) in the front, which is fastened on the small upright shaft (I), and turns the two bevel pinions (2), and the shaft (3), with its small pinion (4), which, working into a rack on the segment of a circle on the fore carriage, gives full power to place the two axles at any angle necessary for causing the carriage to turn on the road, the centre of motion being the perch-pin (I).

"The fore and hind carriage are connected together by a perch, which is bolted fast at one end by the fork, and at the other end is screwed by two collars, which permit the fore and hind wheels to adapt themselves to the curve of the road.

"To ascend steep parts of the road, and particularly when the carriage is used on railways, or to drag another behind it, greater friction will be required on the road than the two hind wheels will give, and there is therefore a contrivance to turn all the four wheels. This is done by a pair of mitre wheels (4), one being on the hind axle, and the other on the longitudinal shaft (6), on which shaft is a universal joint, directly on the perch-pin (I) at (7). This enables the small shaft (7) to be turned, though the carriage should be on the lock. At one end of the shaft (7) is one of a pair of bevel wheels, the other being on the fore axles, which wheels are in the same proportion to one another as the fore and hind wheels of the carriage are, and this causes their circumference to move on the ground at the same speed.

"The patentees, by a peculiar construction of boiler, intend to make it a store of caloric; they propose to heat it from 250 to 500 or 800 degrees Fahrenheit, and by keeping the water in a separate vessel, and only applying it to the boiler when steam is wanted, they hope to accomplish that great desideratum in the application of steam to common roads, of making just such a quantity of steam as is wanted, so that when going down-hill, where the gravitating force will be enough to impel the carriage, all the steam and heat may be saved, to be accumulating and given out again at the first hill or bad piece of road, when, more being wanted, more will be expended.

"The engines are what are called high-pressure, and capable of working to 10-horse power, and the steam is purposed to be let off into an intermediate vessel, that the sound emitted may be regulated by one or more cocks."

In **1824** Mr. W. H. James brought out designs for a steam-carriage, and in **1826** Mr. Goldsworth constructed one. This latter actually made several journeys at the ordinary speed of stage-coaches. The motive power was partly from propellers and partly from a cranked axle on the hind wheels.

An interesting specimen of a steam-coach was built by Mr. David Gordon about this time, of which an illustration is given in Fig. 9. It was worked entirely by propellers, which were supposed to act in the same way as the hind-legs of a horse, being alternately forced out against the ground backwards, and drawn up again. The front wheels were actuated by a hand steering-gear. The propellers were driven off a six-throw crank in the body of the carriage. The rods of the propellers were iron tubes filled

with wood "to combine lightness with strength"! Other
steam-coaches were brought out about this period, but
probably the reader thinks enough time has already been
given to the recital of these crude ideas, which to us, with
our knowledge of the development of the seventy years
that followed, and the present perfection of railway
locomotives, seem childish. We will therefore resume the
history of what we may call the "legitimate locomotive,"

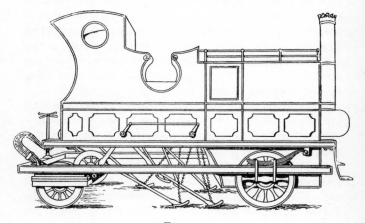

FIG. 9.

remembering, however, that the inventors of these wonder-
fully-conceived land-carriages had no such previous experience to guide them, and giving them at any rate the
credit of their inventive genius, which was of a strikingly
original character.

We now come to the time when Timothy Hackworth's
name first comes to the fore in connection with the
locomotive. He was originally employed on the Wylam
Railway, and had personally assisted in the construction of the

"Puffing Billy." In 1824 he was manager of Stephenson's locomotive factory at Newcastle, and in June 1825 was appointed manager of the Stockton and Darlington Railway, which was opened for passenger and goods traffic in September of that year, an important date in the history of railways and locomotives. To Mr. Edward Pease of Stockton belongs the honour of bringing this undertaking to a successful issue. The opposition to railways at the commencement of their career is now a matter of history, and we can only look back with astonishment at the short-sightedness of our grandfathers; yet we must remember that the views of the general public were guided by persons who were supposed to be experts in engineering science, the majority of whom, in their narrow-minded ignorance and lack of enterprise, did all they could to stamp as folly the ideas of such men as George Stephenson and the other early promoters of railways and steam locomotion.

Adverting to the opening of the Stockton and Darlington Railway, which took place in September 1825, Mr. Henry Pease's speech at the jubilee celebration fifty years after may be quoted. He said—"The scene on the morning of that day sets description at defiance. Many who were to take part in the event did not the night before sleep a wink, and soon after midnight were astir. The universal cheers, the happy faces of many, the vacant stare of astonishment of others, and the alarm depicted on the countenances of some, gave variety to the picture.

"At the appointed hour the procession went forward. The train moved off at the rate of from ten to twelve miles an hour with a weight of eighty tons, with one engine, No. 1, driven by George Stephenson himself; after it six waggons loaded with coals and flour; then a covered coach containing directors and proprietors; next twenty-one coal-waggons fitted up for passengers, with which they were crammed; and lastly, six more waggons loaded with coals.

"Off started the procession with the horseman at its head. A great concourse of people stood along the line. Many of them tried to accompany it by running, and some gentlemen on horseback galloped across the fields to keep up with the engine. The railway descending with a gentle incline towards Darlington, the rate of speed was consequently variable. At a favourable part of the road, Stephenson determined to try the speed of the engine, and he called upon the horseman with the flag to get out of the way, and Stephenson put on the speed to twelve miles, and then to fifteen miles an hour, and the runners on foot, the gentlemen on horseback, and the horseman with the flag were soon left far behind. When the train reached Darlington, it was found that 450 passengers occupied the waggons, and that the load of men, coal, and merchandise amounted to about ninety tons."

The line, after being opened, was worked partly by stationary engines and horse-power, but chiefly by five locomotives, of which four were from Stephenson's factory. After an experience of two years, it was still a matter of discussion which method was the most satisfactory and economical; and it is said that in **1827** a proposition was before the directors to abandon locomotives altogether in favour of horse traction. In this year Hackworth had in the shops one of the company's locomotives constructed by Wilson of Newcastle, and he set to work to alter and improve it. This engine, of which Fig. 10 is an illustration, was turned out in its re-built state in October **1827**, and was called the "Royal George." It is described in Mr. Colburn's book on *Locomotive Engineering:* — "The boiler was a plain cylinder, 13 ft. long and 4 ft. 4 in. in diameter. The return flue of the Wylam engines was adopted, and a liberal amount of heating surface thus obtained. There were six coupled wheels, 4 ft. in diameter, and the cylinders, which were placed vertically at the end opposite to the fire-place, were 11 in. in diameter, the stroke of the pistons being 20 in.; the piston-rods worked downwards, and were connected to the first pair of wheels. These were without

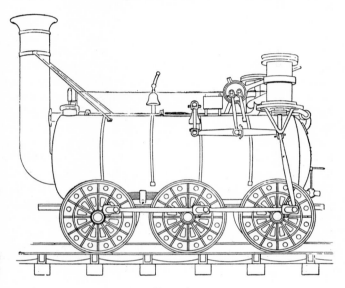

FIG. 10.

springs, so that the pistons should not jump the engine up and down, but the middle and back pairs of wheels carried their load through stout springs.

"Separate smoke-boxes had not then been provided, and the orifices of the exhaust steam pipes opened into the chimney 4 ft. or 5 ft. above the bend. In the single-flue Stephenson engines, the part of the chimney between the bend and the mouth of the exhaust-pipe was often red-hot. The 'Royal George' had a cistern into which a portion of the exhaust steam could be turned to heat the feed-water ; it had also short stroke force pumps worked by eccentrics, adjustable springs instead of weights upon the safety-valves, and a single lever reversing-gear. Most, if not all, of these features were novelties first introduced in this engine. Its maximum performance was that of drawing thirty-two loaded waggons, weighing about 130 tons, at the rate of five miles an hour on the level portions of the line, the speed increasing on gentle descents to nine miles an hour. Its ordinary load in summer was twenty-four loaded waggons, weighing 100 tons; returning with thirty empty waggons weighing forty-five tons, with which load it ascended gradients varying from 1 in 450 to 1 in 100.

"In Messrs. Rastrick and Walker's report to the directors of the Liverpool and Manchester Railway, March 7, **1829**, it was stated, upon the authority of Mr. Robert Stephenson, that this engine had drawn 48¾ tons of goods (exclusive of waggons) for a distance of 2500 yards, rising 10 ft. per mile, and descended again, the average rate of speed over the whole distance both ways being 11·2 miles per hour. Messrs. Rastrick and Walker gave the weight of the engine and tender taken together as fifteen tons, and stated its regular summer load to be 71½ tons on a level at five miles an hour. Estimating, erroneously no doubt, that the tractive force of the engine was inversely proportional to its speed, they considered it capable of drawing only 28¼ tons regularly at ten miles an hour."[1]

[1] *The Locomotive*, by Colburn, p. 21.

CHAPTER II.

THE RAINHILL CONTEST AND SUBSEQUENT DEVELOPMENT.

WE are now approaching the date of the famous contest at Rainhill, which took place in the year **1829.**

Prior to this date, the question of carrying merchandise and passengers upon a railway by steam locomotives was certainly not universally recognized as likely to be brought into general use, either as a practical convenience or a commercial success. Writing on the subject about this time, the *Quarterly Review* said—" As to those persons who speculate on making railways general throughout the kingdom, and superseding all the canals, all the waggons, mails, stage-coaches, post-chaises, and, in short, every other mode of conveyance by land and by water, we deem them and their visionary schemes unworthy of notice. The gross exaggerations of the locomotive steam-engine (or, to speak in plain English, the steam-carriage) may delude for a time, but must end in the mortification of those concerned. We should as soon expect the people to suffer themselves to be fired off upon one of Congreve's ricochet rockets, as trust themselves at the mercy of such a machine going at such a rate."

This being a fair sample of the opinion of the country, it is not to be wondered at that the promoters of the Liverpool and Manchester Railway, which was projected in **1822,** had to cope with the most strenuous opposition. Stephenson had to go before Parliamentary Committees, and was alternately abused and derided for his supposed fanaticism on the subject of railways and locomotives. The self-taught mechanic, however, gave a good account of himself, notwithstanding the gibes of the learned and astute persons, who vied with each other in their endeavours to bring ridicule upon one whom they considered uneducated and illiterate. It is, however, interesting to compare the foresight of this supposed ignorant individual with the wisdom of the learned counsel, who, in summing up the case, declared—" I say there is no evidence upon which the Committee can safely rely, that upon an average more than $3\frac{1}{2}$ or $4\frac{1}{2}$ miles an hour can be done. Consider the nature of the engine : it consists in part of a large iron boiler, and the elastic force of steam is the moving force, and that depends upon the quantity of heat ; the water is enclosed in a boiler of iron, a most rapid conductor of heat, and which must move in storms of snow, in storms of rain, and during times of frost. At all those times it will be extremely difficult to keep up the elastic force of steam ; I do not say impossible, but extremely difficult."

However, eventually the Liverpool and Manchester Railway was completed in the year 1829, and yet the system of tractive force to be employed upon the line was undecided. Indeed, in the spring of that year, the directors were upon the point of adopting fixed engines and ropes, but were induced by two or three members of their board to make a further and conclusive trial of locomotives.

On April 20, **1829**, they decided to offer a prize of £500 in open competition for the best locomotive that could be produced for working the traffic on their railway. On April 25, 1829, this offer was made public, and the following is a copy of the notice issued stipulating the conditions to which the locomotives submitted for trial were required to conform.

"RAILWAY OFFICE, LIVERPOOL.
"*April* 25, 1829.

"STIPULATIONS AND CONDITIONS

On which the Directors of the Liverpool and Manchester Railway offer a premium of £500 for the most improved locomotive engine.

"1. The said engine must effectually consume its own smoke, according to the provisions of the Railway Act, 7th George IV.

"2. The engine, if it weighs six tons, must be capable of drawing after it day by day, on a well-constructed railway on a level plane, a train of carriages of the gross weight of twenty tons, including the tender and water-tank, at the rate of ten miles an hour, with a pressure of steam in the boiler not exceeding 50 lbs. on the square inch.

"3. There must be two safety-valves, one of which must be completely out of the reach or control of the engine-man, and neither of which must be fastened down while the engine is working.

"4. The engine and boiler must be supported on springs and rest on six wheels; and the height from the ground to the top of the chimney must not exceed 15 ft.

"5. The weight of the machine with its complement of water in the boiler must, at most, not exceed six tons, and a machine of less weight will be preferred, if it draw after it a proportionate weight; and if the weight of the engine, &c., do not exceed five tons, then the gross weight to be drawn need not exceed fifteen tons, and in that proportion for machines of still smaller weight; provided that the engine, &c., shall still be on six wheels, unless the weight (as above) be reduced to $4\frac{1}{2}$ tons or under, in which case the boiler, &c., may be placed on four wheels. And the Company shall be at liberty to put the boiler, fire-tube, cylinders, &c., to the test of a pressure of water not exceeding 150 lbs. per square inch, without being answerable for any damage the machine may receive in consequence.

"6. There must be a mercurial gauge affixed to the machine with index-rod, showing the steam pressure above 45 lbs. per square inch, and constructed to blow off at a pressure of 60 lbs. per square inch.

"7. The engine to be delivered complete for trial at the Liverpool end of the railway not later than the 1st of October next.

"8. The price of the engine which may be accepted not to exceed £550, delivered on the railway, and any engine not approved to be taken back by the owner.

"N.B.—The Railway Company will provide the engine-tender with a supply of water and fuel for the experiment. The distance between the rails is 4 ft. 8½ in."

Immediately before the trial the judges issued these instructions—

"TRIAL OF THE LOCOMOTIVE ENGINES ON THE LIVERPOOL AND MANCHESTER RAILWAY.

"The following is the ordeal which we have decided each locomotive shall undergo, in contending for the premium of £500 at Rainhill—

"The weight of the locomotive engine with its full complement of water in the boiler shall be ascertained at the weighing-machine by eight o'clock in the morning, and the load assigned to it shall be three times the weight thereof. The water in the boiler shall be cold, and there shall be no fuel in the fire-place. As much fuel shall be weighed, and as much water shall be measured and delivered into the tender-carriage as the owner of the engine may consider sufficient for the supply of the engine for a journey of thirty-five miles. The fire in the boiler shall then be lighted, and the quantity of fuel consumed for getting up the steam shall be determined, and the time noted.

" The tender-carriage, with the fuel and water, shall be considered to be, and taken as part, of the load assigned to the engine.

" Those engines which carry their own fuel and water shall be allowed a proportionate deduction from their load, according to the weight of the engine.

" The engine, with the carriages attached to it, shall be run by hand up to the starting-post, and as soon as the steam is got up to 50 lbs. per square inch, the engine shall set out upon its journey.

" The distance the engine shall perform each trip shall be $1\frac{3}{4}$ miles each way, including $\frac{1}{8}$ mile at each end, one for getting up the speed, and the other for stopping the train ; by this means the engine with its load will travel $1\frac{1}{2}$ miles each way at full speed.

" The engine shall make twenty trips, which shall be equal to a journey of thirty-five miles, thirty miles whereof shall be performed at full speed, and the average rate of travelling shall not be less than ten miles an hour.

" As soon as the engine has performed this task (which shall be equal to the travelling from Liverpool to Manchester), there shall be a fresh supply of fuel and water delivered to her ; and as soon as she can be got ready to set out again, she shall go up to the starting-post and make twenty trips more, which will be equal to the journey from Manchester back again to Liverpool.

" The time of performing every trip shall be accurately noted, as well as the time occupied in getting ready to set out on the second journey.

" Should the engine not be enabled to take along with it sufficient fuel and water for the journey of twenty trips, the time occupied in taking in a fresh supply of fuel and water shall be considered, and taken as a part of the time in performing the journey.

> "J. U. Rastrick, C.E., Stourbridge.
> Nicholas Wood, C.E., Killingworth. } Judges.
> John Kennedy, Manchester.

" *Liverpool, October* 6, 1829."

The competition was arranged to commence on October 6, 1829, and on the result depended the decision of the important question of the motive power to be used for working the new Liverpool and Manchester Railway.

The following is a list of the competitors ready to enter the field on the date named—

No. 1. Messrs. Braithwaite and Erricson, of London.
> The "Novelty": weight, 2 tons 15 cwt.

No. 2. Mr. Timothy Hackworth, of Darlington.
> The "Sanspareil": weight, 4 tons 8 cwt. 2 qrs.

No. 3. Mr. Robert Stephenson, of Newcastle-upon-Tyne.
> The "Rocket": weight, 4 tons 3 cwt.

No. 4. Mr. Brandrith, of Liverpool.
> The "Cyclopede": weight, 3 tons, worked by a horse.

No. 5. Mr. Burstall, of Edinburgh.
> The "Perseverance": weight, 2 tons 17 cwt.

The engines may be thus briefly described—

No. 1. The "Novelty" (which is illustrated in Fig. 11) was a tank-engine carrying its own supply of fuel and feed-water. It had four wheels, each 4 ft. 2 in. in diameter, intended to be coupled by a chain, which was, however, not used during the trial. There were two vertical cylinders 6 in. in diameter and 12 in. stroke, fixed on to the framing, and the motion was communicated to the driving-wheels underneath them. The pistons worked through the top of the cylinder cover on to cross-heads, which were connected to rods by bell cranks. These latter were connected by other rods to a crank axle on one pair of wheels. The boiler was rather a complicated affair: partly vertical, and partly horizontal; in the vertical portion was the fire-grate, surrounded by water space. The ash-pan was air-tight, forced draught being produced by a pair of bellows worked by the engine. The fire

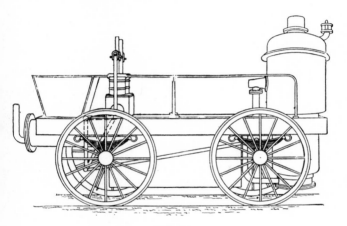

FIG. 11.

was fed from the top (as in old-fashioned coke stoves), and the gases generated were conveyed by a tortuous pipe, about 36 ft. long, through the horizontal part of the boiler to the chimney.

No. 2. The "Sanspareil" (illustrated in Fig. 12) was a four-wheeled, coupled engine with two vertical cylinders, 7 in. diameter and 18 in. stroke, working on to the wheels underneath them by an ordinary piston, cross-head, and connecting-rod. The boiler was cylindrical, 4 ft. 2 in. in diameter and

6 ft. long, with two large flues, in one of which the grate was placed, the flames returning to the chimney through the other. The chimney and fire-hole door were both at the same end of the boiler, the cylinders being at the opposite

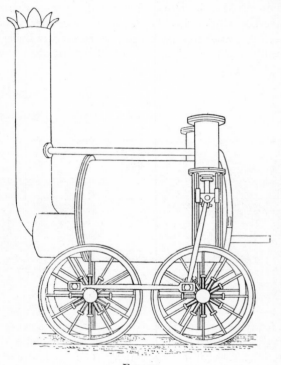

FIG. 12.

end. The wheels were 4 ft. 6 in. in diameter, and were coupled by an ordinary coupling-rod.

No. 3. The "Rocket" (illustrated in Fig. 13) was a four-wheeled engine, mounted on springs. The driving-wheels were 4 ft. 8½ in., and were at the leading or front end of the engine. They were connected by rods to the cross-heads on the piston-rods of outside cylinders, which were fixed to the boiler near the fire-box in an inclined position. The

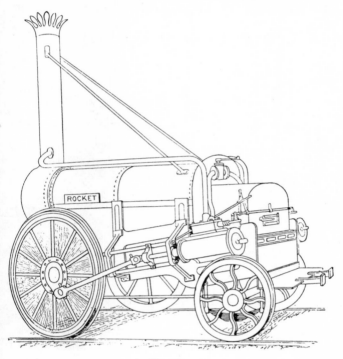

FIG. 13.

cylinders were 8 in. in diameter, and the stroke 16½ in. The exhaust steam was turned into the chimney. The boiler was cylindrical, 6 ft. in length, with twenty-five 3-inch copper tubes in the lower half of it. At one end was a rec-

tangular fire-box, with water space at the top and sides, the
chimney being at the other end. The communication
between the water space round the fire-box and the boiler was
by external pipes. This was, therefore, the first introduction
of the principle of the locomotive boiler in its present
form.

No. 4. The "Cyclopede" was disqualified from entering

FIG. 14.

the competition, as the motive power employed did not
agree with the "stipulations" and "conditions." The idea
of the machine (of which a sketch is given in Fig. 14) was,
however, thoroughly original. The horse, which was to
provide the motive power, was yoked to a frame, and underneath its feet was a kind of endless belt made of planks.
The unfortunate beast had to trot along on these planks,
which worked round drums geared to the driving-wheels,
and thus impart motion to the vehicle in treadmill fashion
without moving out of his stall.

No. 5. The "Perseverance" was, in the details of its machinery, akin to Messrs. Burstall and Hill's steam-coach, described previously. This engine was found unfit to take part in the contest, the highest speed it could attain being five or six miles an hour.

The trials were made on a level piece of line, $1\frac{1}{2}$ miles long, at Rainhill, near Liverpool; $\frac{1}{8}$ mile being allowed at each end of the run for getting up and slackening speed. It was arranged that each engine should run twenty times each way over the course, in two sets of ten double trips. This was to correspond with a journey from Liverpool to Manchester and back. The observations of speed were confined to the distance between the posts, $1\frac{1}{2}$ miles apart, neglecting the overlapping ends of the course for starting and stopping.

The "Rocket" was the first engine tried. Its load was two waggons of stones weighing altogether 9 tons 10 cwt. 3 qrs. 26 lbs., the total moving weight being 17 tons. The engine pushed the waggons in one direction and drew them in the other. The first ten double trips were accomplished without mishap at an average speed of 13·42 miles an hour between the posts, the highest speed attained being 21·43 miles an hour. The average speed while drawing was 14·43, and while propelling 12·54 miles an hour.

The engine then entered on the second series of trips, which were again safely accomplished with the following results—

Average speed between mile posts, 14·2 miles an hour.
,, ,, while drawing train, 15·73 ,, ,,
,, ,, ,, propelling train, 12·93 ,, ,,
Maximum speed attained, 24 miles an hour.

The "Novelty" was tried on October 10. After making two runs in each direction, some part of the boiler joints gave way, and the engine had to be stopped. The average speed maintained between the posts was $14\frac{3}{4}$ miles an hour. The total moving weight of engine and train was 10 tons 14 cwt. 0 qrs. 14 lbs.

In the trial of the "Sanspareil," on October 13, the total weight of engine and train was 19 tons 2 cwt. No sooner had the engine started than one of the cylinders cracked, which caused it to work under considerable disadvantage. After running $22\frac{1}{2}$ miles between the posts, the pumps supplying the feed-water failed, and this disaster brought to an end the experiment so far as the "Sanspareil" was concerned. Had it not been for these mishaps, which were after all of a purely accidental character, the engine might have proved a formidable rival to the "Rocket." The average speed maintained between the posts was 13·88 miles an hour; $15\frac{1}{2}$ while drawing and 12·4 while propelling the load. The highest speed attained was 17·47 miles an hour.

Thus the famous Rainhill contest resulted in a victory for the "Rocket," which settled once and for all the much-debated question of the adaptability of steam locomotives to the purposes of working railways.

Having briefly sketched the history of the locomotive up to the important epoch marked by the success of the "Rocket" at the Rainhill contest, it will be as well to note the improvements that have gradually been effected from that date up to comparatively recent times.

To show the difference in the requirements of modern engines as compared with the early practice on the Liverpool and Manchester Railway, it may be here mentioned that in 1834, the trains run on that line weighed on an average, exclusive of engine, about 47 tons, and ran at a speed of twenty miles an hour.

The weight of a London and North-Western express train of the present day frequently exceeds 250 tons, and this weight has to be run through the country, mile after mile, on many parts of the line at a speed of sixty miles an hour.

The first engines used for working the traffic on the Liverpool and Manchester Railway were of the same type as the "Rocket," but were larger and heavier. They weighed from 6½ to 7 tons, had 5 ft. driving-wheels, with larger cylinders and a longer stroke. They also had outside cylinders fixed to the fire-box end, as had the original "Rocket," but not so much inclined. These engines had ninety 2-in. tubes in the boiler, and were fitted with a smoke-box. The boiler pressure was 50 lbs. to the square inch.

In **1830** Timothy Hackworth designed an engine for the Stockton and Darlington Railway, which embodied certain improvements now recognized as vital principles in the construction of modern express passenger engines. The cylinders, which were placed inside and worked on to a cranked axle, were horizontal, thus doing away with the unsteadiness caused by the depressing and lifting of the springs at every stroke of the piston, which occurred with inclined or vertical cylinders. The engine was also fitted with a steam dome. This was spherical in shape, and gave the name to the engine, which was called "The Globe." This engine is said to have attained a speed of fifty miles an hour, upon a level road with a load of twelve waggons. It was, however, destined to come to an untimely end, as the boiler exploded at Middlesbro'-on-Tees in 1839.

In **1830** there were three types of horizontal inside cylinder engines at work—

The "Liverpool," by Mr. Jas. Kennedy, commenced work on July 22, 1830, on the Stockton and Darlington Railway.

The "Planet," by Messrs. Stephenson, commenced work Oct. 4, 1830, on the Liverpool and Manchester Railway.

The "Globe," by Timothy Hackworth, commenced work
on the Stockton and Darlington Railway shortly after the
"Planet" on the Liverpool and Manchester Railway.

The "Liverpool" had four coupled 6 ft. wheels, the
largest diameter yet employed, and horizontal cylinders
side by side. It was actually at work on the line before

FIG. 15.

the other two, although Hackworth first made designs for a
locomotive on this system.

The "Planet" was the first engine which combined all the
following improvements—

Horizontal cylinders.

Cylinders encased in smoke-box.

Multitubular boiler.

It may therefore be taken as the first locomotive definitely representing the principles, and indeed many of the more important details, which have been adhered to with very slight alteration up to the present day. Fig. 15 illustrates an engine built by Fenton in 1834, and may be taken as a general type of the " Planet " class.

The subsequent ideas of various locomotive engineers, and the gradual structural developments succeeding this

FIG. 16.

date, cannot be better understood than by referring to the sketches given and the accompanying notes—

1833. Richard Robert's locomotive (shown in Fig. 16). This engine had outside vertical cylinders connected on each side by cross-heads and side-links to bell crank levers, transmitting the power to the driving-wheels. One of these engines was worked upon the Liverpool and Manchester line, and three on the Dublin and Kingstown Railway.

1834. Forrester's locomotive (shown in Fig. 17).   It had six wheels, single driving-wheels, outside horizontal cylinders, and outside cranks some distance from the face of the wheels, which caused unsteadiness in running, as the wheels were not balanced (see p. 226).

1835. Bury's engine (Fig. 18).   This engine had 5 ft. driving-wheels, and a round-backed, dome-shaped fire-box.

FIG. 17.

There were still some of these engines employed in hauling materials about Crewe Works only a few years ago.

In **1836** Mr. T. E. Harrison (who was subsequently chief engineer of the North-Eastern Railway) patented an engine, the idea of which was to carry the boiler on a separate carriage from the cylinders and driving gear ; and Messrs. Hawthorn, in **1837,** constructed two engines on this plan for Brunel.   The engine piston acted on a fly-wheel, which communicated the motion to the 6 ft. driving-wheels by spur gearing. Messrs. Hawthorn constructed a second engine, called the "Hurricane," on the same plan, but in this case the piston acted direct on a pair of 10 ft. driving-wheels.

The last three engines mentioned never really got beyond the experimental stage, and from **1835** to **1845**, although there was a continual advance in the weight and speed of

FIG. 18.

locomotives, there was practically no deviation from the lines on which the "Planet" and Bury's engines were constructed.

During this period many engineers had been at work scheming various forms of reversing gear and valve motions for the expansive working of steam; but it was not till **1845** that the general adoption of variable expansive gear began.

This important part of the machinery of a locomotive will be specially described hereafter; and we will now pass on to the consideration of a few more types of engines bridging over the period between the year 1845 and the locomotive of the present day.

In **1845** the heaviest engines on the London and Birmingham Railway did not weigh more than $12\frac{1}{4}$ tons, and of the ninety engines then possessed by the Company, all but one ran on four wheels only. The passenger engines had 12 in. cylinders, 18 in. stroke, and $5\frac{1}{2}$ ft. wheels. They weighed $10\frac{1}{2}$ tons in working order, and worked trains weighing 42 tons at an average speed of 25 miles an hour. In some cases a speed of 50 miles an hour is said to have been attained with a train weighing $37\frac{1}{2}$ tons.

About this date, a special run from Liverpool to Birmingham and back was made by an engine of this kind with the following results—

Distance, 190 miles.

Average speed, $29\frac{1}{2}$ miles per hour.

Weight of train, 60 tons (12 carriages).

Consumption of coke, 37·1 lbs. per mile.

Evaporation, 5·7 lbs. of water per lb. of coke burned.

About the year **1847**, Messrs. Sharp, Roberts & Co. commenced building a number of engines of the pattern shown in Fig. 19, and this for many years represented a standard type of English locomotives.

In **1847** Mr. F. Trevithick, locomotive superintendent of the London and North-Western Railway Works at Crewe (the son of the famous Cornish engineer), constructed an engine now well known in locomotive history. It was called the "Cornwall," and had single driving-wheels, 8 ft. 6 in. in diameter. Its chief feature was that the axle of the driving-wheels was above the barrel of the boiler, the idea being to keep the centre of gravity as low as possible, and thus get a large boiler area and heating surface, at the same time ensuring complete safety in running at high speeds. It was thought at this time by most locomotive engineers that a large boiler fixed in the ordinary way made the engine top-heavy, and was not compatible with safety in narrow gauge engines running at high speeds, an argument which was always adduced in favour of the 7 ft. gauge. Trevithick's engine had 17½ in. cylinders with a stroke of 24 in.

Fig. 20 shows the general arrangement and design of the

FIG. 19.

engine. The eccentric was on the outside of the driving-wheel, being slightly larger in diameter than the throw of the crank. The regulator-rod passed over the top of the boiler, and entered the smoke-box below the chimney. The "Cornwall," as originally constructed, was not a success, and it was subsequently rebuilt at Crewe, and fitted with an ordinary type of boiler above the axle. It is still running on the London and North-Western Railway, although not able to work main line express trains of the

present day.   Fig. 21 illustrates this engine in its present
form.

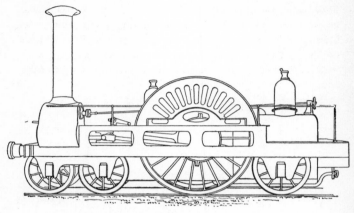

FIG. 20.

The four wheels coupled engine (illustrated in Fig. 22)
was also designed and built by Trevithick at Crewe Works.

FIG. 21.

It had outside cylinders 15 in. × 24 in., and carried a boiler pressure of 120 lbs. per square inch. Engines of this class were for many years employed in working the goods traffic on the London and North-Western Railway, and some of them, known as the old Crewe goods class, are still working on the line. They are, however, not powerful enough to work modern goods trains, as they only weigh about twenty-two tons, and those that survive are chiefly used on local passenger trains. A number of these engines were sub-

FIG. 22.

sequently rebuilt by Mr. Ramsbottom, and converted into tank engines.

In **1848** Mr. Crampton brought out a novel locomotive called the "Liverpool." This engine excited a good deal of attention at the time, and although the type was not adopted to any great extent on English railways, still it achieved a considerable success in other countries.

The "Liverpool" had a pair of 8 ft. driving-wheels behind the fire-box, with outside cylinders fixed horizontally behind the fire-box and smoke-box. The cylinders were

18 in. in diameter with a 24 in. stroke. The engine was reckoned equal to a load of 180 tons at fifty miles an hour, and comparing this with the general performance of other contemporary engines, it may perhaps claim to have been the most powerful of its time. It was certainly the largest that had been constructed, but its weight (thirty-five tons) played havoc with the inferior permanent way then in use, and no doubt this militated against its favourable reception by railway engineers.

It may here be mentioned that in 1847 began the great

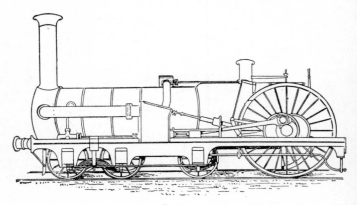

FIG. 23.

"battle of the gauges," which finally resolved itself into a question between 7 ft. and 4 ft. 8½ in., although up to this time the gauges of many smaller railways varied in width. The following is a list of them—

FT. IN.

The Ballochney Line (in Scotland) 4 6
The Liverpool and Manchester, Grand Junction,
    London and Birmingham, and other lines,
    built by Messrs. Stephenson 4 8½

	FT. IN.
The London and Blackwall, Eastern Counties, and Northern and Eastern Lines	5 0
The Dundee and Arbroath, and Arbroath and Forfar Lines (in Scotland)	5 6
The Ulster Railway (in Ireland)	6 0
The Great Western Railway	7 0

Mr. Brunel, of the Great Western Railway, had built engines with 18 in. cylinders, 24 in. stroke, and 8 ft. driving-wheels, running on a 7 ft. gauge, but until Trevithick brought out the "Cornwall," it was thought that nothing on this scale was practicable on a 4 ft. $8\frac{1}{2}$ in. gauge. It is probable that his experiments in the construction of larger narrow gauge engines had a great deal to do with the ultimate decision in their favour. The Great Western Railway, however, clung to their 7 ft. gauge, and indeed the splendid runs of their West of England express trains, which were performed on the broad gauge line till within a year ago, have up to the present time never been surpassed either in punctuality or speed.

The engines recently doing this work were built from the designs of Sir Daniel Gooch in April **1846**,[1] and magnificent engines they were; but unfortunately there is no longer any track on which they can display their powers, for the last remnant of the broad gauge line in this country has been done away with. There must be but few railway men who can help regretting that such a step has had to be taken, but the Great Western Railway Company has been forced to it by the absolute necessity of having all railway stock in the country interchangeable from line to line. Had the requirements of the present day as regards speed and power been foreseen in the year 1847, it is quite possible that broad gauge lines would now have been in the ascendancy, instead of which the last length of line on which these

[1] The engines of this class working in 1892 were built in the year 1851.

time-honoured services were rendered was swept away in May 1892.[1]

The Great Western Railway broad gauge engines of **1846** (as illustrated in Fig. 24) had single driving-wheels 8 ft. in diameter, inside cylinders 18 in. bore and 24 in. stroke. The following were their other leading features—

Fire-grate, 21 sq. ft. ; fire-box surface, 153 sq. ft. ; number of tubes, 305, 2 in. in diameter, 11 ft. 3 in. long ; heating

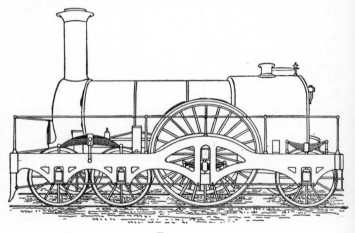

FIG. 24.

surface, 1932 sq. ft. The boiler pressure was 120 lbs. per square inch.

The most powerful rival this engine had on the narrow gauge lines was the " Bloomer " class, designed by Mr. McConnell (the locomotive superintendent of the southern division of the London and North-Western Railway) in **1850**.

---

[1] The last broad gauge train to leave London was the 11.45 a.m.— "Flying Dutchman"—on May 20. The conversion of the line from broad to narrow gauge occupied thirty-one hours.

These engines had 16 in. inside cylinders, with 22 in. stroke and 7 ft. driving-wheels. They weighed 28¾ tons. The fire-box had 142 sq. ft. of heating surface, and contained 195

FIG. 25.

tubes, 12 ft. long, the heating surface of which was 1152 sq. ft. The pressure employed was 120 lbs. per square inch. An illustration of a "Bloomer" is given in Fig. 25.

FIG. 26.

In **1853**, powerful broad gauge tank-engines (as illustrated in Fig. 26) were constructed for the Bristol and Exeter Railway. The following were their leading features—

Cylinders, 16½ in. bore by 24 in. stroke.

Single driving-wheels, 9 ft. in diameter.

Diameter of boiler, 4 ft. 0½ in.

Number of tubes, 180, 1$\frac{5}{16}$ in. diameter, 10 ft. 9 in. long.

Weight of engine, 42 tons.

The leading and trailing ends were carried on two trucks of four wheels each, 4 ft. in diameter. There were no flanges on the driving-wheels. It is reported that an engine of this class has been known to attain a speed of 80 miles

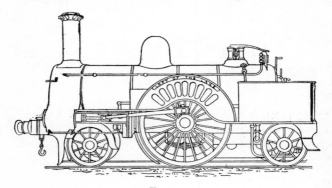

FIG. 27.

an hour, and in ordinary working the coke consumed was only 21¾ lbs. per mile.

In the year **1858** Mr. Ramsbottom designed and built for the London and North-Western Railway Company at Crewe, the express passenger engine illustrated in Fig. 27. This engine excited a good deal of interest at the time. It embodied all the then known improvements in the locomotive, combined with simplicity, compactness, and, it may be said, elegance of design, if such a word can be applied to a locomotive ; for this was certainly one of the prettiest engines ever built. It was and is still known as the " Lady of the

Lake " class, as one of them bearing that name was exhibited at the International Exhibition of 1862 and obtained a gold medal.

The chief features of the engine were —

Driving-wheels, 7 ft. 6 in. in diameter.

Leading and trailing wheels, 3 ft. 9 in. in diameter.

Outside cylinders, 16 in. bore by 24 in. stroke.

Weight, in working order, 27 tons 5 cwt.

Grate area, 15 sq. ft.; heating surface, 1068·3 sq. ft.

Many engines of the " Lady of the Lake " class are still working on the London and North-Western Railway, and are capable of running at as high a speed as any engine constructed up to the present time, although not strong enough to work heavy passenger trains. It may be mentioned that " Marmion," a sister engine to the " Lady of the Lake," ran the Scotch express between London and Crewe during the famous race to Scotland between the east and west coast routes in the summer of 1888, when the train was an exceptionally light one, but the speed required was exceptionally high.

Before the time these engines were built it had become generally recognized that locomotives for goods and passenger trains required certain different capabilities. The former must be able to take heavy loads ; the latter to run at high speeds. For a long time, single-wheeled engines were generally in vogue for working passenger trains, but the adhesion of a single pair of driving-wheels was not sufficient to move the goods trains, whose weight gradually increased. Some engineers coupled four wheels of medium diameter, and used engines of this pattern for mixed goods and passenger traffic ; indeed, this practice even now obtains to a certain extent.

It, however, came to be recognized that six coupled wheels of smaller diameter gave the best results for working heavy goods trains, where power is a greater consideration than speed ; and this system is now generally adopted by all large railways on which the goods and passenger traffic is kept separate.

Mr. Ramsbottom designed and built an excellent goods engine with six coupled wheels (illustrated in Fig. 28), which he first put on the line in **1859**.

These have for many years been the standard London and

FIG. 28.

North-Western Railway goods engines, though now Mr. Webb has built more powerful and faster engines for working the more important goods traffic, and stronger low speed engines for the heavy coal trains.

The chief features of Mr. Ramsbottom's goods engines were—

Weight, in working order, 31 tons 5 cwt.

Six coupled wheels, 5 ft. in diameter.

Cylinders, 17 in. diameter by 24 in. stroke.

Heating surface, 1074·6 sq. ft.; grate area, 17·1 sq. ft.

These engines have perhaps done more all round service in the working of goods traffic on a large railway than any other class ever built. The London and North-Western Railway have 626 of them, of which all the different parts are interchangeable.

In Mr. Ramsbottom's time, his goods and passenger engines may fairly be said to have represented the favourite types in use throughout the country, although of course there were great variations in detail. These. engines have since been rebuilt by Mr. Webb and improved in many ways. They have larger boilers, and the pressure has been increased from 120 to 140 and 150 lbs. per square inch, thus greatly increasing their power and efficiency.

During the latter part of his career with the London and North-Western Railway, Mr. Ramsbottom constructed passenger engines with four 6 ft. 6 in. coupled wheels and inside cylinders. The 7 ft. 6 in. single engines did not always work satisfactorily on the Chester and Hoiyhead Line, which is in parts exposed to furious gales, especially along the North Wales coast and across the bleak island of Anglesea. The high driving-wheels were greatly affected by the wind, and the trains were occasionally brought completely to a stand. Coupled engines were put on this part of the line, and were much more successful in combating with the special difficulties which arose from this cause.

The history of the locomotive has now been traced down to engines in use and doing good work at the present day, although of course it must not for a moment be thought that all engines that may claim a page in locomotive history have been mentioned. The endeavour has been to allude to all the most important ones of the early days, when the locomotive, as we know it, was in embryo, and when each improvement on the first crude and half-formed ideas was a distinct step in the development of the wonderful machine, which may be said to have been born in the days of George Stephenson. Ever since then it has been gradually growing, until it has now reached the prime of life in the shape of the magnificent express engines running on our English railways to-day.

After the Liverpool and Manchester Railway was opened in 1829, a great many locomotive builders entered the field, and it would be impossible to follow all their different ideas, or to enumerate all who have rendered valuable service in bringing the locomotive to its present state of perfection.

During the last half-century the locomotive has steadily increased in size, weight, and power, besides being much more complicated in detail, but this has been a natural growth, as the puny babe in time attains to the vigour of manhood.

Mr. Webb, at the head of those who have been aiming at increased efficiency and economy in this direction, has made a new and important departure in the introduction of compound locomotive engines, which he has successfully adopted for general practice on the London and North-Western Railway. These will be considered later on, but, with this important exception, the vital principles have in no way altered ; and though workmanship, detail, and design have improved and continue to improve, little of importance has been discovered in recent years.

CHAPTER III.

THE ACTION OF THE STEAM IN THE CYLINDER.

THIS chapter will be devoted to a simple description of the most elementary principles of the steam-engine, in the hope of enlightening the non-professional reader as to how the power of steam is brought to bear upon the wheels of a locomotive, causing them to revolve, and thus impart motive power to the engine.

It is perhaps unnecessary to state that the boiler is the source of stored power where the steam is generated and kept in confinement ready for use when required. This power is always there so long as steam is up, but it is only applied when wanted, and can be turned on to and off from the mechanism of the engine by the " regulator," that is to say, the valve controlling the exit of steam from the boiler to the steam-chest and cylinders. When this valve is opened the steam pressure in the boiler is put in direct communication with the cylinders, and it is its action in the latter which constitutes the whole motive power of the non-condensing steam-engine, whether locomotive or otherwise.

The cylinder, as its name implies, is a cylindrical vessel made of cast-iron and bored out perfectly true inside. It is closed at each end by covers, and steam is admitted to each end alternately to press upon a circular block called the piston. The piston is made steam-tight in the cylinder by means of packing rings, and the intermittent action of the steam causes it to be kept in motion backwards and forwards, from one end of the cylinder to the other. Secured to the centre of the piston is the piston-rod, a circular bar of steel or iron which passes through the back cylinder cover and is made steam-tight by packing secured in a recess in the cover called the "stuffing-box." Perhaps one of the most familiar forms of cylinder is illustrated by an ordinary syringe. The "sucker" is the piston, and the rod to which the handle is attached is the piston-rod, the end of the barrel of the syringe through which the rod passes representing the cylinder cover. Instead of the piston being actuated by the handle or piston-rod, as in the syringe, it is, in the steam-engine, made to move by the introduction of steam into the cylinder. The steam being admitted at one end of the cylinder forces the piston to the other end, and is then exhausted or let out through the same passage through which it entered. At the same time steam is admitted at the opposite end of the cylinder and forces the piston back again. This process of forcing the piston backwards and forwards is indefinitely repeated so long as the engine is at work, and thus the motive power is communicated to the mechanism of the engine. It will be observed that the movement of the piston in the cylinder is in a straight line, and before the power thus developed can be practically applied, the backwards and forwards straight line movement (called a reciprocating rectilineal motion) of the piston must be converted into the rotary movement of the wheels. For this purpose the connecting-rod and crank are employed. The former is a rod coupled at one end to the piston-rod, and at the other to the crank. The latter is an arm projecting from the axle of the driving-wheel. This arm is at right angles to the axle, and upon it is a pin called the "crank-pin," which is parallel with the axle, and forms a journal or bearing surface upon which the end of the connecting-rod works. The length between the centres of the arm is called the "throw" of the crank, and must be just half the distance which the piston is required to travel in the cylinder. The crank-pin centre describes a circle round the outside of the driving axle, and the diameter of this circle, called the "stroke" of the engine, is equal to the whole distance travelled by the piston. The connecting-rod communicates the pressure on the piston to the crank-pin, and causes it to revolve in a circle round the driving axle. This in turn causes the axle itself to revolve, and consequently the wheels, which are secured at each end of it.

Again, to illustrate by familiar every-day examples, the lady's treadle sewing-machine and the apparatus of the itinerant knife-grinder may be quoted as examples of an up-and-down stroke converted into a rotary motion. The action of the locomotive connecting-rod is similar to that of the attachment between the treadle and driving-crank of the sewing-machine.

The next thing is to understand how the steam is made to enter and leave the cylinder at alternate ends at the commencement and end of each stroke of the piston. This is brought about by means of a valve called the slide valve, which moves to and fro over the openings or ports which form the steam passages connecting the steam-chest with the cylinder. The metal surface between these openings is made perfectly flat and true, and the valve, which is a hollow box, has projecting ends planed true to slide over this flat surface. The pressure of steam in the steam-chest at the back of the valve keeps the smooth faces of the slide valve and of the ports together.

In most valve motions the movement of the slide valves is controlled by the eccentrics, of which there are two, one for forward and the other for back gear.

The eccentric is a circular disc or sheaf, about $16\frac{1}{2}$ in. in diameter, fixed on to the driving axle. In this disc is a hole about $2\frac{1}{4}$ in. out of the centre. The driving axle fits into this hole, and the fact of its being out of the centre makes the sheaf project some $4\frac{1}{2}$ in. more from the centre of the driving axle on one side than on the other. This eccentricity of motion works the slide valve backwards and forwards over the ports. The motion of the eccentric sheaf itself is simply that of a crank with a very large crank-pin or journal. The travel of the valve being small in comparison with that of the piston, the crank required to produce that travel must have a much shorter throw than the main crank of the engine.

There are two cylinders for every locomotive engine, with a backward and forward valve gear for each. Each cylinder therefore requires two eccentrics or cranks for working the slide valve, one for the forward and one for the back gear, making four in all. It is manifest that it would be out of the question to so construct an axle as to have on it such a number of cranks. The eccentric, therefore, is a mechanical subterfuge for producing exactly the same action as the crank by a device fixed on the crank shaft without weakening it in any way. Fig. 29 represents a section of a crank shaft or driving axle enclosed by two halves of the eccentric. The outer circle or bearing surface of the eccentric acts simply as an enlarged crank-pin, the throw of which is from A to B. Supposing this throw to be $2\frac{1}{2}$ in., the travel of the valve would be 5 in. Owing to the large bearing surface of the eccentric, there is considerable loss of power attending their use, and for this reason various other forms of valve gear, in which the eccentric is dispensed with altogether, have of late years been introduced, but it is still more used than any other system, on account of its simplicity, convenience, ready action, and capability of being easily adjusted in its required position on the axle.

Eccentrics cannot be cast in one piece, as the cranks are forged on the axle, and they have therefore to be put on in two halves.

It will be noted that the duty of the eccentric is exactly the reverse of the crank, being to convert the rotary motion of the crank axle into the rectilineal reciprocating motion of the slide valve, thereby causing it to move backwards and forwards over the port holes, and so regulate the admission and egress of the steam to and from the cylinder. The movement of the eccentric sheaf on the axle is communicated to the valve by the intermediate mechanism of the eccentric-strap, eccentric-rod, and valve

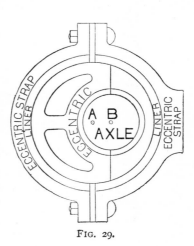

FIG. 29.

spindle. The eccentric-strap is made in two halves, which work on the bearing surface of the sheaf, being bolted together at top and bottom. The eccentric-rod is secured at one end to the eccentric-strap, and at the other is connected to the valve spindle or rod which is attached to the slide valve.

The general arrangement of all the parts named, and the shape of the valve and its position with regard to the ports, will be best understood by referring to the diagram (Fig. 30), which represents a sectional view of an imaginary steam-engine. The diagram illustrates the action of one simple engine with no reversing gear, imaginary because only the working parts are shown, all details being omitted so that the principle of the action of the engine can be easily seen without any accessory complications. The steam is admitted *to* the cylinder from the steam-chest (SC) above or outside the slide valve (SV), and passes out *from* the cylinder underneath the slide valve, the hollow part of which forms a connection from the steam port to the exhaust port when the valve is in certain positions.

It will be observed that the engine is travelling in the

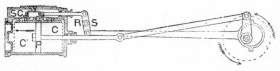

FIG. 30.

direction indicated by the arrow which, with a locomotive, would be going forwards, as the cylinders are in front of the driving-wheel.

The steam-chest (SC) is always full of steam direct from the boiler so long as the regulator is open. With the crank in the position shown, this steam is finding its way through the steam port (SP) into the cylinder (C), and forcing the piston (P) in the direction indicated by the arrow. The steam on the opposite side of the piston in the cylinder at C is escaping through the steam port (SP) through the hollow part of the valve (SV) into the exhaust port (EP), whence it passes to the exhaust pipe and away through the chimney into the atmosphere.

It will be observed that the slide valve covers this port against the steam in the steam-chest, so that the steam from the boiler is only in communication with the end (C) of the cylinder, and acting on one side of the piston only. As the piston proceeds in the direction of the arrows, the turning of the axle and consequent movement of the eccentric causes the valve to slide over the ports, and the steam port (SP) to gradually close, and (SP') to gradually open, the opening of the latter taking place when the piston has been forced by the steam to the end (C') of the cylinder. At this time the steam port (SP) is opened to the exhaust port, and the piston is forced back in the opposite direction by the steam entering the cylinder at SP'.

The amount of steam admitted to the cylinder and used by the engine is controlled by the slide valve, and the

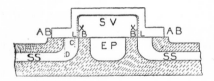

FIG. 31.

eccentric gear or "valve motion" controls the movement of the valve in the steam-chest.

Before describing the relation existing between the valve motion and the distribution of steam in the cylinder, it will be as well first to note how the construction of the valve itself affects the question.

Fig. 31 shows a section of a locomotive slide valve and ports with the valve at the centre of its stroke. SV is the slide valve; SS the steam passages or ports connecting the steam-chest with the cylinder; BB are the flat surfaces, called the "bridges," between the ports upon which the flat surface of the valve works; and EP is the exhaust port. It will be noticed that the inside edges of the valve are exactly in line with the inside edges of the steam ports, and the outside edges of the valve overlap or project beyond the outer edges of the ports. The inside edges being in line with the edges of the ports bring about this result, viz., that the moment the valve cuts off the exhaust from one end of the cylinder, it opens the other end of the cylinder to exhaust. Sometimes, however, the inner edges of the valve project beyond the inside edges of the ports, as shown by the lines XX. This causes the exhaust to take place later, as the valve has so much further to travel before the port is uncovered. It also causes the exhaust from the other side of the piston to be cut off sooner, as the edge of the valve covers the port before the valve has reached its central position. When the inside edges project in this way, the valve is said to have *inside lap*. The later release brought about by giving this inside lap causes a higher back pressure, and the earlier closing of the exhaust port from the same cause makes the remaining steam in the cylinder to be compressed before the end of the stroke, through the closing of the port cutting off the steam from the exhaust port.

This compression is called "cushioning," and it has a useful result, as it prevents strain on the working parts of the engine which would take place if the piston were forced right up to the end of its stroke without any check.

In engines where the valve has no inside lap (which is the case with locomotives), the cushioning is brought about by admitting steam to the cylinder just before the commencement of the stroke, that is, allowing the steam port to slightly open on the exhaust side of the piston just before the end of the stroke. This is called giving the slide valve "lead."

With some engines, but not with locomotives, the inner edges of the valve when at mid-stroke do not cover the edges of the exhaust ports, as shown by the lines LL. This

is called " negative lap " or inside clearance, and is used for
very high speed engines where it is necessary to give as early
a release as possible, and to keep the exhaust port open
during the whole of the stroke to give the steam as free an
exit as possible.

The distance (AB) which the edges of the slide valve
overlap the steam port at the outside edges is called the
" outside lap " of the valve.   The dotted line represents
the full opening of the port for the admission of steam
when the valve is at the end of its stroke.   The reason of
this distance being less than the width of the port, as it
frequently is, is that the same passage serves for the steam
to pass *to* and *from* the cylinder, and although this space is
sufficient for the admission of the steam, the whole width of
the port is necessary for the passage of the exhaust steam,
which should be got out of the cylinder as freely and quickly
as possible, to avoid what is called " back pressure."

The line D shows the amount that the valve is open at
the commencement of the stroke of the piston for the
admission of steam, which, as before stated, is called the
" lead."

The function of the valve motion is twofold, being to
regulate the amount and the direction of the steam
admitted to the cylinders as well as to reverse the engine.

When an engine is starting a train, the steam is allowed
to exert its full pressure upon the piston for about three-
quarters of the stroke before being cut off.   When speed is
attained the momentum of the train helps the engine, and
the valve gear is " notched up," which causes the cut-off to
take place earlier in the stroke, the elastic properties of the
steam admitted during the earlier part of the stroke being
sufficient to actuate the piston for the whole stroke.

The sectional diagrams on Plate I. illustrate this elastic or
expansive working, and also show the action of the steam at

various parts of the stroke, and the relative positions of the piston, crank, and slide valve.

The steam from the boiler enters the steam-chest (SC) through the steam pipe (SP). All the parts of the diagram coloured pink represent space filled with high-pressure steam in direct communication with the boiler. These diagrams must now be examined separately in the order in which they stand.

Fig. 1 shows the engine at the commencement of the stroke, the crank-pin (CP) is in the position in which it is nearest the cylinder, and the piston at the end of its travel in the cylinder. The valve (SV) has just slightly opened at L to give the lead, and steam is passing through the steam-port (SPA) to the end (A) of the cylinder. For convenience of reference, the left-hand end of the cylinder where the steam acts on the left side of the piston will be called A ; and the right-hand end, where the steam acts on the right side of the piston, will be called B. The space coloured blue shows the exhaust steam, and it will be noted that it is escaping from B, through the steam-port (SPB), into the hollow part of the slide valve, and thence to the exhaust port (EP), from whence it passes through the exhaust pipe into the atmosphere.

The steam at A forces the piston from left to right, and Fig. 2 must now be examined to see what is taking place when the piston has travelled to the position indicated by this figure. It will be seen that the piston has travelled about one-fourth of the length of the cylinder ; the crank has described a little more than one-eighth of a revolution, and the valve has completely uncovered the steam-port (SPA), so that the full pressure of steam is being delivered into the cylinder at A, and is acting upon the piston. The opposite port (SPB) is still open to the exhaust. The valve has now come to the end of the stroke, and commences to

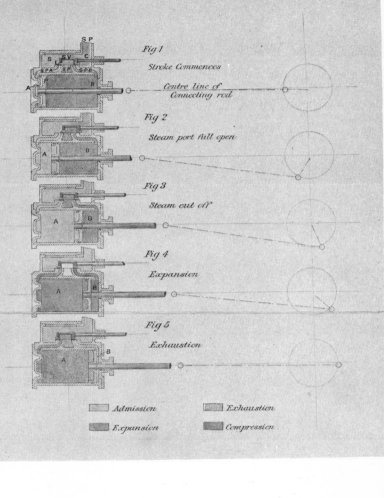

Fig 1

Stroke Commences

Centre line of
Connecting rod

Fig 2

Steam port full open

Fig 3

Steam cut off

Fig 4

Expansion

Fig 5

Exhaustion

Admission   Exhaustion

Expansion   Compression

travel back in the opposite direction, and gradually closes the port (SPA), as shown in Fig. 3. Up to this time steam has been finding its way through the port to A, and exerting its full pressure upon the piston, but now the direct supply is cut off, and the power necessary to complete the remainder of the stroke must be by the elastic property of the steam already in the cylinder at A. The piston has travelled about two-thirds of its stroke ; the exhaust port (SPB) is still open to the exhaust, and the crank has travelled between one-fourth and three-eighths of a revolution.

The distance the piston travels between Figs. 3 and 4 is, by the action of the steam, working expansively, and the grey colour in the latter figure shows the steam in this condition. The piston has now travelled about seven-eighths of its stroke, and the valve is at the centre of its travel, so that *both* the steam and exhaust ports are closed. As the piston finishes the stroke, the remainder of the exhaust steam, having no exit, is compressed at B, and thus cushioning takes place ; the orange colour shows the compressed or "cushioned" steam. Directly after the valve, still moving to the left, passes over its central position, the port (SPA) begins to open for the release of the steam from A, and by the time the piston gets to the end of the stroke (as shown in Fig. 5), this port is fully open to the exhaust, and SPB has just opened, giving the lead for the admission of the steam at B, to commence the return stroke of the piston. One stroke of the piston and half a revolution of the crank is now completed, and the process described again takes place in exactly the same way with the piston travelling in the opposite direction, and goes on with each backward and forward stroke of the piston so long as the regulator is open and the steam-chest supplied with steam from the boiler.

The various technical terms it has been necessary to use

in the foregoing description are enumerated below, and should be thoroughly understood to properly grasp the principles of the working of an engine.

Outside Lap. The amount by which the outside edges of the valve overlap the steam ports when the valve is at the middle of the stroke.

Inside Lap. The amount by which the inner edges of the valve overlap the inner edges of the steam ports when the valve is in the same position.

Lead. The amount of the opening of the steam port at the commencement of the stroke of the piston.

Travel. The distance the valve moves to and fro at each stroke of the piston. This is equal to twice the outside lap plus the lead or opening to steam, and also to twice the throw of the eccentric.

Point of admission. When the valve commences to open the port to admit steam from the steam-chest to the cylinder.

Point of cut-off. When the valve closes the port to stop the admission of steam from the steam-chest to the cylinder.

Point of release. When the inside edge of the valve opens the port to the exhaust for the steam to pass from the cylinder to the exhaust port.

Point of compression or cushioning. When the valve covers the port against the exhaust steam, causing the remainder of the steam on the exhaust side of the piston to "cushion" or be compressed in the end of the cylinder by the advancing piston.

The action of the eccentric gear or "valve motion" must now be more fully explained, to show how it causes the valve to travel backwards and forwards over the ports and regulate the steam in the manner that has been described.

If the throw of the eccentric be at right angles to the crank, when the piston is at the end of its stroke it is manifest that the slide valve will be exactly at the centre of *its* stroke, and it has been shown that when in this position the ports are both closed, and no steam can pass from the steam-chest into the cylinder.

It has also been shown that the valve at the commencement of the stroke of the piston must be slightly open to give the necessary lead.

It therefore follows that the eccentric must be secured on the axle with the throw slightly in advance of the rectangular position in relation to the crank in order to give the required opening of the port.

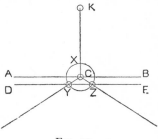

FIG. 32.

This advancement, viz., the number of degrees by which the eccentric is carried forward beyond the position at right angles to the crank, is termed the angular advance of the eccentric. In Fig. 32, the lines CY, CZ show the centre lines of the eccentrics, keyed on the shaft with the angular advance to give the necessary lead. CK is the centre line of the crank in a vertical position, the crank-pin being at K above the shaft.

The line AB passes through the centre of the crank axle at right angles to the crank.

The line DE is drawn parallel to AB at a distance below it, equal to the outside lap of the slide valve plus the required lead.

The circle XYZ is equal to the circumference of the

eccentric sheaf, the centre of which, in the diagram, coincides with the centre of the crank axle.

The line CY drawn from the centre C through the point Y, where the line CD cuts the eccentric circle, gives the centre line of the throw of the forward gear eccentric, and the line CZ the centre line of the back gear eccentric.

The lead being given at the commencement of the stroke, the valve precedes the movement of the main crank throughout the revolution, giving the cut-off, release, and compression at the proper points in the stroke.

The forward and back gear eccentrics are fitted to the

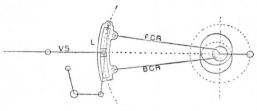

FIG. 33.

crank shaft side by side. The two ends of the eccentric-rods are coupled together by a slotted link, in which works a block connected to the valve-rod. Fig. 33 represents in diagram form the simplest form of link motion. The link (L) being lowered, the forward eccentric-rod (FGR) is placed in connection with the valve spindle and valve at VS, causing the engine to run in the forward direction. When the link is lifted, the eccentric-rod (BGR) is placed in connection with the valve, and a reverse motion obtained, the other eccentric being thrown out of gear.

The original idea of two eccentrics coupled by a link at the end of the eccentric-rod was by a simple arrangement to throw each one in turn in gear with the valve, so as to enable the engine to work backwards and forwards as

required, and more than this simple result was not con-
templated in the original discovery of the link. It was
subsequently however found that by means of this link,
the cut-off of the steam could be so regulated that the
power could be adjusted to the work required.

Now it is obvious that when the link is placed in such a
position that the centre of it is opposite to the valve
spindle, as shown in the diagram, neither of the eccentrics
are in gear, and the valve remains in its neutral position
without uncovering the ports. By moving the link into any
intermediate position, up or down, between the centre of
the link and the end of the eccentric, the valve is actuated
by the eccentric-rod nearest to the valve spindle.

The eccentric, however, not being in line with the valve
spindle, and the link acting so to speak as a lever, the
fulcrum of which is the end of the eccentric-rod not in
gear, the valve has a shorter travel than if it were in direct
line with the eccentric.

This travel is lengthened or shortened according to the
position of the valve spindle with regard to the eccentric-
rod. The nearer it is to the rod the longer the travel of
the valve, and the nearer to the centre of the link, the
shorter the travel. Thus we have an apparatus for controlling the travel of the valve and regulating the point of
cut-off of the steam to the cylinder.

Upon the foot-plate of the engine is a lever working in a
quadrant. When the lever is pushed right over to the
extreme end of the quadrant in one direction, the eccentric-
rod is opposite to the valve spindle and the full travel of
the valve obtained. When it is required to shorten the
travel of the valve and cause the engine to work expansively,
the lever is pulled towards the centre of the quadrant,
and can be fixed in any position required by notches in
the quadrant and a catch on the lever. Pulling the lever

towards the centre of the quadrant, or "notching up" as it is called, brings the valve spindle towards the centre of the link, reducing the travel of the valve, cutting the steam off earlier in the stroke, and thus causing the engine to use less steam and work more economically.

When the lever on the foot-plate is pulled beyond the central position in the quadrant, the back gear eccentric is put in communication with the valve, and when pulled right over to the opposite end of the quadrant, the engine is in full back gear, that is to say, will move backwards on steam being admitted to the cylinder.

With every locomotive engine there are two sets of link motions, one for each cylinder. Both are controlled by the same lever from the foot-plate and work simultaneously, and thus a complete reversing gear and apparatus for expansive working is provided.

The whole question of valve motion will be treated of more elaborately in the next chapter, but it is hoped that this elementary description will have enabled the reader to grasp some idea of its general principles and relation to the distribution of steam in the cylinders.

CHAPTER IV.

In the foregoing chapter the elementary principles of the action of the steam in the cylinders and steam-chest of a locomotive have been described in as simple a manner as possible with a view to explaining to the uninitiated reader how the power of the steam generated in the boiler is brought to bear upon the mechanism of the engine, causing the wheels to revolve, and thus impart motion. This is the A B C of all things appertaining to the steam-engine, and the chapter has probably been "skipped" by the reader whose walk in life has in any measure brought him into contact with some elementary form of engineering. These elementary details have, however, the author hopes, not been entirely devoid of interest to those who may scan these pages with the object of obtaining some general information upon the subject of locomotive engines regarded from a non-professional point of view, seeing what an important part this machine plays in the history of nations, and in the individual life of every member of any civilized community. Such a person may perhaps find it more to his taste to skip this chapter, for in it the author proposes to review historically a very important feature in locomotives which is almost entirely of a technical character.

Long before the introduction of steam for locomotive

purposes was ever thought of, its application to cause a wheel to revolve, and so to communicate power to various kinds of machinery, was an accomplished fact. But that fact being accomplished was in itself sufficient for most purposes to which the power was applied. When its application to locomotives came to be considered, other points in connection therewith arose, and problems hitherto too unimportant or unnecessary to consider had to be grappled with and solved.

A locomotive engine, to be of any practical value, must be able to run backwards or forwards ; moreover, greater power has to be exerted in starting a load than in keeping it moving afterwards, and it became apparent that a locomotive engine must be capable of exerting its powers both as a slow speed engine in starting a heavy load from a state of rest, and as a high speed engine in producing and maintaining a high number of revolutions per minute after the initial slow speed power has been exerted in starting a train.

To do this, many different forms of reversing gear and valve motion for working the steam expansively have been contrived, and the various developments of these schemes have a very important bearing upon the history of the locomotive, and its ability to fulfil the tasks now imposed upon it.

The functions of the valve motion may be briefly stated as follows—

To regulate the movement of the slide valves which control the admission and egress of the steam to and from the cylinders.

To reverse the engine, that is, to cause it to run backwards or forwards as desired.

To enable the engine to be worked *expansively ;* that is, to cut off the steam at any required portion of the stroke of the piston, so that the amount of steam supplied to the engine may be in proportion to the work to be done.

The action of the slide valve having been already described, it is now proposed to review historically the various devices which from time to time have been introduced by engineers for producing the required variations of movement of the valves in the steam-chest.

The link motion, as now almost universally used, like all other great inventions, has been of gradual development, and is the product of the minds of many thinking men, whose attention has been given to the matter. All these different ideas, however, tended in the same direction, which was to produce an apparatus perfect in its design, and capable of fulfilling satisfactorily the important part the valve gear plays in the work of a locomotive engine.

In the early engines of Trevithick steam admission to the cylinders was regulated by a four-way cock automatically actuated by means of a rod and tappet.

The arrangement of the cam and ring introduced in **1820** may be considered the precursor of the eccentric motion for valves which was introduced a little later, and which was a great improvement on the earlier plan and better adapted for the higher speeds at which locomotive engineers at once began to aim.

Mr. Wood, of the Killingworth Engine Works, used a valve gear having a loose eccentric and fixed stop, which has been thus described.

" Fixed upon and revolving with the axle was a lever or crank, having at its end a stud, which slid freely in a concentric groove cut in the eccentric. As the axle turned, the stud found its way to one end of the groove, and determined the position of the eccentric for forward or back gear."

This arrangement is practically the same as that adopted by Mr. Webb in his " Teutonic " class of compounds in the single eccentric reversing motion for the low-pressure valve. This gear is illustrated in Fig. 48.

In **1818** Carmichael of Dundee, in his steam ferries, introduced an arrangement with arms at the end of the eccentric-rods. These arms projected on either side to engage with a rocking-shaft, and this arrangement was afterwards modified and used for locomotive engines by Cavé of Paris in **1835**.

In **1830** Melling, the locomotive superintendent of the Liverpool and Manchester Railway, introduced the gear illustrated in Fig. 34, by which the valve-rod received its

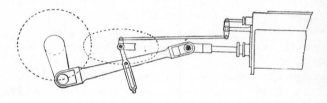

FIG. 34.

motion from a pin fixed to the connecting-rods, working in a slotted lever ; but it was not generally adopted.

Fig. 35 shows the valve-gear brought out by Hawthorn in **1838**. The connecting-rod had a stud (S), on which was fixed a block (B) working in the slotted lever (SL). This lever had arms (A A) at right angles by which the motion was communicated to the rocking-shaft (RS), and thence to the valve-rod (VR). It was rather a complicated arrangement, but is said to have given some fairly good results. These three motions—viz. " Carmichael's," " Melling's," and " Hawthorn's "—may be considered the parent gears of the present Radial type, which has come so much into use during recent years, chiefly through the instrumentality of Mr. David Joy.

His radial motion, brought out in **1879**, was successfully

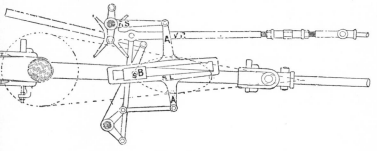

FIG. 35.

adopted first of all by Mr. Webb, and subsequently by other locomotive engineers. This motion will be fully described later on.

Fig. 36 illustrates an arrangement of gab motion used

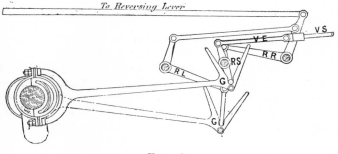

FIG. 36.

on engines constructed by Messrs. Stephenson & Co. prior to **1838**. In this case, four eccentrics were used; it was a very similar gear to the motion brought out by Messrs. Sharp & Roberts in **1842**. The gab ends of the forward and back-gear eccentrics were in turn raised to the rocking-shaft lever by a combination of levers, the action of which will easily be seen on referring to the sketch.

G G, gabs; RS, rocking-shaft; RL, reversing levers; VE, valve link; VS, valve spindle. In Messrs. Sharp & Roberts' arrangement, one gab was raised and the other lowered into position.

Fig. 37 illustrates the improved arrangement of gab motion introduced in **1840** by Mr. Robert Stephenson;

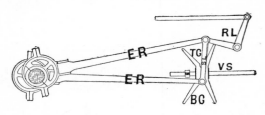

FIG. 37.

this was a much simpler gear than any previously in use, and constitutes one of the most decided steps in the direction of the last and most simple of all, the link motion.

It will be seen that a top and bottom gab (TG and BG), forming a kind of cross-head, were fixed in the end of the valve spindle (VS). The ends of the eccentric-rods (ER) were connected by a straight-link (SL), and were moved up down by the reversing lever (RL) in the same way as the eccentric-rod ends coupled together by the slotted link are moved in the modern link motion.

In **1839** Mr. John Grey introduced his variable expansion gear. It was applied to the " Cyclops," one of the Liverpool and Manchester Railway engines, and is said to have

effected a saving of fuel estimated at 12 per cent. Moreover, it allowed a large variation in the lead. The
exceeding complexity of the arrangement was however
against it, and although it was again introduced on the
London and Brighton Railway in **1846**, it was ultimately
abandoned in favour of the link motion.

In September **1839**, Dodds of Rotherham and Owen of
York introduced and patented the " wedge motion," which
is illustrated in Fig. 38. This arrangement consisted of
two eccentrics, one for each valve, mounted on the axle,
and prevented from sliding laterally by means of keys or

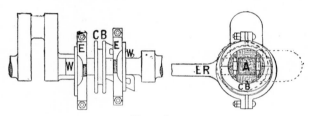

FIG. 38.

guides attached to it. The wedges (W) were allowed to
slide laterally upon the axle (A), which was square on the
part over which the wedges worked. Attached to the
wedges was a clutch-box (CB), by whose action on the
wedges the eccentrics (EE) were forced into the required
position for forward and back gear. The inventors proposed to alter the movement or travel of the valve, but
made no arrangement for expansive working. By a subsequent and more practical arrangement of the late Mr.
Henry Dubs of Glasgow, this was effected. The illustration
shows the motion as used on No. 55 saddle tank-engine on
the North Stafford Railway from **1871** to **1880**.

Dodds was followed by Fenton of Leeds, who, in **1842**,

introduced a combination of link motion and sliding eccentrics, which were attached to a collar. This collar moved laterally by means of a clutch-box and ring. The eccentrics were guided into the various positions for forward and back gear, and for different degrees of cut-off, by means of a spiral feather on the shaft.

In February **1842** Crampton patented an arrangement of variable valve motion, in which the single fixed eccentric was proposed; it was, however, rather a complicated gear,

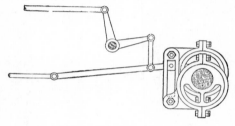

FIG. 39.

and does not play a very important part in the history of the valve motion.

We should here notice the arrangement proposed by Williams of Newcastle in **1842**, as illustrated in Fig. 39. It was undeniably ingenious, and shows that the inventor had got the idea of the slotted link in much the same form as now used; but as Williams did not employ eccentric-rods to couple up to his link, the contrivance proved impracticable; indeed, it was a mechanical impossibility.

Fig. 40 illustrates the famous link motion invented by Howe of Newcastle, and applied by Messrs. Stephenson & Co. in **1843**. This invention stands, in relation to the various valve-gears used on locomotives, much in the same position as that in which the "Rocket" stands with regard to locomotive engines. As the "Rocket" solved the problem of the possibility of the practical use of steam-power for land-carriages, so did the link motion solve the problem of working the steam expansively. Its simplicity of construction and the favourable results at once obtained have never yet been to any very great extent improved upon, and in spite of the multitudinous arrangements of link or radial motion since introduced, it still maintains its supremacy, and is the most extensively used of all valve-

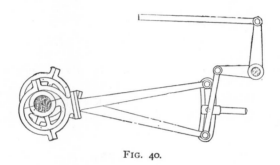

FIG. 40.

gears. The details are described in the illustration of the more modern application of this type of motion.

Fig. 41 illustrates the Gooch or stationary link motion which was brought out by the late Sir Daniel Gooch, locomotive superintendent of the Great Western Railway, and used on engines of the "Great Britain" and "Pyracmon" class in the year **1848**. In this motion it will be seen that the expansion-link (EL), the concave side of which is towards the valve spindle, is hung from the bracket (B) by the swing-link (SL). The change in the position of the valve-link (VL) and die-block (D) is effected by the reversing-shaft (RS), operated from the foot-plate. The link (VL) is raised or lowered to alter the grade of expansion or to reverse the engine as required. This motion was used by Mr. McConnell on various types of engines

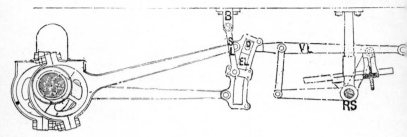

FIG. 41.

constructed by him for the London and North-Western Railway.

In **1855** Mr. Alexander Allan, locomotive superintendent of the Scottish Central Railway at Perth, invented and

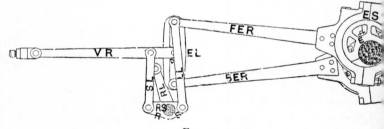

FIG. 42.

patented the straight-link motion (illustrated in Fig. 42). In the earlier arrangements he brought out, Mr. Allan used a "box"-link, but subsequently adopted an open link which worked in the forked end of the valve-rod. The link here slides upon a die-block, which is kept in position by a pin through the fork end. Mr. Allan's arrangement may be considered a combination of the shifting and stationary link motions, a simultaneous and contrary movement being given to the eccentric-rods and link, and to the valve connecting-rod, by levers working on opposite sides of the reversing-shaft. This double movement necessitated the use of a straight-link instead of the usual form of curved-link. In reversing it will be seen that part of the action is produced by the up-and-down movement of the straight expansion-link (EL), and part by the valve-rod (VR) and die-block (D) moving in the opposite direction and towards it. The combination of levers is very simple, and can be easily understood from the sketch. With the short fixed levers the reversing-shaft motion round its own axis is less, and the reversing-lever can thus be proportionally lengthened and a large increase of power obtained, generally three times that of the ordinary motion. The advantage of this is obvious, as the gearing can more easily be moved to and fixed in the required position, and the expansion regulated with the full steam-pressure on the slide-valves. Balance-weights are dispensed with ; the links and eccentrics being coupled to the short lever (S) and the valve-rod to the longer lever (RS), they balance each other. This gearing requires less room and allows the boiler to be placed lower than with the shifting link motion. The angular position of the valve-rod is less, and the valve-rod moves during reversal through one-half of the space traversed in the fixed link motion. It is accurate in its working as regards lead and equal distribution of steam in both sides of the cylinder in back and forward gear. The only fixed portion is the reversing-shaft, which may be above or below the link as most convenient. The illustration shows Allan's motion as applied by Mr. Webb to the express passenger and other locomotives on the London and North-Western Railway.

The valve-rod (VR) is supported by the short suspension-links (SL), which are coupled at one end to the long lever (R) of the reversing-shaft. The short lever (S) is coupled to the long suspension or lifting-links. These latter are attached at the other end to the forward eccentric-rod (FER), and to the top of the expansion-link (EL); the back gear eccentric-rod (BER) being attached to the other end of the expansion-link. E,E are the eccentrics of cast-iron, the eccentric-rods being of Bessemer steel, fastened by screws and riveted to the cast-iron eccentric-straps (ES). D is the motion-block or die-block, which slides in the straight-link, and is fixed to the end of the valve-rod (VR) by means of a pin. RL is the reversing-shaft arm (or lever) which is operated from the foot-plate by the reversing-screw, as used by Mr. Webb, or by any other suitable arrangement.

The essentials of a good valve-gear may be here stated. It is necessary that when employed to work expansively, it should admit steam *freely* to the cylinder during that period of the stroke when the admission is required, the ports being properly uncovered during the whole time of admission to allow the free passage of the steam to the cylinders, and so prevent wire-drawing or gradual reduction of pressure.

The cut-off should take place as quickly as possible, and the expansion should be as long as is consistent with satisfactory working. The release of steam from one side of the piston, and the compression of the remainder in the cylinder on the other side, should take place at such a point in the stroke as to avoid unnecessary back pressure; and yet provide sufficient resistance to balance the pressure of steam equally at both sides of the piston at the end of the stroke. By this means the momentum of the crank is allowed to overbalance the dead point at the end of the stroke. The pre-admission should be just sufficient to allow the steam to gain its full pressure on the piston at the commencement of the stroke.

Fig. 43 illustrates the arrangement of curved Howe-Stephenson shifting link motion as applied by Mr. Ramsbottom, and adopted on the London and North-Western Railway for many years. This same type of motion, varying slightly in accordance with the ideas of various locomotive superintendents, is also used on many railway lines throughout the world.

FE and BE are the forward and back-gear eccentrics;

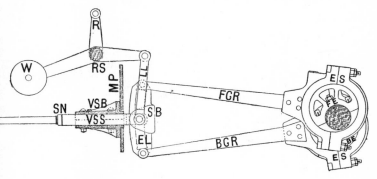

FIG. 43.

ES the eccentric-straps of cast-iron, and FGR and BGR the eccentric-rods by which the motion of the eccentrics is transmitted to the curved expansion-link (EL).

The latter has a suspension-pin and bracket (SB) attached to one side, connected by the lifting-link (LL) to the weighbar or reversing-shaft (RS), upon which is the balance-weight (W). VSS is the valve spindle, to which is attached a die-block sliding in the curved-link. VSB is the valve spindle slide-box made in two halves, faced inside with white metal, and bolted to the motion plate (MP). In some arrangements of gearing this plate also carries the reversing-shaft, but in the example illustrated the shaft is supported by brackets fixed to the main frames of the engine. The motion is reversed from the foot-plate by a screw arrangement connected by a rod to the lever (R) on the shaft (RS). On the end of the valve spindle slide is a screw and nut (SN), which forms the attachment to the valve-rod, and at the same time adjusts it to the required length.

Fig. 44 illustrates a type of this same motion in use on the

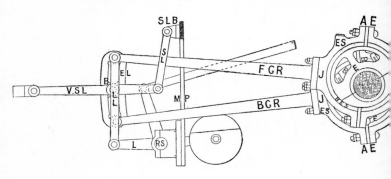

FIG. 44.

North Stafford Railway, in which there are some differences of detail. It will be seen that the curved expansion-link (EL) is the same as that originally adopted in the Howe-Stephenson gear. The eccentric-rods are coupled to the ends of the centre line of the link. The top of the expansion-link (EL) is coupled to the forward gear eccentric-rod (FGR), and to the top end of the lifting-link (LL) at the same point. The bottom end of the lifting-link is coupled to the lever (L) on the reversing-shaft (RS); the latter is carried on brackets attached to the motion plate (MP). The swing-links (SL) are attached at one end to the bracket (SLB), and at the other to the end of the valve spindle-link (VSL). This link is slotted at the end, and the expansion-link works up and down in the slot, sliding on the block (B). It will be seen that the eccentric-straps (ES) are attached to the eccentric-rods (FGR and BGR) by studs and nuts, and in setting the valves the adjustment is effected by means of liners at the joints (J). The eccentric-straps are of wrought-iron, having brass liners (BES) to form the bearing surface on the eccentrics (E), and liners (AE) to adjust for wear.

The wedge motion has already been described, but next in chronological order comes a type of this motion introduced in **1871** by Mr. T. W. Dodds, engineer of permanent way on the North Stafford Railway. From the illustration (Fig. 45) it will be seen that the crank axle (CA) is planed flat on two sides, perpendicular with the centre line of the right-hand crank. On these planed surfaces the wedges (W,W), which formed part of the clutch- or reversing-box (CB), were allowed to work in a lateral direction, being forced through the eccentric (E), thereby bringing it into the relative positions for forward and back-gear. The eccentric (E) was prevented from moving laterally on the axle by the keys (K,K), which were fixed on the shaft in grooves and pinned down. These keys acted as guides for the eccentric in its transverse movement across the shaft, which was due to the action of the wedges.

Both eccentric-straps worked on the one eccentric; the right-hand eccentric rod (RER) was coupled direct to the valve spindle-slide. The left was a short rod (SER), the end of which was connected to the arm (X) of the bell crank lever (BCL) on the balance-shaft (BS). The other lever arm (Y) was coupled to the left-hand valve spindle-slide by the coupling-rod (VCR). The balance-shaft (BS) was carried at either end by an arrangement of compensating levers (CR) attached to brackets (BB). The back lever on each side (BCR) was

connected from A to the axle-box, thereby keeping the shaft
(BS) in line with the crank axle, and preventing undue strain

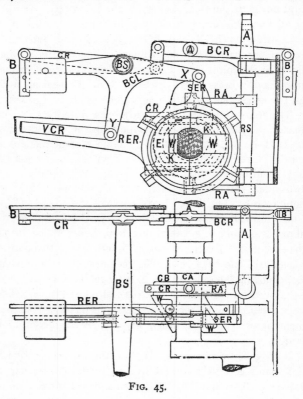

FIG. 45.

on the gear.   The pillar or reversing-shaft (RS) carried two
arms (RA), which were connected to the clutch-ring (CR).
The reversing-shaft was operated from the foot-plate by a
screw reversing-gear, which was connected to it by a rod
to the arm (A).

Theoretically, perhaps, the wedge motion is as nearly perfect as can be imagined. One eccentric does for forward and back-gear, and by simply sliding it up and down on the parallel sides of two wedges the eccentric-sheaf can be fixed in any required position for forward or back-gear, or expansive working. In practice, however, one great drawback manifested itself in the tendency of the wedges to stick, and so prevent the driver from manipulating the gear. An accident attributable to this cause took place on the North Stafford Railway, and the motion, which had never had the approval of Mr. Angus, the locomotive superintendent, was then finally condemned by the Government inspector, so that its introduction proved a costly experiment to the company.

We now come to an important point in the history of the valve motion, which belongs to more modern times. In March **1879** Mr. David Joy brought out and patented the gear known as the "Joy" valve-gear. This arrangement entirely dispenses with the four eccentrics and rods of the link motion, the necessary movement being obtained from the connecting-rod. The construction of locomotives to meet the demands for increased speed and power has necessitated the employment of larger cylinders, which, owing to the impossibility of altering the distance between the main frames, prevents the valve-chest being placed between the cylinders.

Now the "Joy" motion allows the valve-chest to be placed either above or below them, and also permits of larger bearing surfaces being used for the driving-axles. Among the advantages claimed for this motion are—

The number of working parts reduced ;

The weight of the gearing reduced ;

All the strains are central.

Its operation is more correct and reliable, and gives the

nearest approach to a theoretically correct distribution of
steam in the cylinder.   Mr. Webb saw the benefits likely to
be derived from this motion, and he was one of the first to
practically apply it to locomotive engines.   He first fitted it
to a number of six-wheels coupled goods engines with 18 in.
cylinders with the most satisfactory results, and subsequently
to the compound engines built at Crewe.

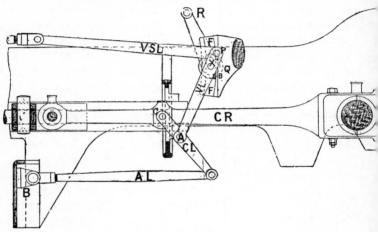

FIG. 46.

Fig. 46 shows the "Joy" valve-gear as adopted by Mr.
Webb for the low-pressure valve of a compound express
passenger engine.

Q is the quadrant-shaft, of cast-steel, carried by brackets
fixed to the frames; the quadrant guides or facings (FF) are
bolted to the shaft; working in the grooves of the quadrant
guides are brass slide-blocks (SB) carried by the valve lever
(VL).   At the point P the top joint of VL is attached to
the valve spindle-link (VSL), whilst the lower joint is attached
to the connecting-link (CL) at the point A.   The connect-

ing-link is coupled to the connecting-rod of the engine (CR) at C, and at the other end to the anchor-link (AL), which is attached at the other end at the bracket (B). This attachment is the only fixed point about the motion; the bracket is bolted to the guide-plate of the leading radial axle-box. It is interesting to notice that while the point (C) of the connecting-rod (to which the connecting-link is

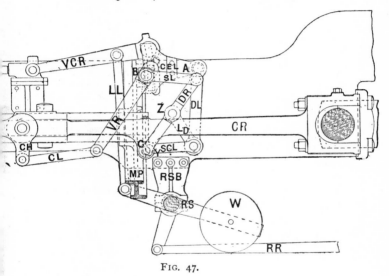

FIG. 47.

attached) describes an oval, the point (A) of the latter describes a flattened ellipse, thereby imparting an equal motion to the point (X). The motion is reversed by the lever (R), which is fixed to one end of the quadrant-shaft (Q). The direction of the engine and the travel of the valve is regulated by the position in which the quadrant-shaft is placed.

The valve motion, illustrated by Fig. 47, was invented and

patented in **1884** by the late Mr. Bryce Douglas, manager of the Naval Armaments Company, Barrow-in-Furness, and first applied to a locomotive by Mr. D. Drummond, locomotive superintendent of the Caledonian Railway, in **1886**, on an express passenger engine. It will be noticed that there are two attachments on the line of motion, viz., at C on the connecting-rod, and at CH on the cross-head. At this joint is coupled one end of the connecting-link (CL), the other end being coupled to the vibrating-rod (VR), which oscillates on fixed centres at the point B, where it is supported by brackets fixed to the motion-plate (MP).

Above these centres the rod (VR) carries a curved expansion-link (CEL), which has the usual sliding-block. To this block the valve spindle is connected by the valve connecting-rod (VCR), which is adjusted in position and supported by the lifting-links (LL). These links are coupled at the lower end to the reversing-shaft lever, at the opposite end of which is the balance-weight (W). The reversing-shaft (RS) is carried by means of brackets (RSB) fixed to the main frames. RR is the reversing-rod actuated from the foot-plate.

In addition to the to-and-fro motion of the vibrating-rod (VR), the expansion-link (CEL) has an oscillating motion imparted to it by coupling the arm (A) at the back to the driving-link (DL). The lower end of the latter has two attachments; first by the short connecting-link (SCL) to the fixed point (Y) on the motion-plate, and secondly by the connecting-link (LD) to the point (L) on the driving-link (DR). The lower end of this rod is coupled at the point C to the connecting-rod (CR), whilst its upper end is attached to the supporting-link (SL), by which it is connected to the bracket (B). This valve motion is said not to have worked satisfactorily, and it was subsequently discarded for the ordinary link motion.

Fig. 48 illustrates an arrangement of loose eccentric used

for the low-pressure valve by Mr. Webb in some of his
latest compounds.   With these engines the low-pressure
cylinder is always worked in full back or forward gear as the
case may be.   The two high-pressure cylinders (to which
either the Joy valve-gear or link motion may be fitted) are
powerful enough to give the engine the initial start.   The
loose eccentric, which is an exceedingly economical and
simple arrangement, answers very well, and altogether dispenses with the intricacies of a valve motion for the low-

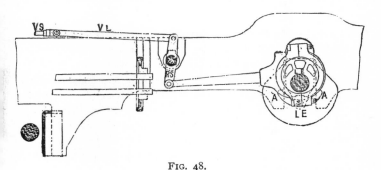

FIG. 48.

pressure cylinder.   As the engine starts the axle revolves
without the eccentric moving until its proper position is
reached for forward or back-gear, as the case may be.   LE is
the loose eccentric, in which is a slot terminating at either
side at the points AA.   S is a stop fixed on the axle.   This
stop works freely in the slot between the ends AA.   When
the axle has revolved far enough for the stop to come in
contact with A, the eccentric begins to move, and actuates
the valve.   The motion is transmitted through the rocking-
shaft (RS) to the valve spindle (VS), through the link (VL).

CHAPTER V.

THE BOILER.

LIKE every other steam-engine, a locomotive consists of the machinery of the engine, and the boiler for generating the steam which supplies the motive-power.

With stationary engines, the engine may be a considerable distance away from the boiler, and the general design of each may be worked out to suit the place in which it is to be fixed; or the engineer, in many cases, may have *carte blanche* to carry out his own ideas in the matter of design, the place where his engine is to be fixed being specially built to accommodate it.

It is therefore easily seen that the designer of locomotives is restricted in many ways that have not to be considered at all by the builder of stationary engines. Among these considerations are the following—

Height.—No part of a locomotive can be more than 13 ft. 6 in. above rail level, and that maximum must only be reached just above the centre of the space between the rails.

Width.—Its greatest width must not exceed about 8 ft. 6 in.

Length.—The wheel-base, that is, the distance from the centre of the front pair of wheels to the centre of the rear pair of wheels, must be so constructed that the engine may be able to travel round curves without strain, and without any danger of its leaving the rails.

Weight.—The weight must be correctly distributed, it should not exceed about eighteen tons on any one pair of wheels, and the centre of gravity must not be too high, or the engine would be top-heavy, and unsafe for running at high speeds.

There are many other such restrictions ; and when it is remembered that all the complicated details of a modern high-pressure or compound engine, capable of exerting something like 1400 horse-power, together with a powerful boiler for maintaining steam at a uniform pressure and driving that machinery, have to be compressed in such a limited space, and that they have to be specially constructed to stand the wear and tear of travelling over a metal road at upwards of sixty miles an hour, it will be recognized that the design, material, and workmanship of a locomotive engine must all be the most perfect possible of their kind.

Generally speaking, the boiler of a locomotive may be said to consist of four principal parts—

1. *The Barrel;* that is, the cylindrical part extending from the fire-box to the smoke-box.

2. *The Fire-box Shell,* or casing, adjoining the barrel at one end, and rectangular in shape except at the top, where it is a continuation of the upper half of the barrel. The bottom part extends below the barrel, and is joined to the lower half of the barrel by the shoulder-plate.

3. *The Fire-box,* a square chamber inside the fire-box shell, with four walls and a roof, having an open space at the bottom for the fire-grate.

4. *The Tubes,* a number of small cylindrical flues extending through the barrel for conveying the gases generated by the fire to the smoke-box and chimney.

Fig. 49 is an outline section through a locomotive boiler, and shows the position of the fire-box and tubes.

FB is the fire-box, TT the tubes, of which only two are shown so that they can be more clearly defined. The space between them is in reality filled with tubes, the number being usually about 200. The grate is at G, the fire-door at FD. The shaded part shows the water space, the steam space being above the water at SS.

The inside surface of the tubes and the fire-box plates

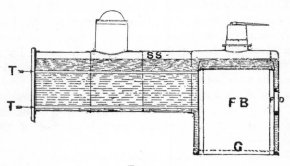

FIG. 49.

comes directly into contact with the flames of the fire, and is called the *heating-surface*. It is absolutely necessary that these plates and the tubes should (as shown in the diagram) be always surrounded by water when there is a fire in the fire-box. The space between the walls of the fire-box and the fire-box shell, and round the outside of the tubes, is called the *water space*.

It may be here stated that the outer plates, namely, those forming the barrel and the fire-box shell, are always made either of the best Yorkshire iron or of mild steel, while the fire-box plates are almost invariably copper, on account of its high conductivity for heat, and its ability to stand alternate expansion and contraction from heat and cold without cracking.

Since Bessemer steel has attained its present state of perfection, making it available for boiler plates, some enterprising engineers have tried to use it also for fire-box plates in locomotives. A measure of success has attended these experiments, but the general result has been to demonstrate that the very best copper that can be procured is far superior to any other metal for the purpose.

The temperature in a locomotive fire-box varies to a great extent, the variations at times being very sudden and covering a great range. At one moment an engine is dragging a heavy train at a high speed with the fire urged by a fierce blast and fed by a strong draught from below. Under such conditions the furnace is developing the maximum heat it is capable of producing. The next moment steam is shut off and the blast ceases, the damper is shut and there is no draught from below, all possible means being used to check the heat and prevent the generation of steam not then required for working the engine. Steel fire-box plates will not stand such sudden strains, and although they are much cheaper than copper in the first instance, the enduring powers of the latter under the conditions described, and its superiority as a conductor of heat, have proved it again and again to be the most economical in the long run. Steel has come very much to the front in recent years for the outer plates of locomotive boilers, although many engineers still prefer to use the best Yorkshire iron. Mr. Webb has been a great pioneer in the introduction of steel, and to show the important part it now plays in the construction of locomotive boilers, the following quotation is given from a speech he made to the Institution of Naval Architects in 1886.

Speaking of the manufacture of steel boiler plates at Crewe, he said—" Since commencing to make steel plates, we have made in the works 2752 locomotive boilers, working at pressures varying from 120 to 180 lbs. on the square inch. We have also made 230 stationary and marine boilers for ourselves, and of all the material used, not a single plate has ever failed."

The tubes are usually made of brass, although copper, steel, and iron all have their advocates as being suitable for the purpose. Of course the two latter have the recommendation of being much cheaper than brass or copper, and on some railways they have been successfully used. However, it is generally conceded by the majority of locomotive engineers that in the long run brass tubes prove the most economical and satisfactory.

The usual thickness of the boiler plates and tubes is as follows, varying slightly under certain conditions—

Steel plates, barrel and fire-box shell, $\frac{1}{2}$ in. when pressure exceeds 140 lbs. per square inch.

Yorkshire iron, barrel and fire-box shell, $\frac{9}{16}$ in.

Steel plates, barrel and fire-box shell, $\frac{13}{32}$ in. when pressure is less than 140 lbs. per square inch.

Copper plates, fire-box, exclusive of tube-plate, $\frac{1}{2}$ in.

    ,,   ,,   ,,   tube-plate, $\frac{7}{8}$ in.

Tubes, 10 W. G. (wire gauge).

Tubes external, diameter from $1\frac{1}{2}$ in. to $1\frac{7}{8}$ in.

As already stated, this book does not profess to be a scientific work; its purpose being more to give the reader, who may not feel disposed to dive into figures and calculations, some information about locomotives in a condensed and intelligible form. It is therefore not intended to mathematically consider the various strains to which boiler plates are subjected, nor to analyze scientifically the strength and composition of the materials used in boiler construction. The writer will, in this chapter, simply endeavour to set forth some part of the general modern practice in respect to locomotive boilers. He may be pardoned if in this and other matters he refers more especially to that which obtains on the London and North-Western Railway, with which his experience is connected, and which may be considered not only one of the foremost lines in the kingdom at the present day, but one of the oldest in existence. The engineers on this line have benefited by the intricate calculations and experiments made by the many eminent men who have been connected with the undertaking, since George Stephenson's "Rocket," the first locomotive with a multitubular boiler, ran on what is now a part of the London and North-Western Railway.

It may first be premised that it is very essential for all plates used in boiler-making to be of the very best quality. They have to pass through various processes which inferior plates cannot undergo without probable injury and deterioration. Among these processes are the following—

Flanging.—Turning the edge over at right angles to the rest of the plate, to form a surface to rivet another plate to.

Dishing.—Working the plate into any other required form to make a joint with another plate.

Punching.—Stamping holes in the plate for the reception of the rivets.

Rolling.—Putting the plate through a roller-mill and bending it into a circular form, such as is required for the plates in the barrel of the boiler.

The last two operations are performed when the plates are cold.

Fig. 50 shows a section through the back plates of the fire-box and fire-box shell of one of Mr. Webb's boilers, with *flanges* at FF, to which the top plates of the fire-box shell and fire-box are riveted; holes at H, punched for the rivets fixing the side plates and the plates *dished* at D, to form a circular orifice called the fire-hole, through which the fuel is put on the fire.

Until the introduction of soft mild steel, wrought-iron was

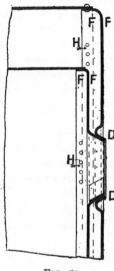

the only metal possessing the necessary tenacity, toughness, and ductility for undergoing these operations, as well as the power of resisting sudden strains and alternations of temperature.

Steel has a much higher tensile strength than iron, and for that reason steel boilers may be made of thinner plates, and accordingly much lighter. Good mild steel also possesses a superior ductility to wrought-iron, and therefore is more suitable for flanging. On the other hand, it requires greater care in heating, and in the regulation of the temperature at which it is worked. Also it must always be annealed after being

Fig. 50.   punched.

In flanging steel plates, the whole operation should if possible be performed in one heat ; this is done at Crewe by means of a powerful hydraulic press, with dies for all the different forms of plates required. As the machine shapes each plate in a few seconds and performs the operation with perfect accuracy, this method is far superior to the old system of doing the work with sledge-hammers, which necessitated each plate being heated a great number of times. Indeed, there is no doubt that the success achieved by Mr. Webb with his steel boilers is in a measure due to the superior appliances he has introduced at Crewe for the treatment of the plates.

The tensile strength of the various materials used for making boiler plates is here given—

Ordinary Wrought-iron.—Twenty-one tons per square inch along the grain, and eighteen tons per square inch across.

Best Yorkshire or Low Moor Iron.—Twenty-four tons along the grain, and twenty-two tons across.

Steel.—Twenty-six to thirty-two tons per square inch.

The different plates composing a locomotive boiler are fastened together by rivets. The rivet-holes in the plates are brought opposite each other, and the rivet, which is first made white-hot, is put into the hole as shown in Fig. 51. The head (H) is held firmly up against the plate (P), and the end of the rivet is then hammered or pressed by hydraulic pressure so as to form another head (H') pressing on the plate (P'), as shown in Fig. 52.

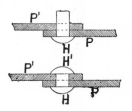

FIGS. 51, 52.

There are two systems of riveted joints: (1) *Lap Joints*, and (2) *Butt Joints*. The different kinds of "lap" and "butt" joints are shown in Diagram A, and are given in the order of their relative strength.

(1) Single lap.
(2) Double lap.
(3) Single butt, one strip.
(4) Double butt, one strip.
(5) Single butt, two strips.
(6) Double butt, two strips.

It will be observed from the diagrams that in the case of double riveted joints the rivets are placed zig-zag, the reason being that the joint made is tighter than if the rivets were immediately opposite each other. When placed in the latter position (as shown in Fig. 7), the joint is called a

" chain riveted butt-joint." In actual strength this form of
joint is the better of the two, but it is not much used in

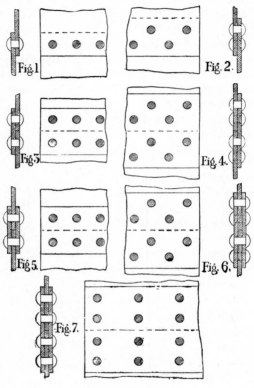

DIAGRAM A.

practice, because it is not so tight. The usual thickness
of rivets in locomotive boilers is $\frac{3}{4}$ in.

Lap-joints are generally used for making the circum-
ferential joints in the cylindrical plates forming the barrel

of the boiler, but some engineers prefer butt-joints for the purpose. The longitudinal joints in these plates are always butt-joints, with inside and outside strips. The strips should be made of the same plate as the boiler itself.

Rivet holes may be drilled, but in general practice with locomotive boilers they are punched when the plates are cold. Each method has advantages of its own. The chief argument against punching is that the plates are, to a certain extent, weakened by the process, and before the introduction of mild steel it was considered unwise to punch holes in steel plates; now, however, mild steel plates are successfully treated in this way.

One advantage of punching is that the edges of the holes are not sharp, as is the case when they are drilled, therefore there is less cutting action on the rivet. It has been found by experiment that when the plates are punched *the rivets are stronger*, although the plates are weakened to a greater extent than when drilled. When, on the other hand, the holes are drilled, the plates are not so much weakened, but the shearing tendency of the sharp edges of the holes lessens the strength of the rivet. The process of punching holes is of course very much more expeditious and less expensive than drilling, and the former method has practic· ally altogether superseded the latter in the manufacture of locomotive boilers.

The plates must be very carefully marked out and punched in exactly the right place, or when they come to be put together they may be found not to correspond. Should this be found to be the case with any of the holes, a drill is put through the two holes and a slightly larger rivet used. This difficulty in getting the holes exactly true is one of the chief arguments in favour of drilling. By putting the drill through both plates after fixing them in position, the holes are of course bound to be exactly fair with each other.

The holes formed by punching are always a little tapered through the action of the die-block, and when the plates are put together, the larger edges of the holes should be outside and the smaller next each other. This makes a tighter joint, as the expansion of the body of the rivet in the taper holes during the act of riveting tends to bring the plates more closely together than the mere pressure on the rivet heads would do. It should also be here noted that the contraction of the rivets in cooling exercises an irresistible force in pulling the plates together, and making the joint thoroughly steam-tight.

Formerly, all riveting was done by hand, but a number of ingenious machines for riveting by hydraulic power are now constructed, and are so designed that they will reach all parts of the boiler. The work done by these machines is very much superior to hand riveting, as the pressure comes gradually on to the whole rivet and presses it fully into the hole before forming the head. With hand riveting, each blow from the hammer acts upon the metal where struck, and consequently the shoulder or head begins to be formed before the body of the rivet becomes any larger in the hole. Generally speaking, steel rivets should only be used when the riveting is done by hydraulic power, as they chill too rapidly when hammered ; moreover, there is a risk of their overheating and burning.

Having explained the method of fastening the plates together, the various forms of plates used and the position they occupy, the component parts of the boiler may now be noted.

The barrel is made of three plates, which fit into each other telescopically.

The Back Plate is riveted inside the crown of the fire-box shell and shoulder plate.

The Middle Plate is riveted inside the back plate.

The Front Plate is riveted inside the middle plate.

The Smoke-Box Tube Plate is a circular vertical plate, which forms the front end of the barrel. It is $\frac{3}{4}$-in. thick, and is fastened to the front plate of the barrel by a circular angle-iron.

The plates of the fire-box shell are arranged as follows—

One long plate forms the two sides and semi-circular top or crown. The back plate is flanged forward and riveted inside the last-named plate. The front or shoulder plate is flanged back and riveted inside the fire-box casings. The semi-circular top edge of this plate is flanged forward and riveted to the outside of the lower half of the barrel. This is a very important plate ; it is subjected to severe strains, and great care must be taken when flanging not to damage it.

Having seen how the outside plates are arranged, a longitudinal section through the boiler (Fig. 53) must be studied to gain some idea of its interior construction.

D, is the dome ; F, cast-iron flange riveted to dome ; DC, dome cover ; DCF, dome cover flange. The cover is secured to the dome by two flanges, which are fastened together by studs (or bolts) and nuts.

The use of the dome is to afford additional steam space. The supply of steam to the cylinders is taken from near the top of the dome with the object of getting it from as high a point as possible above the level of the water, to avoid *priming*, a term used to describe the state of affairs when water enters the steam-chest and cylinders along with the steam from the boiler. The dome mostly in use at the present time is a vertical cylinder made of steel plates the same thickness as the boiler.

The top and sides of the fire-box are made of one plate in a similar way to the top and sides of the fire-box shell, but in this case the top is flat instead of semi-circular. The front plate (TP) is flanged backwards and riveted to the top and sides. It is called the *tube-plate*, and is perforated with holes for the reception of the tubes in that part of it which is opposite the barrel.

Fig. 54 is a half cross section and end view of the fire-box, which must be studied in connection with Fig. 53 to understand the position of the various parts named.

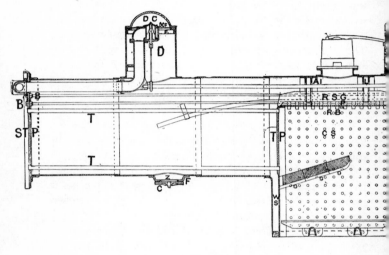

FIG. 53.

The smoke-box tube-plate (STP) is perforated with corresponding holes. These holes in both plates are drilled before the plates are riveted in their respective places. The top and bottom row of tubes are shown at TT.

The back fire-box plate (BFP) is flanged forward and riveted to the top and sides in a similar way to the tube plate. All the flat surfaces of the boiler plates have to be secured by stays; the only plates that do not require staying being the cylindrical ones forming the barrel. The space (WS) between the walls of the fire-box and the fire-box shell is usually about 3 in., and the distance from the top of the fire-box to the crown of the fire-box shell, 14 in. Round the fire-box, at a distance of 4 in. apart, are copper stays (CS). The stays have threads on them at each end, one end being screwed into the fire-box plate, and the other into the shell. After the stays are screwed into position, three-eighths of an inch projects beyond the outside of each plate, and these ends are riveted over.

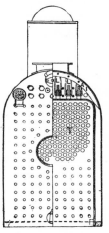

Fig. 54.

In the boiler shown in the sketch there are 198 tubes, $1\frac{7}{8}$ in. in diameter. The holes in the tube-plate are large enough for the tubes to fit them easily. The tubes are put in from the smoke-box end, and when in position, the ends are expanded in the tube-plates by a *drift* or *tube-expander*, and thus made steam-tight in the tube holes. They are further secured at the fire-box end by ferrules driven tightly into the ends of the tubes.

The tubes themselves act as stays to the tube-plates, thus making them perhaps the strongest part of the boiler. Above the tubes are longitudinal stays; long iron rods screwed into the fire-box shell at AA, and into the smoke-box tube-plate, at BB, above the tubes.

These rods stay the flat surface of the smoke-box tube-plate above the tubes, and the flat surface of the back plate of fire-box shell above the fire-box, where it is not secured by the copper stays, which strengthen all the other parts of the shell.

The flat top of the fire-box has to be securely stayed, which may be done in various ways. In the boiler shown in Figs. 53 and 54, it is done by strong wrought-iron girders (RSG) placed longitudinally across the top of the box ; $\frac{7}{8}$ in. bolts (RB) are screwed steam-tight through the top fire-box plate into the girders, making the roof of the fire-box thoroughly rigid and strong.

The girders are secured by links (L) to an angle iron (AI)

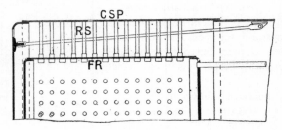

FIG. 55.

riveted round inside the crown of the fire-box shell. This arrangement is shown by the cross section (Fig. 54). With a long fire-box there are two rows of these links, one at each end of the girders.

Sometimes the stay bolts extend from the fire-box roof to the crown of the shell, into which they are screwed, as shown in Fig. 55. RS, roofing stay bolts; FR, fire-box roof; CSP, crown shell plate. This is a good arrangement, as the stays do not impede the circulation of the water over the top of the fire-box.

It is most important that the roof of the fire-box should be efficiently stayed. There is a great pressure on this plate; with 140 lbs. pressure per square inch it amounts to 150 tons. It is subjected to a fierce heat from the fire, and in case of the boiler running short of water, it is the first plate that is left exposed.

In the centre of this plate, therefore, is screwed a hollow brass plug filled in with lead. This is called a fusible plug, and constitutes a safeguard against the collapse of the top of the fire-box, in the event of the driver allowing the boiler to run short of water. A section of the fusible plug is shown in Fig. 56. (BB, brass; L, lead.) Directly the water gets below the level of the top of the plug, the heat from the fire causes the lead to melt, and the steam rushing through the orifice, puts the fire out. These plugs must be frequently examined and changed, as they gradually waste away, and if allowed to remain in too long, the lead is liable to be blown out and cause a failure.

FIG. 56.

The usual thickness of the copper plates of the fire-box is $\frac{1}{2}$ in., except the tube-plate, which is $\frac{7}{8}$ to 1 in. Iron rivets, $\frac{3}{4}$ in. thick, are used for making the joints between the fire-box plates.

The following are details of the various riveted joints used for the parts named—

Fig. 57. Joint between barrel and smoke-box tube-plate. BP, barrel-plate; A, angle iron; T, tube-plate; SBP, smoke-box plate.

Fig. 58. Joint between top of fire-box shell and back plate of fire-box shell. SS, top of shell; BP, back of plate of shell.

Fig. 59. Joint between top of fire-box and back plate of fire-box. T, top; B, back plate.

Fig. 60. Longitudinal butt-joint of cylindrical plates of barrel.

In designing a locomotive boiler, care should be taken to arrange that all the different parts may be easy of access, in order that they may be taken apart with as little cost as possible.

The proportion of the heating surface to the fire-grate area should vary from 60 : 1 to 90 : 1. The relative value of the heating surface of the tubes and that of the fire-box is— Fire-box, $\frac{1}{5}$; tubes, $\frac{4}{5}$. The proportion of heating surface of the tubes to that of the fire box is generally between 10 : 1 and 12 : 1. With an ordinary-sized locomotive, the heating

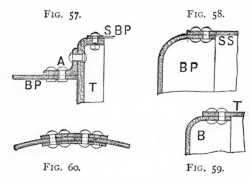

Fig. 57.　　　　　　　Fig. 58.

Fig. 60.　　　　　　Fig. 59.

surface of the fire-box is about 110 sq. ft., and of the tubes 1100 sq. ft.

The rule given for finding the required heating surface of a locomotive boiler in feet is as follows—

$$\text{(Diameter of one cylinder in inches)}^2 \times 4.$$

Thus, if the engine has a cylinder 18 in. in diameter, the total heating surface should be $18 \times 18 \times 4 = 1296$ sq. ft.

In Hutton's *Practical Engineers' Handbook*, the standard proportion of heating surface of locomotive boilers on various English railways is given as follows—

Railway.	Diameter of Cylinder.	Fire-grate Area.	Heating Surface.		
			Fire-box.	Tubes.	Total.
	In.	sq. ft.	sq. ft.	sq. ft.	sq. ft.
Great Northern Railway ...	18	17·6	122	1043	1165
Brighton Railway	17	17·8	102	1080	1182
Brighton Railway	18¼	20·65	112	1373	1485
Brighton Railway (Tank Engine)	17	16	90	858	948
Midland Railway	18	17·5	110	1096	1206
Great Western Railway (B.G.)	18	21	153	1800	1953
Great Western Railway (N.G.)	17	16·25	97	1216	1313
Great Western Railway (N.G.)	18	17	133	1145	1278
London & North-Western Ry.	16	15	85	1013	1098
London & North-Western Ry.	17	15	89	1013	1102
London, Chatham, & Dover Ry.	17½	16·3	107	962	1069
South-Western Railway ...	18½	17·5	104	1112	1216
Great Eastern Railway	18	17·3	117	1083	1200
Manchester S. & L. Railway ...	17½	17	87	1057	1144

The work done by hydraulic riveting machinery in the construction of locomotive boilers has been alluded to in a previous part of this chapter, and through the kindness of Mr. R. H. Tweddell, the writer is enabled to give the accompanying diagrams (Fig. 61), which illustrate the Tweddell hydraulic riveting machinery as used for the different parts of a locomotive boiler.

The illustration is reproduced from the *Proceedings of the Institution of Civil Engineers*, March 6, 1883, when Mr. Tweddell read a paper on this subject.

After the shell and most of the fire-box has been riveted in the stationary hydraulic riveter, the boiler is turned over and placed on supports, as shown. It is then ready for the portable riveting machines. The one shown at letter A is used to close the rivets in the smoke-box front, the gap being deep enough to reach over the corners of the plate where the cylinders are placed. This machine is also shown in another view. The same riveter is used for riveting-up locomotive frames and other odd work.

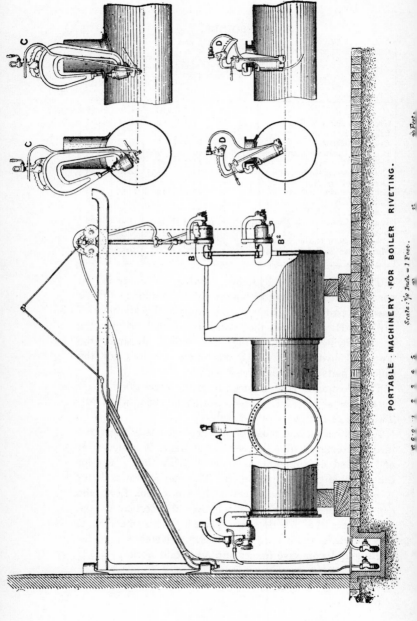

PORTABLE · MACHINERY · FOR · BOILER · RIVETING.

Scale ⅛ Inch = 1 Foot.

At letter B is shown a very compact form of machine for riveting the foundation rings. This machine is shown suspended by the hydraulic lift to the travelling monkey or carriage on the gib-crane. By means of the walking-pipes shown, pressure is conveyed to the riveters and can work them over two or three locomotives. Any of the portable riveters can be suspended to the lift according to the work to be done. This portable riveter (B) has a very small gap, which, while quite sufficient for the foundation rings, also allows of it being applied to riveting the fire-hole door rings. The ordinary plain ring fire-hole is shown, but the machine can also rivet the type of flanged fire-hole introduced by Mr. Webb. (See Fig. 50.)

The two views of the portable riveter shown at C explain themselves—as also those at D. Practically, every rivet can be put in a locomotive boiler by the Tweddell riveters, and Mr. Webb has stated (see p. 39, *Proceedings of Mechanical Engineers*, 1883) that "in the ordinary locomotive boiler of the London and North-Western Railway Co., there was not a single rivet that could not be put in by hydraulic pressure, and hand riveting had been entirely abandoned"; and, in the same paper, Mr. Webb made some very appreciative remarks as to what locomotive engineers owe to Mr. Tweddell.

CHAPTER VI.

THE fire-bars may either be made of cast or wrought-iron; perhaps, on the whole, the former is most extensively used. They extend horizontally from front to rear of the fire-box and are vertically taper, the thin edge downwards to allow free passage of air up to the grate surface. The bars are held in position by racks or carriers extending from side to side of the bottom of the fire-box. A plan and sectional elevation of fire-grate with cast-iron bars is shown in Figs. 62 and 63.

The fire-bars (FB) rest upon the carriers (CC): two of these carriers are made of cast-iron and extend from side to side of the fire-box, one at the front underneath the tube-plate and the other at the back under the fire-hole. The central carrier is made of wrought-iron, and extends across the centre of the box. The front and back carriers are held in position by the bolts (B) which pass through the foundation ring and are riveted over at R. These bolts project some 4 in. into the fire-box, and upon them are fixed the washers (W) to keep the carriers away from the side of the box.

The carriers are screwed up by the nuts (N) against the washers, and are thus kept firmly in position.

The central carrier is supported by brackets (X), which

are riveted to the fire-box plate through the foundation ring.

The table (p. 110) shows the proportion of air space to

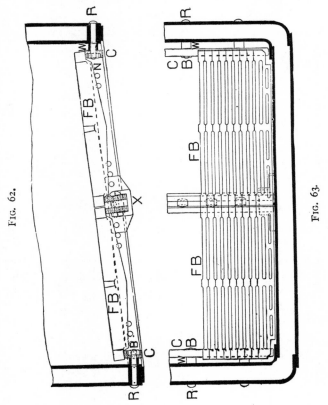

FIG. 62.

FIG. 63.

the grate area, with the fire-bars of different railway companies' locomotives.[1]

[1] This information was obtained about five years ago, and may not now be quite up to date.

Class of Engine.	No. of Fire-bars.	Air Spaces.				Total Grate Area.			Remarks.
		No.	Dimension of each Space.	Total Area of Spaces.		In square feet.	In square inches.	Proportion of Air Space Area to Total Grate Area.	
				In sq. ft.	In sq. in.				
L. & N. W. 6′ 6″ coupled	26	27	24—4¾ × ½″ / 25—4 10¼ × 5/16″	4·1	600·5	17·09	2461	1 to 4·1	1 row of bars, 1 air space between each row
Great Northern Express Passgr.	56	112	11″ × 7/16″	3·7	539·0	16·1	2328·7	1 to 4·5	2 rows of bars, 2 air spaces between each row
Midland Express Passgr.	50 single	132	100—12″ × 9/16″ / 32—various	6·1	891·5	17·7	2551·5	1 to 2·8	Ditto
Great Eastern Express Passgr.	4 double 68	136	1 3/8 × 5/16	4·0	579·0	17·0	2449	1 to 4·2	Ditto
South-Western Express Passgr.	double bars 27	112	12″ × 9/16″	5·2	756·0	17·7	2562	1 to 3·3	2 rows of double bars / 2 lengths of air spaces in each length of bar
Great Western Express Passgr.	24 single bars	25	23—67½ × 7/16 / 2—¾ ×	7·0	100·7	19·6	2829	1 to 2·8	1 row of bars / 1 air space between each

Below the bars is the ash-pan, which is made of wrought-iron, and is attached by bolts to the foundation ring. The ash-pan is rectangular in shape, being about 12 in. deep, and in plan the same size as the fire-box.

At the front of the ash-pan, and also at the back with engines that have to work trains either way without turning, is a door called a damper. This door is hinged at the top, and is actuated by a rod from the foot-plate. In the rod are notches which fit into a catch, so that the damper may be set in any required position. The function of the damper is to admit and regulate the supply of air below the fire.

Inside, up against the tube-plate and side of the fire-box is a brick arch, which extends partly across the fire-box. This is made of ordinary fire-bricks; the ends of the arch rest on studs projecting from the sides of the fire-box, and the bricks are kept in position by the spring, which is generally about 4 in.

The object of the arch is to deflect the gases as they arise from the furnace, and thus cause a more perfect combustion before they escape away through the tubes, than would take place if they found their way direct into the tubes without any obstruction. The arch has also the effect of sending the gases up towards the top of the box, and thence through the top rows of tubes.

The fire-hole door is an important part of the boiler, as by it the draught to the top of the fire is regulated.

There are various forms of door in use. One rather favourite device is to have the door in two halves, made to slide in a frame fitted with grooves at the top and bottom. The two halves are rectangular wrought-iron plates about ½ in. thick, connected to a handle by a simple arrangement of levers, which, when the handle is moved, causes the plates to shoot outwards to expose the fire-hole, or come together to close it. The handle should be so placed that the driver can actuate it without moving from his position on the foot-plate.

Inside the fire-box, immediately over the fire-hole, is a

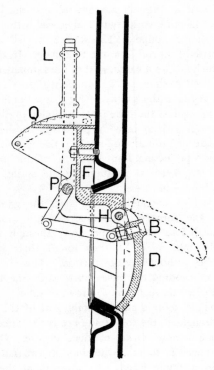

FIG. 64.

deflecting plate extending downwards part of the way across the fire-box. When the door is opened, cold air rushes into the fire-box, and the object of this plate is to deflect it downwards on to the fire, and prevent it striking right across the box on to the tube-plate.

Mr. Webb has introduced an ingenious fire-hole door, which acts both as door and deflector-plate, of which an illustration is given in Fig. 64. The door (D), which opens inwards, is hung upon the hinge (H) which forms part of the cast-iron frame (F). The links (I) connect the door to the lever (L), which works on the pivot (P). The lever is cranked at P, and works in a small quadrant (Q). This quadrant is fitted with teeth as shown, so that the door can be set in any position required. The door is shown closed, but when open occupies the same position as a deflector-plate, which is indicated by the dotted line. These doors wear out rather quickly from being constantly exposed to the action of the fire, but they are very easily renewed, and being made of cast-iron, inexpensive ; and after all they do not wear away any quicker than an ordinary deflector-plate. The cast-iron frame is not affected by the fire, and when a new door is required, the old one has merely to be detached by removing two bolts (B).

The smoke-box is in shape a continuation of the barrel of the boiler towards the front of the engine, and is the same length as the cylinders. It is formed by two bent wrought-iron plates, usually $\frac{5}{16}$ths of an inch thick, with a joint at the top. The plates are riveted or bolted to the flanged edge of the smoke-box tube-plate, and fastened by screws to the frame-plates at the bottom edges.

Riveted round inside the front edges of the plates is an angle iron, to which the front of the smoke-box is riveted. The front is made in one piece, $\frac{1}{2}$ in. thick, with a large aperture in it, over which the door fits. This aperture is about 3 ft. 10 in. in diameter, and at the side of it are hinges upon which the door hangs. Across it are two strong iron stays or cross-bars, about $1\frac{1}{2}$ in. apart. The door is convex from the outside, and when shut its outer edges must be a good fit against the smoke-box front, so as to prevent any entrance of draught except through the fire-box.

Through the centre of the door is a rod, at one end of which is a dart-shaped catch, which passes between the cross-bars. At the other end of the rod is a handle, which, when the door is closed, is turned through a quarter of a circle, bringing the catch across the bars and making the door fast.

The outer end of the rod has a screw-thread, and upon this screw is a second handle, acting as a nut which, when screwed tight up against the centre of the convex door, presses its edges close up against the front of the smoke-box, thereby making an air-tight joint. The smoke-box door gives access to that part of the engine for cleaning and repairs.

The safety-valve is one of the most important fittings of a steam boiler, whether it be that of a locomotive or any other class of engine. As its name implies, the function of the valve is to secure immunity from the explosions which might arise from an excessive pressure of steam.

In the earlier days of locomotives such explosions were by no means rare events, and many treatises have been written upon their cause and cure. At the present time the construction of boilers is so well planned, and the strength of materials so accurately calculated, that an explosion is happily a very rare occurrence indeed, notwithstanding the fact that since the days of the "Rocket" the ordinary working pressure has gradually increased from 50 to, in many cases, 180 lbs. per square inch.

A modern engine running a heavy express train develops steam as fast as it can be passed through the cylinders. The maximum height of water is maintained, and also the maximum steam pressure; therefore, all the steam used in working the engine and escaping from the boiler through the cylinders is over and above that indicated by the pressure-gauge.

Now when a driver has to make a quick stop unexpectedly, he shuts the regulator with the boiler working under these conditions, and the consequence is that the steam, which is being generated as fast as the boiler is capable of producing it, is suddenly denied the outlet through which it was passing. Hence comes a rapid accumulation of steam in the boiler, and consequently an enormous increase of pressure.

Were there no other outlet to relieve this pressure during the first minute or so after closing the regulator, while the fire is still under the influence of the blast, it would rise to more than any ordinary boiler could stand, and an explosion would be the result were it not for the safety-valve.

When making a regular stop, for which preparation is made in the ordinary course, such a great increase of pressure can be prevented by a process to be explained hereafter. But emergencies may arise in which the safety-valve must be able to discharge steam as fast as it is possible for it to be generated, when the boiler is working at the maximum pressure. However rapidly the steam is being generated, the pressure must never be allowed to exceed by 10 per cent. that at which the safety-valve begins to act. Of course this is a matter of calculation based upon experiments and previous experience, the results of which show that the lift of a safety-valve with a flat face should be equal to one-fourth the diameter of the valve, to make the opening for the outlet of steam equal to the area of the valve.

Some time ago Mr. Webb made some experiments with a locomotive boiler to ascertain the size of the orifice through which it was possible for all steam the boiler was capable of generating to pass, with the result that he found a pipe 1¼ in. in diameter was sufficient to discharge it as fast as generated without raising the pressure.

The two kinds of safety-valves most generally used with locomotive boilers are the spring-balance and Ramsbottom's duplex safety-valves. The former is the outcome of the

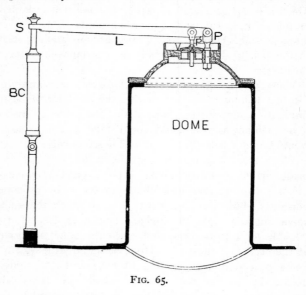

FIG. 65.

old weighted-lever still frequently used with stationary boilers—the spring acting on the lever instead of a weight—and the latter consists of a strong spring exerting its power directly upon the valves against which the steam presses.

With the spring-balance the spring acts upon the long arm of a lever with a very short purchase, so that a strong spring is not required. Fig. 65 illustrates a safety-valve of this description. The lever (L) has a fixed point (P), and extends to S, where its upward movement is resisted by the spring in the balance-casing (BC), which can be adjusted so as to bring any required power to act upon the end of the lever. The steam acts upon the valve (V), forcing it against the lever at the point (P). With a safety-valve of this description the lever is generally so divided that 1 lb. at its extremity balances 1 lb. per square inch of the valve surface.

The form of Ramsbottom safety-valve in use on the

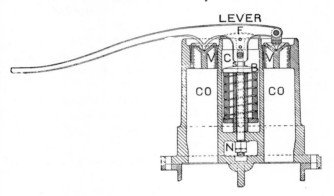

Fig. 66.

London and North-Western Railway engines is shown by Fig. 66. In the original form of this valve the steam escapes through two brass pillars with a mushroom valve at the top of each, the spring being between the pillars, coupled at its lower extremity to a fixed eye-bolt, and attached at the top to the centre of the lever which crosses above the pillars.

As a less expensive and equally effective arrangement, Mr. Webb has adopted the plan of making one casting with two cylindrical outlets (CO) for the steam, in place of the brass pillars. Each of these outlets is fitted at the top with a valve (V). The spring, which can be adjusted by the nut (N), fits into a chamber (C) between the two outlets, and is connected at its lower extremity by a stirrup-link (SL) to (F) the centre of the lever. This will be readily understood on referring to the illustration.

The top of the spring presses against the large circular head of a bolt (B), whose lower end is attached to the main casting, and thus the valves (V) are kept pressing tightly down on their seatings. The lever is prolonged so as to be within the driver's reach, and if there is any question of the valve sticking, by pressing the lever down he relieves the pressure of the spring upon the valve furthest away from him, and by raising it the pressure is released on the nearer valve.

The valves are three inches in diameter; the spring has six coils $2\frac{7}{8}$ in. internal diameter, made of steel $\frac{11}{16}$ in. by $\frac{29}{32}$ in. The usual position of the safety-valve is just in front of the cab on the top of the boiler, but sometimes it is placed on the top of the dome, or between it and the chimney.

Another important adjunct to the locomotive boiler is the apparatus by which the feed-water for generating the steam is conveyed into it. Every locomotive carries a supply of water in a tank, in addition to that which is being converted into steam in the boiler. There are two systems by which the water is conveyed from the tank to the boiler, viz. by the pump and by the injector. The former is simply an ordinary force-pump usually driven by an eccentric fixed upon one of the axles. At one time this was the only known way of introducing water into a steam boiler.

A locomotive feed-pump is illustrated by Fig. 67. The ram (R) moving forward in the direction of the arrow by the action of an eccentric fixed upon one of the axles, opens the ball-valve (V), through which it draws from the

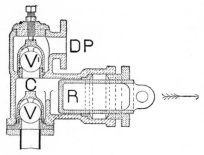

FIG. 67.

tank the water which fills up the chamber (C) behind the ram. After going the full length of the stroke, the ram moves back in the opposite direction, and the pressure of the water closes the valve (V) and forces open V1, through which the water passes into the delivery-pipe (DD) and thence to the boiler through the clack-box.

An ordinary form of clack-box is illustrated in Fig. 68. The water enters at W, forcing up the valve or clack (V), and passing through the passage (P) into the boiler. In the event of anything going wrong with the pump, the pressure in the boiler keeps the

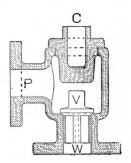

FIG. 68.

valve (V) closed. The cover (C), which acts as a stop for the clack, is screwed into the clack-box, and can be taken off when required for purposes of examination. The water is supplied to the pump from the tank through the feed-pipe below the valve V (Fig. 67).

The more recent system of introducing water into the boiler by means of an injector is more difficult to describe. A simple form of this apparatus is illustrated by Fig. 69. Steam is conveyed from the boiler to the injector by the branch-pipe (S). The space coloured pink is pure steam, which is admitted to the injector through the conical nozzle (N). The amount of steam admitted is controlled by screwing up or down the spindle (V), which is actuated by the steam regulating wheel (SRW), and can be screwed right into the nozzle, thus closing the orifice altogether when required.

The water enters the injector at W, and the space coloured blue is all pure water. The admission of the water is controlled by the cone (C), which is moved up and down by the pinion (P), actuated by a small cog-wheel and rack, controlled by the hand-wheel (WRW). The steam and water meet in the cone (C), and the mixed jet of steam and water coloured purple, discharged through the delivery-pipe (D), forces back a valve and so gains entrance into the boiler. If the injector is not working properly, the water, instead of entering the boiler, finds its way into the overflow-chamber and out through the pipe (O), thus indicating to the driver that there is something wrong. In such cases the steam and water-cones must be adjusted until it is found that the water is being delivered into the boiler.

The principle upon which the injector works may be thus briefly stated.

The velocity of a jet of steam forced through an orifice under a certain pressure is much greater than the velocity of a jet of water forced through a similar orifice under the same pressure. The jet of steam forced into the injector

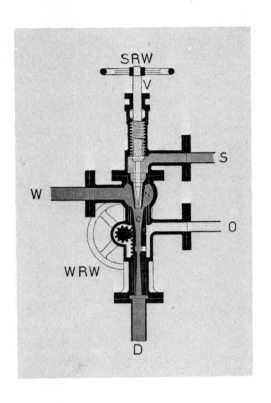

from the boiler is condensed into water by coming into contact with the cold water at C, but *although condensed into water, its velocity is not reduced* to that of a jet of water under the same pressure, and therefore the jet is able to overcome the pressure in the boiler.

When once the injector has started, the condensation of the water causes a vacuum, and more water rushes in through W, keeping up a continuous jet, which is forced into the boiler. A good injector will lift its own water supply 10 to 20 ft., and each pound of steam used should carry with it about 18 lbs. of feed-water into the boiler. Most injectors will not work with hot water, although the temperature of water in passing through the injector is raised about 100 degrees Fah. The feed-water should enter the boiler through a pipe, the discharge from which should be a little below the working level of the water, but above the level of the top of the fire-box. Being colder and heavier than the water in the boiler, it descends by gravitation, and thus promotes circulation. If the discharge is below the level of the furnace crown, in case of failure of the injector-valve, the water may be forced back through the delivery-pipe and expose the fire-box plates to the action of the fire.

Of late years many improved forms of injector have been brought out, the more recent ones having the special advantage of being able to inject hot water. The chief advantages claimed respectively for the pump and injector may be thus briefly summed up—

An injector can be worked at any time whether the engine is standing or moving, whereas with a pump no water can be got into the boiler unless the engine is in motion. This was the cause of many difficulties in past times, when it was frequently necessary to run engines up and down sidings, and sometimes on the main line, for no other purpose than to pump water into the boiler. When an engine was hemmed in by other engines or vehicles so that there was no room for it to move, the plan often resorted to was to oil the rails, screw the tender-brake hard on, and open the regulator. This caused the wheels to fly round on the slippery rail, and thus work the pump and fill up the boiler, to the great detriment, however, both of the engine and of the rails upon which the wheels revolved. A further advantage is that the injector absorbs less power, and is only in action when required. Also it is always possible to tell whether it is working or not.

In favour of the pump, it may be observed that it will pump hot water into the boiler, and can therefore be worked without appreciably reducing the pressure of steam. Also that it is on the whole more certain in its action, and is not subject to climatic influences, whereas the injector often gives trouble and sometimes causes absolute failures in hot weather.

The late Mr. W. Stroudley, locomotive superintendent of the London, Brighton and South-Coast Railway, always upheld the old system of pumps. He used no injector, but fed his boilers with water heated in the tender-tank by exhaust steam, and there is no doubt his engines compared well with many others in point of economy of fuel.

The only way to get the full benefit of pump and injector would be to fit an engine with one of each, the pump to be used while running, and the injector when standing. In that case there should be two separate tanks, one to carry hot water for the pump, and the other cold for the injector. The usual plan is to fit engines either with two pumps, or with two injectors, so that in case of one failing the other can be used to keep up the supply of water to the boiler. Many injectors are now coming into the field that work with fairly hot water, and it is likely that feed-pumps will soon be altogether superseded. Indeed, the immense advantage the injector has of being able to work when an engine is standing almost outweighs every argument in favour of the pump.

The action of the injector may almost be called phenomenal, when it is considered that steam taken *from* the boiler is actually able to drive water *into* the same boiler against a pressure greater than its own.

The injector was invented in the year **1858** by the late M. Henri Giffard, a French scientist[1] who thus has the honour of having made one of the most important discoveries of modern times in connection with the steam-engine. Since its first introduction there have been many improvements made and patents taken out in connection with injectors, but the principle is the same with all.

Fig. 70 illustrates an improved pattern of injector brought out by Messrs. Gresham and Craven. The advantages claimed for it are that it is perfectly automatic in its action and starts to work instantaneously upon opening the steam and water-cocks, and should it cease working from any cause, such as the momentary stoppage of steam or water in locomotives occasioned by shunting or passing over crossings, it will re-start itself automatically. The cones can easily be taken out and cleaned without breaking any pipe-joints. Its action is thus briefly described by the makers—

A is the steam-nozzle ; BB the combining-cone, which is divided into two parts as shown ; C is what is known as the throat or smallest diameter of the cones, and D is the receiving or delivery-cone ; E being the back pressure valve, the other valves, as well as the various branches, being clearly marked upon the engraving. The combination-injector is completely self-contained, having combined in one instrument, along with the nozzles, the whole of the

[1] The injector was first brought out in this country by Messrs. Sharp Stewart and Company.

valves for regulating and starting, the valves being as follows :—Steam-valve, back pressure valve, stop-valve for closing off when back pressure valve requires cleaning or grinding, water-regulating cock, and overflow or warning-cock.

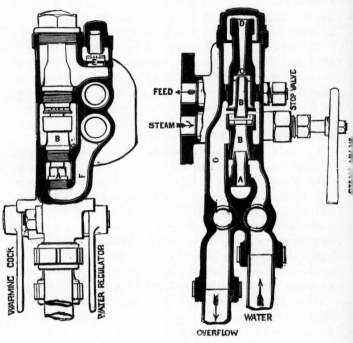

FIG. 70.

By the use of this injector there are no pipes whatever under pressure, and consequently its action can never be interfered with through burst pipe-joints. It is fixed upon the fire-box of the locomotive, which is the handiest position for manipulation, as it can be worked easily without the driver's attention being taken off the signals. The steam is conveyed from the dome to the opening in fixing-flange marked "Steam," the feed-water being carried from the opening marked "Feed" by means of an internal pipe over the fire-box, and into the water space of the boiler.

The operation and action of the injector are as follows— First open the steam-valve and the water-cock, the steam will then flow along the passage marked F, and entering at the steam-nozzle pass out of it at a great velocity, and through the first part (B) of the combining-cone, escaping at the opening between BB into the overflow-chamber (C), and out at the overflow-pipe, thus creating a suction in the water-pipe which causes the water to be lifted and brought into contact with the steam. The steam and water now combine together in the cone B, and also pass up through cone B′, thus allowing this latter cone to fall upon the valve seating at the top of B, the two cones then becoming practically one.

Should too much water be passing into the injector to be in proportion to the quantity of steam due to the boiler-pressure, there will be a loss of water at the ordinary overflow opening, i. e. the space at the top of cone B, and between it and the throat (C). This waste of water at the overflow-pipe is an indication that the water admission requires adjusting by means of the water-cock. When this adjustment has been made there will be no escape at the overflow-pipe, and the jet will pass through the overflow space, entering the receiving cone (D), and thence through the back pressure valve (E) into the boiler.

As will be readily seen by the engraving, it is a simple matter to remove the back pressure valve-clack, either for cleaning or re-grinding, and by means of a special key to take out the whole of the cones of the injector for examination if needed.

Fig. 71 illustrates an injector introduced by Mr. Webb, and similar in construction to the standard pattern used on London and North-Western engines. It is simple in design, neat in appearance, and gives very little trouble in its working. The following is an index of its various parts, which can be readily understood by comparing them with those already described—

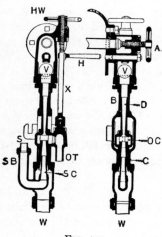

FIG. 71.

W = Water supply.
SB = Steam-branch.
S = Steam-pipe.
SC = Steam-cone.
B = Barrel.
OC = Overflow-chamber.
C = Combining-nozzle.
OT = Overflow-tap.
D = Discharging-nozzle.
X = Rod for overflow-tap.
H = Handle of overflow-tap.

HW = Hand-wheel for raising or lowering the combining and discharging nozzles.

V = Ball-valve or clack.

A = Stop-cock, to prevent back flow of water in case of failure of injector valve.

The valve for admitting and regulating the supply of steam from the boiler to the cylinders of a locomotive is called the regulator. There are various types of regulator, one of the most favourite being that adopted by Mr. Ramsbottom (as shown in Fig. 72). It consists of a double-

seated valve (V), fixed vertically in the dome on the end
of the steam-pipe (SP). Attached to this valve is a rod
(R), which extends downwards, and is connected to an
eccentric-rod (ER) by the pin (P). The eccentric (E) is

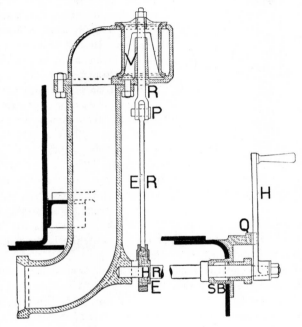

FIG. 72.

fixed on the end of a long rod (HR), which extends
horizontally through the barrel of the boiler, above the fire-
box and through a stuffing-box (SB) on the back plate of
the fire-box shell.

At the end of this rod, working in a quadrant (Q) affixed
to the boiler-plate, is a handle (H), by means of which

the driver moves the rod, thus causing the eccentric to revolve in the segment of a circle, and transmit the movement to the regulator-valve, opening or shutting it to the extent to which the handle is moved.

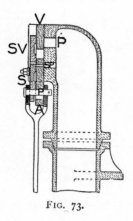

FIG. 73.

An early type of regulator, and one still commonly used, is shown in Fig. 73. In this instance the admission of steam to the steam-pipe is controlled by a flat valve (V), working on a face with ports in the same way as the slide-valve, which admits steam from the steam-chest into the cylinder. On the back of this valve, kept in position by the spring (S), is the small valve (SV), which receives the first movement of the eccentric, and causes the steam to be admitted through the small port (SP). On the pin (P) coming in contact with the valve (S) at the point A, the larger valve is actuated and the port opened.

The object of the small port is to prevent steam being admitted too suddenly into the cylinders. When the piston-head is suddenly subjected to the full steam-pressure, a great strain is put upon the working parts of the engine, to avoid which, steam should always be applied very gradually in starting.

The valve of this type of regulator is usually actuated by an eccentric in the same way as with the Ramsbottom regulator. The arrangement will be understood by referring to the sketch.

The pipe for conveying the steam from the regulator to the cylinders is usually made of copper, and is $4\frac{1}{2}$ in. in diameter. This pipe extends horizontally inside the boiler from the dome to the smoke-box tube-plate, through which it passes into the smoke-box, and is jointed on to a vertical pipe, which is fixed by studs to the top of the steam-chest.

The position of these pipes will be best seen by referring to the sectional drawing (Fig. 53, p. 100).

In order to show the height of the water in the boiler, a water gauge is fixed to the back plate of the fire-box shell in a convenient position, to be well within sight of the men on the foot-plate. This gauge consists of a strong glass tube fitted into the sockets of a brass stand at top and bottom. These stands are fixed by studs and nuts to the boiler-plate; the upper one is about 3 in. above the working level of the water, and forms a passage for the steam from the boiler into the top of the glass, the lower stand is level with or just above the top of the furnace-crown, and by it water enters the bottom of the glass. Each stand is fitted with a cock to shut off the steam from the glass in case it should break. The pressure in the gauge-glass is the same as in the boiler, and the level of the water in the glass tube correctly represents the height of water in the boiler.

The bottom stand is fitted with another cock below the glass which, when opened, allows steam and water to blow through from the boiler, thus keeping clear the steam and water passages, and maintaining the gauge in proper working order.

This cock should be opened occasionally during a trip to prevent the passages getting choked up. The cocks used are generally ordinary plug-taps, and if a glass breaks (a not unfrequent occurrence) there is often a difficulty in shutting them, owing to the rush of steam and water from the broken glass, and many more or less serious scalds have resulted from the operation.

To obviate this, Mr. Webb has introduced an ingenious contrivance, by means of which the taps close automatically in the event of a gauge-glass breaking. An illustration of one of these gauges is shown in Fig. 74.

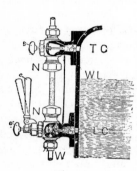

FIG. 74.

The working level of the water in the boiler is shown by the dotted lines. This may vary, but it is best to keep the water at such a height under ordinary circumstances that the gauge-glass is nearly full. The water enters the gauge-glass through the lower opening (LC) and the steam through the top opening (TC). With the gauge shown in the illustration, instead of these openings being fitted with ordinary plug-taps, the small balls (A) and (A') are used. They are shown in the position they occupy when the gauge is working. If the glass breaks, these balls are forced by the pressure in the boiler into the position shown by the dotted circles, like the ball in a patent soda-water bottle, and thus prevent water or steam from entering the gauge.

After a new glass has been put in, the plungers (B and B') are pressed inwards and force the balls off the seatings, allowing steam and water to enter the glass. The pressure in the glass then becomes the same as in the boiler, and the balls remain in their normal working position. To get a "blow through," the handle (C) is pulled into the position shown by the dotted lines. This opens the seating (V), and allows steam and water to pass through to the waste-pipe

(W). The glass is kept steam-tight by india-rubber packing rings inside the nuts (NN).

Many locomotive engineers fit all their engines with two water gauges, so that in the event of one failing the driver can finish his trip without inconvenience. Two gauges also have the advantage of at once indicating if one of them is not working correctly, as the levels shown do not agree. Engines not so fitted must, in addition to the one water gauge, have two test taps fixed to the boiler plate, one about level with the top of the gauge-glass and one with the bottom. By them the height of the water can be approximately gauged. So long as water issues from the bottom tap there is enough in the boiler; directly it gets below that level, so that only steam appears on its being opened, the boiler is getting short and the water down to the level of the furnace crown. When working with the test taps, the water should always be kept about level with the top one. The worst feature about test taps is that they are apt (notwithstanding instructions to the contrary) to get neglected. When a driver goes a long time with his gauge-glass working satisfactorily, if a mishap occurs, it too often is found that the test taps are out of order and unworkable.

The steam pressure is recorded by a gauge with graduated dial and pointer. It is fixed in a convenient position in the cab where the driver can best see it when standing at his proper post. The steam is conveyed to the pressure gauge by a small pipe about $\frac{3}{8}$ in. internal diameter. The pipe is fixed to the boiler in any convenient place above the water level, and the steam from the boiler comes in contact with a small piston which acts upon a spring which is part of the mechanism of the gauge. This spring in turn causes a small vertical rack to move upwards and actuate a cog-wheel carrying the needle or pointer, which is thus made to travel round the face of the

FIG. 75.

dial and record the pressure. The movement of the spring, and consequently of the needle, depends upon the force acting upon the small piston, and hence the varying pressure is shown.

Fig. 75 illustrates an ordinary pressure gauge of the usual type.

Before leaving the subject of the steam-gauge, our readers may be interested in the following copy of a letter which appears in Smiles's *Life of George Stephenson*—

"*Tapton House, Chesterfield,*
"*October*, 1847.

"A most important invention has been submitted to me for my approval, patented by a Mr. Smith of Nottingham, and intended to indicate the strength of steam in steam-engine boilers. It is particularly adapted for steam-boats, and can be placed in the office of every manufactory where a steam-engine is used, at a considerable distance from the boiler. I am so much pleased with it that I have put one up at my own collieries. It is some distance from the boiler, in another house, and works most beautifully, showing the rise and fall of the steam in the most delicate manner. The indicator is like the face of a clock, with a pointer making one revolution in measuring from 1 lb. to 100 lbs. upon the square inch upon the pressure of steam.

It is quite from under the control of the engineer, or any other person, so that its indications may be relied upon ; and the construction is so simple that it is scarcely possible for it to get out of order.   I might give a full explanation of the machine, but I think it best to leave that to the inventor himself.   The numerous and appalling accidents which have occurred through the bursting of steam-boat boilers have induced me to give you the observations which I think desirable to lay before the public.   I may state that I have no pecuniary interest in the scheme, but, being the first person to whom it has been shown, and the first person to make use of it, I feel it a duty I owe to the inventor, as well as to the public, to make it as universally known as possible.   The indicator is put up at Tapton Colliery, near Chesterfield, and may be seen any day by any respectable person.

" (Signed)   GEORGE STEPHENSON."

A large tap, called the " blow-off cock," is fixed to the lower part of the fire-box shell.   It is turned off and on by a handle from the foot-plate, and is used to let the water out of the boiler when necessary to empty it, or to lower it if required, should the boiler be too full.   Of course the water must never be allowed to sink below the top of the furnace crown when the engine is in steam.

The London and North-Western Railway boilers have underneath the barrel an aperture called the " man-hole," which is shown in Fig. 53, p. 100.   A flat cover (C) is attached by studs to the flange (F).   Upon this cover inside the boiler at Z is placed a circular piece of zinc, which acts chemically upon the water, having a deterrent effect upon the formation of scale on the boiler plates and tubes.   The man-hole also enables sediment and scale which may fall from the tubes to the bottom of the barrel of the boiler to be cleared out.

In various convenient parts of the boiler plates are holes about $1\frac{1}{2}$ in. in diameter. These are for washing out, and are called "mud-holes"; they are tapped with a very fine thread, and solid brass plugs are screwed into them in the same way as the fusible plug is screwed

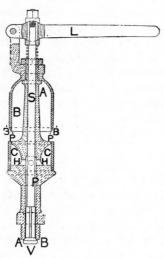

FIG. 76.

into the furnace crown. The plugs are taken out when the boiler is washed out, and a continuous stream of cold water is kept circulating through the boiler, being put in through the topmost hole and finding its way out through the lower ones. While the water is thus circulating, copper rods are thrust through the holes and scrape out the dirt. The boiler of a London and North-Western engine has altogether about a dozen of these wash-out plugs.

The whistle is made of brass, and is fixed at the top of the boiler near the cab. The steam should be conveyed to it from as high a point as is convenient, so as to get it pure and free from water, otherwise the sound is not clear. Fig. 76 illustrates the section of a whistle used on the Furness Railway. Steam enters through AB into the chamber (P), from whence it passes through the holes (H) into the outer chamber (C), and up through the narrow circular passage

(P). The bell (B), which is screwed on to the pillar (A), is turned true at its outer edge, which edge is about ¾ in. above and exactly over the narrow passage (P′), and the steam striking the thin edge of the bell at B′, causes it to vibrate and produce a shrill sound in a similar manner to the action of an organ-pipe. The lever (L) depressing the valve (V) by means of the spindle (S), admits the steam to P.

The blower, or steam-jet, is a pipe fixed in the chimney. A handle on the foot-plate is connected usually by a rod extending along the side of the boiler to a steam-cock at the side of the smoke-box, which turns the steam into the blower-pipe. This pipe sends a jet of steam up the chimney, and causes an induced draught on the fire, acting in exactly the same manner as the blast-pipe. It is used to urge the fire, if necessary, when getting up steam ; and also, when turned slightly on, prevents the emission of smoke from the chimney if an engine has to stand at a station with a strong fire, or one that has recently had coal put on.

CHAPTER VII.

CYLINDERS, PISTONS, AND CONNECTING-RODS.

WHEN the cylinders of a locomotive are placed side by side between the main frames, the engine is known as an *Inside Cylinder Engine.* This position necessitates the employment of cranks upon the driving axle to communicate the steam pressure to the driving-wheels.

An *Outside Cylinder Engine* has the cylinders outside the main frames on either side of the engine, and the pistons and connecting-rods work on to crank-pins fixed to the driving-wheels. With this arrangement the axle between the driving-wheels is straight, no cranks being needed.

These are the two standard positions for the cylinders of locomotive engines, some engineers preferring " outside " and others " inside " cylinders. If the steam-chest is placed centrally between them, the diameter of inside cylinders is restricted, because the distance between the frames is unalterable, and cannot exceed 4 ft. 2 in., as it depends on the fixed 4 ft. 8½ in. gauge. In the earlier days of locomotives, the usual internal cylinder diameter was about 12 in., but this has gradually increased until a maximum of 20 in. has been reached with some ordinary high-pressure cylinders. Seventeen inches is a diameter frequently used, and if inside cylinders are larger than this, the steam-chest is generally either above or below them, owing to the limited space between the frames.

Fig. 77 shows, in diagram form, a cross section of a pair of inside cylinders with the steam-chest (SC) placed midway between them. The slide valves move in a vertical plane in the steam-chest. The cylinder castings project at either side and are bolted to the frame-plates (FP) at A. The section (in this and the other similar illustrations) is taken through the exhaust pipe (E), so that the steam-port does not appear. As a rule each cylinder is cast separately, and they are afterwards bolted together, the line CD, which passes

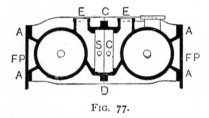

FIG. 77.

through the centre of the steam-chest, representing the joint between them.

The two surfaces where the castings come together must be faced up exactly true, and be well fitted together, so as to make an absolutely steam-tight joint. This is very important, because it is a difficult and expensive job to re-make this joint when the engine is once put together. As the same letters are used for each part in the different sketches, it will be unnecessary in each case again to refer to all of them.

Fig. 78 shows a pair of 19-inch inside cylinders with the steam-chest above them, as constructed by Mr. Johnson for certain classes of Midland Railway engines. In this case each valve is placed horizontally with the flat surface downwards, the ports being immediately above each cylinder. The steam-chest can be similarly constructed *below* the cylinders, the faces of the valves being upwards. When the steam-chest is above or below the cylinders, the valves—unless

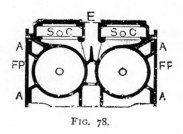

FIG. 78.

inclined — are not in a plane with the driving axle, and an intermediate gearing must be used, to connect the valve spindles to the eccentric rods. The rocking-shaft (RS, Fig. 30, chap. iii.) is an example of such intermediate gear.

Another form of inside cylinders is shown in Fig. 79. This time the steam-chest is neither directly above nor below the cylinders, but has a V section, the apex of the V being midway between the centre lines of the cylinders. This arrangement allows more room in the steam-chest than

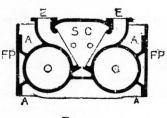

FIG. 79.

when it is placed exactly between the cylinders, and at the same time admits of a direct acting motion between the slide valves and eccentrics. Mr. Webb uses this form of steam-chest with his straight-link type of express passenger engines which have **17** in. cylinders, and are fitted with the link motion illustrated in Fig. 42, chap. iv. In this case also, the steam-chest may be similarly placed below the cylinders with the apex of the V upwards. Although it is usual with inside cylinders to cast each cylinder separately, and bolt them together, as explained in Fig. 77, Mr. Webb prefers to cast both cylinders in one piece; and this is the case with those shown in Fig. 79, and the casting is an excellent piece of workmanship.

Fig. 80 is a cross section of the 18-inch outside cylinders of the Great Northern Railway express passenger engines, constructed at Doncaster by Mr. P. Stirling.

It will be seen that they are outside the frames (FP) at either side of the engine, each cylinder having a separate steam-chest on the inner side of the frame. The frames in this case are of different design to those of an engine having inside cylinders, so as to allow space for this special form of

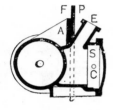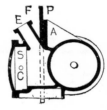

FIG. 80.

casting. Whether the cylinders are inside or outside, they are always kept in position by being securely bolted to the main frames, as shown at A in the different diagrams.

Fig. 81 gives four views illustrating the details of a pair of inside cylinders, designed by Mr. Ritches, locomotive superintendent of the Taff Vale Railway. As they are very simple in construction, they afford a good example for descriptive purposes.

FC is the front cover secured by studs to the cylinder casting at the end nearest the buffer plank. The studs are screwed firmly and permanently into the casting all round the cylinder at a distance of about 5 in. apart, and $\frac{3}{4}$ in.

from the edge of the cylinder boring. This latter distance is the width of the joint surfaces. The joint is made of a ring of asbestos packing or other suitable material. The studs project through the corresponding holes in the cylinder cover, which is screwed up tight by nuts. In the centre of

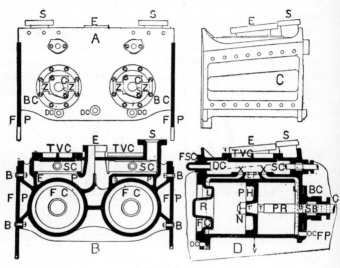

FIG. 81.

the cover is the recess (R), to allow clearance for the large nut (N), which secures the piston-rod to the piston-head.

The main casting of the cylinders forms part of the back cover, and the small cover (BC) is attached to it by studs in a similar way to the front cover. It is never necessary to take the piston out at the back end of the cylinder, and therefore this cover need not be of so large a diameter as the bore of the cylinder, and when the joint is made it should be permanent. This cover also forms the stuffing-box, and has cast into it the brackets (Z) to which the slide-bars are attached.

The stuffing-box (SB) is a recess or chamber for the reception of the piston rod packing.   At the bottom of the stuffing-box is a small recess into which the bush (B) fits. This is a small brass easy-fitting ring slid over the piston-rod after the piston has been put in the cylinder, its use being to act as a guide in keeping the piston-rod central, as well as to prevent the packing from being forced into the cylinder.

There are various kinds of packing used, the most common being hemp saturated with tallow.   The packing is twisted round the piston-rod in folds, and pushed into the stuffing-box up against the bush.   The gland (G) is a brass casting bored out like the bush to be an easy fit on the piston-rod.   In the cylinder cover are two long studs (SS), which pass through corresponding holes in the gland. After the stuffing-box is filled, the gland is pushed up to the packing.   The studs project through the holes, and the gland is screwed down on the packing, compressing it into the stuffing-box, and making a steam-tight joint round the piston-rod. As the packing wears the gland can be adjusted, but care must be taken in tightening the nuts to keep it exactly true on the piston-rod, so that its edge may not cut it.

The front steam-chest cover (FSC), generally called the valve cover, is, like the cylinder covers, attached to the main castings by studs.   It is fitted with a guide or dummy gland (DG), in which the free end of the valve spindle works.   The back of the steam-chest is solid with the main casting, and is likewise fitted with a gland and stuffing-box, through which the valve spindle works on to the eccentric-rod.

The piston-head (PH) is made of cast-iron, and is secured

to the steel piston-rod (PR) by the large nut (N). The piston-rod is taper at the end, which fits into a corresponding taper-hole in the piston-head. This taper is shown at TT', and the rod from T' to the end projects through the piston-head. Upon this projecting part the nut (N) is screwed, thus drawing the taper part of the rod tightly into the hole in the piston-head, and making both perfectly secure and rigid. The nut is prevented from slackening back by a split-pin.

The piston-head is turned to be an easy fit in the cylinder, and round it are cut the two grooves (V) into which the piston rings are fitted. These rings are cast-iron hoops turned to fit easily in the grooves, and about $\frac{1}{8}$ in. larger in diameter than the cylinders. After they are turned, a small piece is cut out of each hoop, leaving the two ends about $\frac{1}{4}$ in. apart, and then by pressing the edges together, the ring is made small enough to fit into the cylinders. The rings are sprung into the grooves in the piston, and the natural tendency they have to spring outwards causes them to make a joint with the smooth surface of the boring, when the piston is in the cylinder. The cuts in the two rings must not be left opposite to each other, or the steam has a direct passage from one side of the cylinder to the other.

The travel of the piston in the cylinder is between the dotted lines (LL); the space between these lines and the covers is called clearance, and is necessary to allow the steam to pass into the cylinder and act upon the piston at the commencement of the stroke. The steam-ports are shown at XX, and the exhaust port at EP. S is the steam entrance where the steam passes from the steam-pipe to the steam-chest (SC), and E is the exhaust. Both these orifices are flanged, the former for the attachment of the steam-pipe from the boiler, and the latter for the blast-pipe. A hole is drilled through the bottom of the cylinder at DC, to let out the water which accumulates from condensed steam. Into this hole is fitted the drain-cock or "cylinder tap," an ordinary form of tap actuated from the foot-plate by an arrangement of levers.

In going through the above explanation, the four views, A, B, C, and D, must be studied conjointly, and the various parts noted in each diagram.

A is the end view of the back of the cylinder.

B, a cross section through the exhaust port, and through the steam passage (SP) which conveys the steam from the steam-port to the cylinders. This view clearly shows the method of fastening the cylinder casting to the frame (FP) by the bolts (B).

C is an outside elevation of the side of the cylinder next the frame, showing the flanges and bolt-holes by which the cylinders are secured. D is a longitudinal section through the cylinder and steam-chest. The top valve cover (TVC) should be noted. This is a plate forming the top cover of the steam-chest. It is secured to the main-casting by studs and nuts, and can be taken off when required for purposes of examination.

The cylinders and covers should all be of the best close-grained cast-iron, free from any defect of material or workmanship. The usual thickness of locomotive cylinders is given below—

Diameter of cylinder, 17 in.; thickness, $\frac{7}{8}$ in.

,,	,,	18 in.;	,,	1 in.
,,	,,	19 in.;	,,	$1\frac{1}{8}$ in.
,,	,,	20 in.;	,,	$1\frac{1}{4}$ in.

A considerable allowance should be made for re-boring, as cylinders gradually wear owing to the high speed of the piston, and sometimes become grooved for want of lubrication, from any defect in the metal, or through ashes getting into them from the exhaust pipe.

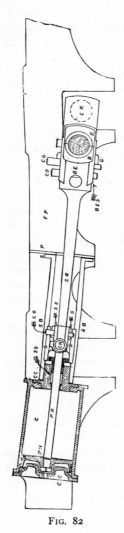

FIG. 82

Fig. 82 shows the section of a cylinder, illustrating its position with regard to the slide-bars, connecting-rod, and crank. This is taken from a London and North-Western six-wheels coupled coal-engine, which has two parallel slide-bars for each piston-rod. The bars (SB) are made of Bessemer steel, and are fixed at one end by studs and nuts to the cylinder cover (CC), and at the other end are bolted to the stay or spectacle-plate (SP). They must be fitted up with great care and accuracy, and be absolutely parallel with each other, and in line with the centre of the cylinder.

At the end of the piston-rod is the cross-head (CH). This is a steel block with a taper hole into which the end of the piston-rod is fitted. At the end of the rod is a thread upon which a nut and lock-nut are screwed, thus securely fastening the piston-rod to the cross-head. The latter has two arms, which project horizontally outside the slide-bars on either side; these arms are called gudgeons, and upon them are fixed gun-metal caps, upon which the small ends of the connecting-rod work. The cross-head has also two vertical arms upon which the slide blocks (S) are fitted. These are made of cast-iron with white metal faces, which fit up against the slide-bars. The slide-blocks must be carefully adjusted by washers on the cross-head, and must be made to work freely between the slide-bars. The slide-blocks and bars take all the strain of the up-and-down pressure when the crank is being forced away from or drawn towards the cylinder. The greatest pressure is against the top bar when running forwards, and against the under one when running backwards. The figure illustrates the type of slide-bar most generally used on the London and North-Western engines, namely, two flat parallel bars, one above and one below the cross-head. It is an arrangement that has been found to work well, and the bars are easily adjusted. It may, however, be here mentioned that there are other kinds of slide-bars; sometimes one strong bar only is used, in which case the cross-head is attached to a box which encloses the bar. A slide-box of this description has an upper and lower bearing-surface working on to the top and bottom of the bar. The Great Eastern Railway engine illustrated in Fig. 110, p. 247, has slide-bars of this description.

A very usual plan is to have four slide-bars for each cylinder, in which case the slide-blocks are at each side of the cross-head. There is an upper and lower bar for each slide-block, and the cross-head is attached to a pin which passes through the two blocks. The cross-head and little end thus move to and fro between the double bars at either side of them. The distance between the top and bottom bars may be much less than when only two are used, as it is not necessary to give clearance for the up-and-down movement of the connecting-rod, which is free to work between the bars. When this arrangement is used, the small end of the connecting-rod is not forked, and has only one bearing on the pin which passes through the two

slide-blocks. Fig 84, in the next chapter, illustrates the
position of the slide-bars when four are used.

Reverting to Fig. 82 ; the connecting-rod (CR) is made
of Bessemer steel, and is attached by the small end straps
(SE) to the cross-head (CH). The small end of the rod
is forked, and the straps are secured to each forked end by
wedges called gibs and cotters—CO is the cotter, and G
the gib. The small end straps may be made of case-
hardened iron or cast-steel. They work on to the gun-
metal caps of the cross-head (CH). The big end (BE)
consists of two brasses (BB), which encircle the journal (J)

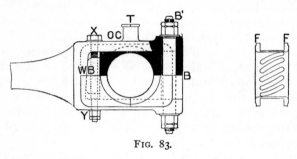

FIG. 83.

of the crank axle (CK). The brasses are enclosed in the
steel straps (BES), and are kept in position and adjusted
by the cotter (CO) and gib (G). The ends of the strap fit
on to the end (BE) of the connecting-rod, and are secured
to it by the butt cotter (CO). The connecting-rod works
to and fro between the slide-bars, through a hole cut in the
spectacle-plate (SP).

Another form of big end for a locomotive connecting-rod
is illustrated in Fig. 83. This is somewhat similar in
construction to the big end of a marine engine ; the end of
the rod is an open fork forming the straps into which the
brasses fit, the straps thus being a part of the rod. After

the brasses have been fitted into the forked end, they are
secured by the block (B) at the end of the fork through
which the bolt (B') passes. This bolt has a slight taper,
and is fitted with nuts at each end, thus enabling it to be
tightened up or withdrawn easily.

The adjustment of the brasses is affected by the wedge
block (WB), into which the bolt (X) is screwed. This bolt
passes through the straps or fork and is fitted at its lower
end with the nuts (Y). To adjust the block the nut is
slackened, and the head of the bolt turned with a spanner,
thus screwing the wedge up and down as required to
tighten or loosen the brasses.

This big end is used by Mr. Webb on the compound
engines. The oil-cup (OC) immediately over the centre
of the brasses is solid with the upper fork. The top (T)
screws into the oil-cup, and in the centre of it is a hole
kept closed by a small button, which is pressed upwards by
a spiral spring. When the cup is being filled with oil the
button is pressed down by the oil-feeder, and closes
automatically when the feeder is withdrawn. This is the
usual form of oil-cup used for big ends, eccentrics, coupling-
rods, &c.

One of the brasses is shown separately. The big end
strap fits in the spaces between the flanges (FF). The
flat surface of the outside of the brass is coated with
white metal and then faced up to the standard size as the
brass wears in the strap. The grooves or ribs are filled
with white metal.

CHAPTER VIII.

GENERAL DETAILS.

THE construction and position of ordinary single frames is explained in chapter ix., in which the method of erecting an engine is described. This is the kind of frame most generally used, and the locomotive engineers of some railway companies, who formerly built all their engines with double frames, are now reverting as far as possible to the single frame system, which is much less complicated. Double frames, however, are still frequently used on account of the additional strength obtained, and in the case of large single-wheeled engines having inside cylinders—such as the latest type of Great Western and Midland Railway engines —which have no outside coupling-rods, they are no doubt more suitable than single frames, the wheels being placed between the two frame plates.

A part plan of double frames and a pair of driving-wheels for a coupled engine is shown in Fig. 84. IF is the inside and OF the outside frame ; both of them extend along the whole length of the engine at either side, and are stayed at intervals by the transverse stay plates (TSB). The driving-wheels (DW) have each two axle-boxes. The inside axle-box (IAB) and the outside axle-box (OAB) work in the horn-plates (HP) in their respective frames. The wheels are shown between the two frames. The axle projects beyond the outside axle-box, and upon the end of it is fixed the coupling-rod crank (OC), to which is attached the coupling-rod (OCR) in the manner shown. CC are the driving cranks and (E) the eccentrics. There are altogether eight journals or bearing surfaces upon this axle without counting the eccentrics, so, as may be imagined, it is a costly piece of work.

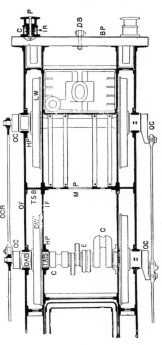

The engine from which the illustration is taken has six coupled wheels, the leading and trailing-wheels having axle-boxes on the outside frames only. The leading wheels (LW) are shown in the diagram, the frame being broken off between the driving and trailing-wheels.

The details of an ordinary form of locomotive buffer are also illustrated in Fig. 84. BP is the buffer plank, C is the buffer casting cylinder in which the plunger (P) works. The plunger fits into the cylinder as shown, and is held in position by the long bolt, which extends

FIG. 84.

through the centre of the plunger and cylinder, and is secured by a nut at the back of the latter. The plunger is kept in its normal position by the three india-rubber rings (IR), between which are wrought-iron washers, $\frac{1}{4}$ in.

thick. After the plunger, cylinder, and india-rubber rings
have been fitted together and the long bolt made fast, the
buffer cylinder is fastened to the buffer plank by bolts
which pass through it and the flange on the cylinder casting. When anything strikes the plunger (P) the india-
rubber rings (IR) are compressed, thus giving elasticity to

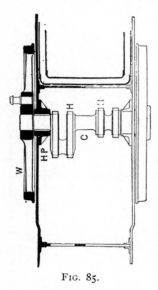

the buffer, and minimizing any
shock sustained. The draw-
bar, to which the coupling is
attached, is shown at DB.

A pair of driving-wheels for
a coupled engine and their
position with regard to single
frames is shown in Fig. 85.
There is one axle-box for each
wheel, and the crank-pin for
the coupling-rod is inserted
in the boss of the wheel (W),
which is specially constructed
for its reception. It will thus
be seen that with single framed
engines no outside crank is
necessary to carry the coupling-
rods. This greatly simplifies

FIG. 85.   the construction of the crank
axle. In this instance the
cranks (C) are strengthened in the web or arm of the crank
by the iron hoops (HH), which are shrunk on to them.
Crank axles are usually made of mild steel, as are also the
straight axles of all locomotive wheels, whether driving or
otherwise.

It will be observed that in the two foregoing illustrations
the horn-plates and axle-boxes hold the wheels rigid with
the frame-plates. Now a long wheel base with rigid axles

and wheels is unsafe for travelling round curves. With
goods engines that have six wheels coupled, the lateral
play in the axle-boxes and horn-plates, and the elasticity of
the frame enables the engine to take any ordinary curves
with safety; but with passenger engines that have to travel
at a high speed it is now becoming the general practice to
have only two pairs of the wheels rigid with the main
frames. In such cases the leading or trailing-wheels run in
bearings that are not rigidly in line with the main framework, so that the engine can take any ordinary curve
without strain. This sometimes applies to both leading
and trailing-wheels when the engine has a long wheel base
and more than six wheels. The two most common contrivances for this are the "radial axle-box" and the
"bogie."

Mr. Webb's radial axle-box is shown in Fig. 86. Stretching between the main frames (FF), and bolted to them in
the manner shown, are the curved guides (GG). These
guides are rigid with the framework of the engine, and so is
the spring frame (SF), which is fixed to the centre of the
guides. The radial axle-box (AA) is made of cast-iron,
and extends across, between and through the frames, being
curved to slide transversely in the guides. Bearings of the
ordinary description are fitted at either end of the radial
axle-box, and the journals of the axle revolve in these
bearings.

Attached to the axle-box in the manner shown is the
rod (R), which passes through the spring frame and is connected to the horizontal spiral springs (HS), which are
coiled right and left round the rod. When the engine
enters a curve the springs are compressed towards one side
and take any shock which may be transmitted through the
wheels from the rails, allowing the box to slide laterally in
the guides. When the engine gets on the straight road

again, the springs resume their normal position, and keep the wheels central.

All the most recent London and North-Western Railway express passenger engines built by Mr. Webb are fitted with radial axle-boxes at the leading end, and some of the eight-wheeled side-tank passenger engines have them fitted to the leading and trailing-wheels.

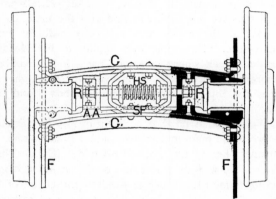

FIG. 86.

				FT.	IN.
Diameter of wheels	...	...	...	3	9
Diameter of journal	...	...	...	0	$7\frac{1}{2}$
Length of journal	...	...	...	0	10
Distance from centre to centre of bearings				3	$8\frac{1}{2}$
Lateral movement	...	...	...	0	$1\frac{1}{4}$
Thickness of guide plates	...	...		0	$0\frac{7}{8}$
Thickness of rod (R)	...	...	...	0	$1\frac{1}{2}$
Outside diameter of spring	...	...		0	$3\frac{7}{8}$

Thickness of spring coils, $\frac{5}{8}$ inch square.

A bogie is a separate carriage with a frame and wheel base of its own. It carries one end of the engine, the weight being pivoted on the centre of the bogie.

An arrangement of bogie, known as the Adams' type,

used by Mr. S. W. Johnson on the Midland Railway, is illustrated in Figs. 87, 87A. The pivot (P) is a circular steel

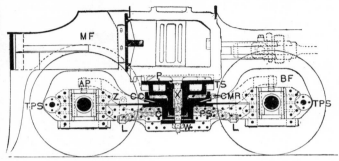

FIG. 87.

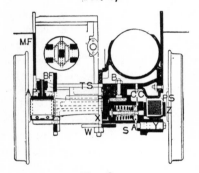

FIG. 87A.

PRINCIPAL DIMENSIONS OF FIGS. 87 AND 87A.

	FT.	IN.
Diameter of wheels	3	6
Wheel base	6	0
Diameter of journal	0	$5\frac{3}{4}$
Length of journal	0	9
Transverse centre to centre of bearings ...	3	7
Distance between bogie frames	2	$7\frac{3}{4}$
Thickness of bogie frames	0	1
Inverted laminated springs, 11 plates		

casting, which is bolted by bolts (B) to the transverse stay (TS). This stay extends underneath the cylinders between the main frames (MF) of the engine, to which it is bolted in the manner shown. It will thus be seen that the bogie-pivot is rigid with the main framework of the engine.

The bogie frames (BF) are made of steel, and are stayed at either end by the transverse pillar stays (TPS), which extend between the frames. The frames are fitted with horn-plates in a similar manner to the main frames.

It must be clearly understood that the bogie is an entirely separate carriage, with its own independent wheel base, wheels, axles, axle-boxes, horn-plates, and all other fittings appertaining to a vehicle constructed to run on a line of rails. The only point at which the bogie comes in direct contact with the main construction of the engine is where the pivot (P) fits into a hole in the centre casting (CC), which rests upon the framework of the bogie-carriage, and forms the floor or seating upon which the weight of the engine is carried. The shape of this casting will be understood upon referring to the illustration. It is not rigidly fixed to the bogie, but slides laterally in the guides (G), which are fixed transversely between the bogie frames. The large bolt (X) passes through the pivot (P) and casting (C), and at the end of the bolt is a large wrought-iron washer (W), held in position by the nut beneath it; this bolt prevents the possibility of the engine and bogie becoming disconnected. The gun-metal ring (GMR) forms a bearing surface between the pivot (P) and the centre casting (CC).

The bogie has two separate movements, namely, a circular motion round the pivot (P), and a lateral traverse between the guides (G). The space (I), which is $\frac{3}{4}$ inch, represents the distance allowed on either side between the centre casting and the bogie frame for the lateral traverse of the bogie in the guides (G). The lateral or transverse movement is controlled by spiral springs at either side of the casting: one of these springs is shown in section at S, at one side of the bogie. When the engine enters a curve the spring on the inner side is compressed, and when it passes from a curve on to a straight road the spring resumes its normal position, and the two springs keep the vehicle central. The weight is transmitted to the axle-boxes through the inverted plate spring (PS), which is attached by the pin (Y) to the bogie frame at A. The ends of the springs rest in the stirrup-links (LL), which are attached to the spring-cradle (Z), which transmits the weight to the top of the axle-boxes through the pillars (AP), which can be screwed up and down to adjust the weight. The spring-cradles (Z) are at either side on the outer side of the bogie frames. Each cradle consists of two wrought-iron plates, between which the spring is fixed. These plates are brought together and welded at the ends, where they are attached to the adjusting pillars (AP). The position of the spring (PS) in the cradle will be best seen in the cross section at one side, and the attachment of the cradle to the axle-box at AP in the same figure on the other side, and at AP in the longitudinal section.

The details of a locomotive wheel are given in Fig. 88. This is one of Mr. Webb's cast-iron wheels used for goods or mineral engines, which do not run at a high speed, and therefore do not require large wheels. The diameter in this case is 4 ft. 6 in. Mr. Webb was one of the first engineers to demonstrate the practicability of using cast-iron wheels for modern locomotives. The excellence of the design and manufacture of those made at Crewe renders them thoroughly trustworthy, and they have given satisfaction in every way, especially as they can be produced at an extremely moderate cost. The tyre (T) is made of Bessemer steel, and shrunk on to the rim of the wheel. The boss or

centre (B) is bored out in a lathe, and the key-way (K) cut
in the hole (H). The end of the axle is turned to be a
tight fit in the hole, and a key-way is cut on the shaft to
correspond with the one in the hole. The wheel is then
forced on to the axle by a powerful hydraulic press, thus
rendering wheel and axle perfectly secure. This is further
effected by a key carefully fitted in the key-ways. After the
wheels are fixed on the axle the tyres are turned in a lathe.
The tyre shown in the sketch is called a lip-tyre, that

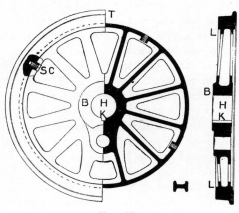

FIG. 88.

is to say, its outer edge projects beyond and encloses a
portion of the rim as shown at L. This lip prevents the
possibility of the tyre working off on the inside of the wheel,
and the flange pressing against the rail renders it equally
impossible for it to work off in the opposite direction. A
further security is also afforded by the set screws (SC),
screwed through the rim of the wheel into the tyre as
shown.

Until recently it was the invariable practice to make all

locomotive wheels of wrought-iron with steel tyres, and some railway companies continue this system. Each spoke is forged separately on to the boss or hub of the wheel, a section of the rim being first welded on to the outer end of the spoke. Each rim section is afterwards welded up between the spokes. Mr. Webb has, however, effected an improvement in the manufacture of passenger engine wheels by making them of cast-steel, which is stronger, and found to answer in every way. The metal itself is of course more expensive than wrought-iron, but the cost of production is so much decreased that they are cheaper in the long run.

An ordinary form of Bessemer steel coupling-rod for a six-wheel coupled engine is shown in Fig. 89. There are

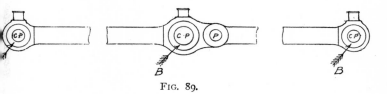

Fig. 89.

two of these rods at each side of the engine, working on to the crank-pins (CP), which are affixed to the wheels. The bushes (B) are rings of white metal or brass, which encircle the journal of the crank-pin. The bushes are hammered or pressed tightly into holes bored in the rods for their reception, and are then bored out, the exact distance between the centre of each bearing being first accurately measured. On the rod which couples the leading and driving-wheels there are two bearings ; the end of the rod projects towards the trailing-wheels, and is connected by a forked joint and pin (P) to the trailing-rod, which has a bearing at the other end on the crank-pin of the trailing-wheel. The use of coupling-rods is to procure increased adhesion to the rails ;

for when the driving-wheels are turned by the steam acting
on the crank axle, the leading and trailing-wheels are made
to revolve with them.

Fig. 90 shows the position of an axle-box in the horn-
blocks, and illustrates the manner in which the weight is
transmitted to the springs.   The axle-box (AB) is made of
cast-iron, and has cast into it the brass step or bearing (BS)
in which the journal of the wheel revolves.   This brass has,
at the top or crown of the bearing-surface, a transverse
groove about 1 in. wide, into which the oil for lubricating

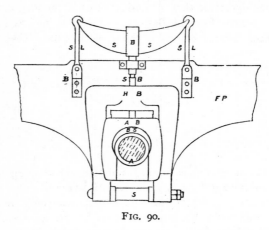

FIG. 90.

the axle is fed ; also recesses cut on either side of the groove,
which are filled with white metal before the bearing is
carefully bedded down to the journal of the axle.

At each outer side of the axle-box are smooth surfaces,
which are carefully fitted into corresponding faces of the
horn-blocks (HB), so as to obtain a good tight fit with a
uniform bearing over the two flat surfaces.   Grooves are cut
on the side of the axle-box to allow oil to pass between it

and the horn-block. There is only a bearing-surface on the upper part of the journal, the lower part of the axle-box having in it the " axle-box keep," which contains a tin in which is a sponge for preventing dirt from injuring the bearing surfaces. This tin is supported underneath by four spiral springs, which keep the sponge up against the journal. The brackets (B) are riveted to the frame-plate (FP), and to these brackets the spring-links or hooks (SL) are secured by pins. The two ends of the spring (S) fit into the hooks as shown. Underneath the spring is the adjusting-pin (SB) working on the top of the axle-box through a guide bracket riveted to the frame. This pin transmits the weight from the axle-box to the spring.

The spring (S) is composed of nineteen steel plates kept in position by the buckle (B). The axle-box is free to work up and down in the horn-block, as the spring is depressed or otherwise, by the movement of the engine, due to irregularities in the road or when passing over points and crossings. The spring plates must be of the very best steel, carefully tempered.

The horn-block (HB) is bolted to the frame (SB), and at its lower end is the stay (S), through which a bolt passes. This stay and bolt strengthen the frame, which would otherwise be weakened by the space cut in it for the reception of the horn-block. They also prevent any strain on the horn-block which might tend to throw the bearing surface out of truth.

This figure illustrates the usual manner in which the weight is carried by the spring of a locomotive; but the spring may be fixed in any other convenient position, either above or below the axle-box.

The large wheels of passenger engines frequently carry the weight on volute or spiral springs fixed below the axle-boxes. By another arrangement the driving and trailing springs are connected to a compensating lever, thus more equally dividing the weight. This lever is pivoted at its centre on to a pin fixed to the main frame; one end of the lever is connected by a link to the driving spring, and the other end to the trailing spring.

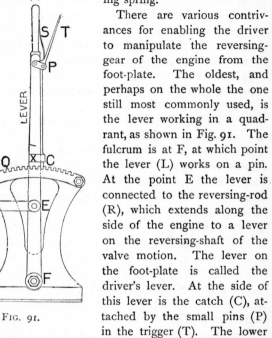

FIG. 91.

There are various contrivances for enabling the driver to manipulate the reversing-gear of the engine from the foot-plate. The oldest, and perhaps on the whole the one still most commonly used, is the lever working in a quadrant, as shown in Fig. 91. The fulcrum is at F, at which point the lever (L) works on a pin. At the point E the lever is connected to the reversing-rod (R), which extends along the side of the engine to a lever on the reversing-shaft of the valve motion. The lever on the foot-plate is called the driver's lever. At the side of this lever is the catch (C), attached by the small pins (P) in the trigger (T). The lower part of the catch slides in a clip (X), and drops into the notches in the quadrant (Q). When the lever has to be moved, the trigger (T) is pressed against the handle (H), and this draws the catch out of the notch, and allows the lever to work free in the quadrant. After moving the lever to the required position the pressure on the trigger is released, and the spring (S) forces the catch into the notch, thus securing the lever.

Very often a screw and wheel are used instead of a lever. This arrangement has the advantage of enabling the driver to set the valve gear exactly in any position required, as he is not dependent upon the position of notches in a quadrant, as with the lever arrangement. The screw, which is actuated by the hand-wheel, also affords a more powerful means of manipulating the valve gear. The reversing-wheel can be turned back when steam is on, whereas with a lever the steam has to be shut off before the driver can notch the engine up, because he has not sufficient power to overcome the pressure of the steam upon the slide valve. The expression to "pull the engine back," or "notch it up," is still retained by railway men when the reversing-gear is moved towards the position for increased expansive working, whatever may be the appliance provided on the foot-plate for the purpose.

Mr. James Stirling, the locomotive superintendent of the South-Eastern Railway, has fitted his engines with a very ingenious arrangement, whereby the valve gear is controlled by a piston working in a small steam cylinder.

This gear is briefly described among other details of one of Mr. Stirling's engines, illustrated on p. 279.

The chimney of a locomotive is usually made of wrought but sometimes of cast-iron. The bottom part of it is dished outwards to form a joint with the top of the smoke-box, to which it is bolted. The upper part of the chimney is cylindrical with a single riveted butt joint from top to bottom, the rivets being counter-sunk on the outside. Round the top edge is a circular casting to afford additional strength and rigidity. The length of the chimney must be determined by the height of the top of the smoke-box above rail level. Its usual internal diameter is about 14 in. or thereabouts, but this varies, and chimneys are frequently made taper, diverging upwards. The relative positions of the chimney and blast-pipe to each other are most important. They must be absolutely vertical with a centre line common to both. If either is at all out of truth, the steam, upon leaving the blast-pipe, instead of coming into equal contact with the whole of the internal circumference of the chimney, will strike it at one side, and the action of the blast will be impeded, producing a detrimental effect upon the steaming of the engine.

The diameter of the orifice of the blast-pipe is an important matter; the smaller it is, the sharper the blast, and the more powerful its action upon the fire. A strong blast causes an engine to steam well, but when the fire is too fiercely urged, a greater quantity of fuel is burned, besides which the contracted orifice for the outlet of the exhaust steam causes a back pressure in the cylinders, and prevents the engine from working freely. The point to be aimed at is to get the blast-pipe as large as possible, consistent with the boiler making steam satisfactorily. There have been many experiments made from time to time in the construction of blast-pipes to determine their effect upon the working of an engine and the consumption of coal. It has been found that the influence exercised by the blast-pipe upon the coal-bill of a large railway company is very great, a variation of no more than an eighth of an inch in the size of the orifice producing most important results. An engine that has the heating surface and grate area properly proportioned to the size of the boiler and cylinders, should, under ordinary circumstances, be capable of making steam with a blast-pipe orifice not less than $4\frac{5}{8}$ in. in diameter.

The top of the blast-pipe is usually about level with, or slightly above, the top row of tubes. It has often been thought that the vacuum in the smoke-box, caused by the blast, has a much stronger effect upon the upper than upon the lower rows of tubes, and therefore that the heating surface proper of the tubes is unequally distributed, the upper rows doing the greater part of the work. This theory is borne out by the fact that the upper rows wear away more quickly than the lower tubes, and more frequently fail from this cause. To obviate this, and distribute the work evenly over the whole of the tube surface, the blast-pipe is sometimes made shorter, and the barrel of the chimney extended downwards into the smoke-box with a bell mouth $4\frac{3}{4}$ in. above the top of the blast-pipe. This is an arrangement lately applied by Mr. Webb to many London and North-Western engines with good results (see CE, Plate II., p. 306).

Mr. Adams, of the South-Western Railway, has brought out a blast-pipe which he claims acts equally upon all the tubes in the boiler. A transverse section of the smoke-box of a South-Western Railway locomotive fitted with the Adams vortex blast-pipe is shown in Fig. 92. It will be seen that the area at the orifice where the steam is discharged is between the two pipes (BP) and (AP). The central pipe extends downwards, and diverges into a large bell mouth in front of the lower rows of tubes, through which the air is directly drawn. The exhaust steam passes from the cylinders through the cylinder exhaust passages (CEP) to the blast-pipe (BP). The lower extremities of the blast-pipe attached to the exhaust passages, instead of converging to the usual cylindrical outlet at the top of the pipe, are so formed that the air passage (AP) passes down the centre of the pipe, the steam discharge being through the circular orifice (CO) which encloses the air passage (AP). The latter being directly acted upon by the blast, has drawn through it the air from the lower part of the smoke-box, and thus the blast is made to act upon the lower rows of tubes. By this arrangement a great saving in the fuel consumed by South-Western engines is claimed. This illustration also shows the ordinary arrangement of steam-pipes in the smoke-box for conveying the steam from the boiler to the cylinders. The cast-iron T piece (TP) is attached by the flange (F) and studs (S) to the tube plate and main steam-pipe running through the boiler to the regulator. The steam-pipes (SP) are made of copper, and are secured by the flanges (F') to the T piece (TP). Passing round the smoke-box at each side, they are secured by studs at their lower ends to the branches (Y), where the steam passes into the steam-chests. This engine, having outside cylinders, there are two steam-chests to be fed with steam from the boiler, and two steam-pipes are required; whereas, with the inside cylinders, illustrated in Figs. 77 and 79, both valves are in one steam-chest, and one steam-pipe only is needed.

Z (Fig. 92) is the blower-pipe through which the steam from the boiler is turned up the chimney to cause a draught on the fire if required when the engine is standing. H is the steam-pipe conveying the steam from the boiler to the valve (V), which is actuated from the foot-plate. By opening this valve the steam is turned into the blower-pipe. EP is the exhaust pipe from the ejector, or apparatus for creating the vacuum for working the brake. The heads of the longitudinal stays, which have been mentioned in the boiler chapter, are shown at L.

Great Western engines are fitted with a device by which the driver can, from the foot-plate, put a cap on the top of the blast-pipe, to contract the orifice and sharpen the blast, if the engine is not steaming properly.

Although the Westinghouse and automatic vacuum brakes (which will be hereafter described) are frequently fitted to locomotives, their use upon the vehicles of the

train does not necessarily imply that the same form of
brake must be fitted to the engine.

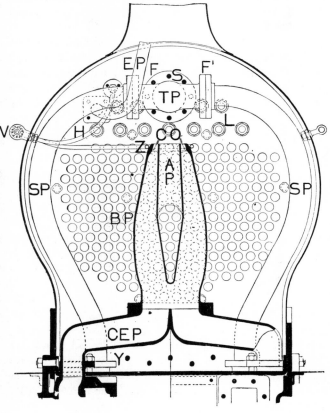

FIG. 92.

Many locomotive engineers had fitted their engines with
powerful steam-brakes, before they thought of adopting a

continuous air-brake. This was the case on the London
and North-Western Railway, and until recently the vacuum
brake on the train and the steam-brake on the engine were
worked quite separately. The diagram (Fig. 93) illustrates
the action of Mr. Webb's steam-brake.

A vertical cylinder (C) is fixed under the foot-plate (FP),
to which it is attached by studs, through the flange (F).
Inside the cylinder is the piston (P), fitted with the usual
form of piston-rings to render it steam-tight. Forming a
part of the piston is the hollow trunk (T), which projects

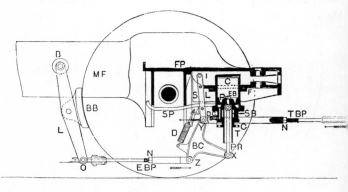

Fig. 93.

downwards through the stuffing-box (SB) and gland (G).
The trunk is packed in the same way as an ordinary
piston-rod. In the centre of the piston-head is fixed the
eye-bolt (EB), to which is attached the pull-rod (PR),
which passes through the centre of the trunk (T), in which
there is room for it to have a lateral movement. The
lower end of the pull-rod is fixed to the bell-crank lever
(BC) at the point X. As will be seen from the drawing,
this lever has three arms, one terminating at X, where it is

attached to the piston pull-rod. Of the other two arms, one projects upwards, and is attached to the tender brake pull-rod (TBP) at Y, where it is also fixed to the suspension link (SL). This link carries the weight of the gear, being attached at its upper end (I) to the foot-plate; the other arm of the bell-crank projects downwards, and is similarly attached at Z to the engine brake pull-rod (EBP).

When the brake is applied, steam is admitted to the cylinder below the piston through the steam-pipe (SP), and forces the piston upwards. This has the effect of drawing up the arm (X) of the lever. The arm (Y) is thus forced in the direction of the arrow, and causes the tender pull-rod (TBP) to close the blocks on the tender-wheels; at the same time, the point Z is forced in an opposite direction, as shown by the arrow, and a tension obtained on the engine brake pull-rod (EBP). This rod is fastened at the opposite end (O) to the lever (L), which swings on the bracket (B) attached to the main frame (MF). This lever being pulled towards the wheel brings the brake block (BB) against the tyre, and the brake is thus applied simultaneously on engine and tender. When the brake is released the application valve on the foot-plate allows the steam to exhaust back through the pipe (SP), and the lever is brought back to its normal position by the spring (D), whose action can be easily seen. The nuts (NN) on the pull-rods are for adjusting the brakes as the blocks wear. The drain-cock (DC) is a small automatic ball valve provided to let the condensed steam out of the cylinder. A small hole in the top of the cylinder casting, and another through the head of the piston to the inside of the trunk, places the cylinder above the piston in connection with the atmosphere.

CHAPTER IX.

HOW AN ENGINE IS PUT TOGETHER IN THE ERECTING-SHOP.

To give the reader a general idea of the construction of a locomotive, or rather of the way in which it is put together, it may be as well to follow step by step the work done in the "erecting-shop." This is the shop to which all the different parts of the engine are brought, after undergoing various stages of manufacture and fitting, to be put together, piece by piece, until the whole structure is completed.

In this description no attempt will be made to go into any details of the parts named, nor would it be possible in a work like this to fully describe all the details of one particular engine, much less to analyze the value of the different ideas held by various engineers in respect to the design and arrangement of the multitudinous fittings of a a locomotive. The more important details have already been described and illustrated in the previous pages, and in this chapter the place they occupy and the functions they fulfil will simply be mentioned.

For the purpose in view it will be as well to select some modern type of locomotive with as few complications as possible, and take a cursory glance at the work done in putting the parts together in the erecting-shop.

Mr. Webb has built at Crewe a large number of "six-wheels coupled" engines for working the heavy mineral traffic on the London and North-Western Railway, which perhaps combine power and simplicity of design as well as any engine in the country. They are called "coal-engines," and the routine of erecting one of them in the Crewe shops will be briefly described.

The *frame-plates* have first to be dealt with. There are two made of Bessemer steel, 1 in. thick, both exactly the same in every respect. They extend along the whole length of the engine at either side. Before being brought to the erecting-shop they are roughed out to the proper shape, the surfaces are ground and made perfectly flat and true, and the edges trimmed round in a slotting machine. This being done, they are fixed by temporary cross-bars into the position they will occupy when the engine is completed. Fig. 94 shows an elevation, and Fig. 95 the frame-plates in plan.

The *cylinders* are fixed between the frames at C. They are cast in one piece, and are of the pattern shown in Fig. 77. They are bolted

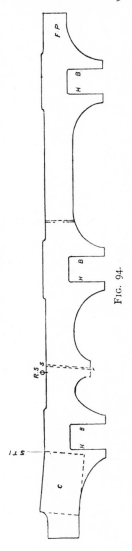

FIG. 94.

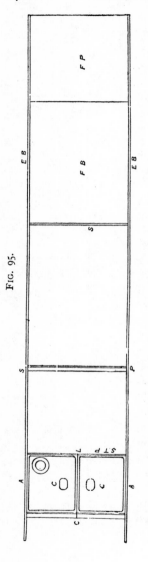

FIG. 95.

to the frames at AA, CL being the centre line through the steam-chest. The cylinders, which are brought to the erecting-shop ready fitted and bored out, are slung into position between the two frames by an overhead crane.

The *spectacle-plate* is fixed between the frames at SP. This is made of cast-steel; it forms a stay between the two frames, and is a carrier for one end of the slide-bars and for the guides in which the valve spindles slide, as shown at VSS, Fig. 43.

A *stay-plate* at S and *foot-plate* at FP complete the rigid groundwork on which the engine is built up. The foot-plate is made of cast-iron, and is the floor upon which the driver and fireman stand.

The *horn-blocks*, or guides for the axle-boxes, are bolted to the frames in the spaces (HB). They are made of cast-iron or steel, with smooth faces at right angles to the frames, and their use is to keep the axle-boxes in their proper position, but allow them to work up and down to the extent that the spring moves with the jolting of the engine (see Fig. 90, p. 158).

After the frames, cylinders, spectacle-plate, foot-plate, and horn-blocks are all bolted together, the accuracy of the work is tested by diagonal, transverse, and longitudinal measurements. This is very important, it being absolutely necessary that the centre line of the cylinder should be perfectly parallel with the frames, and the faces of the horn-blocks square with them. To get the cylinders, frames, and horn-blocks perfectly square is one of the chief points aimed at in building an engine. If not accurately done at this stage, the error can never be properly remedied afterwards. It does sometimes happen that through carelessness or inaccurate measurements, an engine is built slightly on the skew, and if such be the case troubles will always ensue so long as it runs. The driver who has charge of a badly-built engine can never get satisfactory work out of it; axles and journals run hot, and it is a continual source of expense in the matter of repairs.

The method employed in setting the cylinders in position, and the whole engine square, is as follows—The cylinders are fixed temporarily by cramps to the framing, in as nearly the exact position as can be judged. A thin bar of iron is then put across between the driving or middle horn-blocks, the top edge of the bar being exactly in the centre line of the driving axle according to the drawing that is being worked to. A strip of metal is put across the front end of each cylinder. In this strip is a small hole exactly in the centre of the bore of the cylinder. Through each of these holes a wire is passed and extended as far as the trailing horn-blocks, being fastened to a bar between them. This bar is fixed at such an altitude that the wires just touch the top of the bar between the driving horn-blocks. The cylinders are then moved as required until the wires are found to pass exactly through the centre of each. All the measurements for ensuring that the frames, &c. are in proper position with regard to the cylinders, are taken along the length of these lines, and the frame-plates set in any direction required.

After the exact position of the cylinders has been accurately ascertained the bolt-holes in the frame-plates are marked through the bolt-holes which are already drilled in the cylinder casting. The holes in the frame-plates are then drilled, and a "rose-bit" put through them and through the holes in the cylinder casting, thus ensuring that both shall be exactly true to each other and of the same size.

In some cases the bolt-holes in the frame for securing the parts fixed to it are marked from a "template," or pattern, and then drilled by a machine. A "rose-bit" is always put through the frame and the part to be secured to it. The bolts are turned so as to be a good driving fit in the holes.

An angle-iron is riveted along the outside of each frame-plate, the top of it being flush with the upper edge of the frame-plate. To this angle-iron the *side plates* are riveted at right angles to the frame, forming a gangway at each side of the engine. They are strengthened by angle-irons riveted underneath the outer edge, and are supported at intervals by brackets fastened to the frames. The side plates are below the top part of the wheels, and have holes cut in them for the latter to work through. These holes are covered by *splashers* bolted to the side plates.

At the same time the side plates are being riveted up, the *axle-boxes* may be fitted in the horn-blocks. They are in the first instance a shade too large, and are filed to the proper size, being made to fit fairly tight in the horn-blocks with a uniform bearing over the two flat surfaces at each side of the axle-box.

There are flanges on the axle-boxes to keep them in proper position in the horn-blocks, but a little side play is

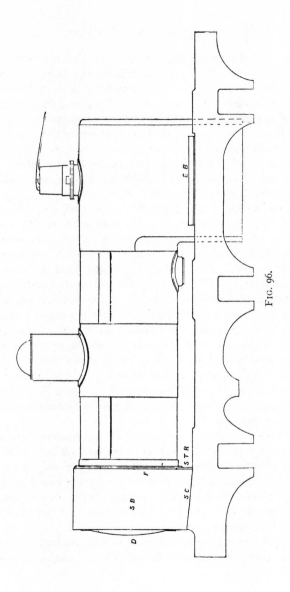

FIG. 96.

allowed between the flange and the edge of the horn-block
to relieve the strain on the frame when travelling round
curves.   After the sides have been fitted in the horn-blocks,
the axle-boxes are taken down again, and their bearing
surfaces carefully bedded on to the journals of the wheels.

Brackets are fixed to the frames, to which the *spring-links*
or hooks are secured by pins.   The springs are not fixed in
position until the engine is lowered on to its wheels.   The
general arrangement of horn-block, axle-box, and spring is
shown in Fig. 90, chap. viii.

The work has now reached a stage when the *boiler* may
be tried on.   It comes ready finished from the boiler-
shop, with all fittings complete and attached.   An overhead
travelling crane brings it over the framework and lowers it
into position.   The fire-box end drops down between the
frame-plates at FB (Fig. 95), and is supported on the upper
edge of the frames at EB (Fig. 96) by brackets riveted to
the outer casing of the fire-box.   These are called expansion
brackets; they are not fastened to the frame-plates, but
simply rest on them, carrying the weight of the boiler at
the fire-box end, and sliding along as the boiler expands
and contracts, which it does to an appreciable extent.   The
total length of the boiler varies some three-eighths of an
inch between the condition of the boiler-plates when under
steam and when cold.

The smoke-box tube-plate projects downwards, and is
bolted to the cylinders at STR, the only place at which the
boiler is rigidly fixed to the main framework of the engine.
The boiler, after being fixed in position, is tested by steam
at its ordinary working pressure (which with this class of
engine is 150 lbs. per square inch) and any necessary
caulking done.

The smoke-box tube-plate is flanged forward at the top
and sides, and to this flange (F) the *smoke-box* (SB) is

riveted. The smoke-box, which is made of sheet-steel, is built up in position in the erecting-shop. It is at the top and sides a continuation of the cylindrical part of the boiler, but somewhat larger in diameter. The bottom part is curved outwards, and secured by set screws to the frame-plates at SC. The door (D) must be carefully fitted and made as near air-tight as possible. The *chimney* is secured by bolts to the top of the smoke-box.

The *steam-pipe*, for conveying the steam from the boiler to the steam-chest, the *steam-jet* or *blower-pipe*, and the *blast-pipe* are in the smoke box. Their position and method of attachment have already been described, and are illustrated in Fig. 92, chap. viii., and although there is a considerable difference in the detail of the smoke-box fittings of a South-Western engine compared with a London and North-Western engine, the general arrangement is the same in each case. In fixing the blast-pipe great care must be taken to set it in such a position that the centre line of the blast-pipe is exactly parallel and central with the centre line of the chimney, as the chimney or blast-pipe being out of truth seriously affects the steaming properties of the engine ; the action of the blast being one of the most important features in the working of a locomotive.

While this work is going on, other fitters may be engaged in putting up the *slide-bars* and other gear underneath the engine.

The slide-bars are fixed at one end by studs to the back cylinder cover, and at the other by bolts to the spectacle-plate. They must be fitted into position with great care and accuracy, to ensure which a string is fixed through the centre of each cylinder and prolonged beyond the length of the bars. This string is the guide which enables the fitter to get the bars exactly parallel with each other, and the centre line between them in line with the centre of the cylinder.

After the slide-bars are fitted up, the *pistons* may be put in the cylinders. They are made of cast-iron, and have the steel *piston-rods* attached to them before they are brought to the erecting-shop. There are three grooves turned in the piston-head for the reception of the *packing-rings*. The rings used by Mr. Webb are not of cast-iron, as in the case of those previously described. Each ring is made of a thin bar of steel set by machinery into a circular form ; about an inch and a half is left between the two ends, and the circle is slightly larger than the bore of the cylinder. The rings are therefore in compression when working in the cylinder, and their natural tendency to spring outwards forms a steam-tight joint with the surface of the cylinder. The ends should almost touch when in the cylinder, and, as has already been explained, in putting them in care must be taken not to let the joints in the rings be opposite to each other. The piston is put in from the front end of the cylinder, and the piston-rod projects through the stuffing-box. The *cross-heads* are then fixed to the piston-rods. Each cross-head has two *slide-blocks :* the bearing surface of one works on the top slide-bar, and of the other on the lower slide-bar. These slide-blocks must be carefully adjusted so as to be a good fit between the slide-bars, but at the same time work freely between them.

After placing the *slide-valves* in the buckles or frames attaching them to the valve spindles, they are inserted in the steam-chest from the front end. The *valve spindles* project through the stuffing-box at the back of the steam-chest, and are connected by the adjusting screw and nut to the *valve spindle-slides*, which work in the cast-iron guide bolted to the spectacle-plate.

In the meantime other men may be engaged on the following work—

Fixing the framework of the *angle-iron* round the barrel

of the boiler and at the top and sides of the fire-box, casing down to the frame-plates. After this framework is completed, a thick layer of *felt* is placed next to the boiler-plates, which has the effect of preventing loss of heat by radiation. The *lagging-plates*, which form the outer covering of the boiler and are made of thin sheet-iron, are then screwed on to the angle-irons, enclosing the felt lagging between them and the boiler.

Bolting the *splashers* to the side-plates, also fixing the *panel-plates*, which form a protection at each side of the foot-plate. Along the top of the panel-plates *hand-rails* are bolted, secured at one end to the *hand-rail pillars* fastened to the side-plates, and at the other end curved round and bolted to brackets on the fire-box casing. The splashers for the rear or trailing-wheels are riveted to the inside of the panel-plates.

Fixing the *cab*, which is the hood protecting the engine-men from the weather. It is bolted to the panel-plates at both sides, the centre of it resting on the fire-box case.

The engine is now ready for the *wheels*, and is lifted by two overhead travelling-cranes (one at each end) off the cast-iron pillars that have supported it under the framework during the process of construction. Mr. Webb's coal engines have cast-iron wheels similar to that illustrated in Fig. 88. The wheels, axles, and tyres are put together and turned up before being brought to the erecting-shop. The axle-boxes have already been bedded on to the journals and fixed by the axle-box keeps on to the axles, and the wheels are run under the engine, which is suspended in mid-air by means of the travelling-cranes. Each pair of wheels is placed in position under the corresponding horn-blocks, and the engine is lowered on to them, a man guiding each axle-box into its horn-block as the engine descends.

The *springs* are placed in the hooks with the *spring-pins* under them in the guides bolted to the frame-plates. These pins, as soon as they touch the top of the axle-boxes, transmit the weight of the engine to the springs.

The trailing-wheels are carried on one large inverted spring which extends from one axle-box to the other, the ends of the spring taking the weight on a friction roller on the top of each box. These rollers prevent strain on the frames when travelling round curves, and allow free play for the spring, which is curved upwards, the top part of it bearing on the centre of the bottom of the cast-iron foot-plate.

After the engine is lowered on to the wheels a *stay-bolt* is bolted through the two lower ends of the horn-plates underneath each axle-box (see S, Fig. 90). This strengthens the frames, which would otherwise be weakened by the spaces cut in them for the reception of the horn-blocks and axle-boxes.

The wheels being in their places, the work of fixing up the *valve motion* and *connecting-rods* may be taken in hand. The connecting-rods are coupled by their *small ends* to the cross-heads, and by the *big ends* to the crank-axle. The small end of the rod is forked, and to the end of each fork a bearing is attached by wedges called "gibs" and "cotters." Each bearing works on a brass cap at either side of the cross-head.

The big end consists of two brasses fixed in a steel "strap." The strap with one brass in it is put on the journal of the crank axle; the second brass is then put in the strap, and the two form a complete bearing round the journal, being also kept in position by "gibs" and "cotters." The ends of the strap fit on to the end of the connecting-rod, being secured to it by another cotter called a "butt-cotter."

The details of the piston, piston-rod, and connecting-rod for an engine of this class have been illustrated in Fig. 82, chap. vii.

The *eccentric-rods* may now be put up, and are fixed in

the manner already described, this engine being fitted with the valve motion illustrated in Fig. 43. The eccentric-sheaves are keyed on to the driving axle before the wheels are brought to the erecting-shop.

The *reversing-shaft* is fixed between the frames at RS (Fig. 94), and works in a boss or bearing surface on each frame. On it near the centre are four levers; two to support the valve motion and move it in the required position for reversing the engine and working the steam expansively; the other two on the opposite side of the shaft, each carrying a heavy cast-iron block, to balance the weight of the motion. Another lever on the end of the shaft, outside the framing, is coupled by a long rod to the *reversing-screw*, which works in a cast-iron bracket fastened by studs to the fire-box casing. On this screw is a wheel, which is the driver's handle for actuating the reversing-gear.

The *outside coupling-rods* are now put up; there are two at each side of the engine, working on the crank-pins. The leading-rods have each two bearings, one for the driving and the other for the leading crank-pins. The trailing-rod works on the trailing crank-pin at one end, and at the other is coupled to the leading-rod by a forked joint and pin (see Fig. 89). The rods are kept in position by large *washers* on the ends of the crank-pins, to which they are attached by *split-pins*.

The process of setting the valves will be described in a succeeding chapter.

The *ash-pan* is bolted to brackets at the bottom of the fire-box casing. It must be made air-tight as far as possible, and the door or damper fitted to the front with a rod extending to the foot-plate, where it works in a rack, thus enabling the driver to set it in any required position.

The *fire-bars* are then put in position, and the *brick arch* built in the fire-box.

The following fittings, which have not yet been mentioned, are added, being put up during the erection of the engine whenever most convenient—

The *cylinder taps* and gear for working them from the foot-plate, for allowing the condensed water to escape from the cylinders.

The *sand-boxes* and gear for putting dry sand on the rails when greasy, to prevent the engine slipping.

The *feed-pipes* for conveying the water from the tender to the injectors, which constitute the apparatus for supplying the boiler with the feed-water, as already described elsewhere.

The *buffer-plank*, *draw-bar*, and couplings are the last things to be put up, and having mentioned them, the general survey of the process of the erection of a locomotive, such as has been described, is completed. It must be understood that allusion has here been made only to the more important parts that have to be put together and handled in the erecting-shop, a detailed description of the various parts, and of the boiler and its fittings, having been already given.

The usual time taken to erect a coal-engine in the Crewe Works is four weeks, but as an experiment, the whole of the work was upon one occasion performed in $25\frac{1}{2}$ hours. An illustration of an engine of this class is shown in Fig. 106.

CHAPTER X.

HOW THE SLIDE-VALVES ARE SET.

AFTER the connecting-rods and valve-gear are put up, the process of " setting the valves " is gone through. This is an important duty, and should only be entrusted to a careful and experienced man.

As already explained, the admission of steam to the cylinders is controlled by the size of the valve and ports, the lead given, and the throw of the eccentric ; but although these may all be correctly calculated and properly constructed, great care is necessary in fitting up the gear to see that the valve is so placed in the steam-chest as to afford an equal distribution of steam to each end of the cylinder. If the eccentric-rod or valve spindle are not exactly of the right length, the steam admission is greater at one end of the cylinder than at the other, and "setting the valves" is the term used to describe the operation by which the correct length of the valve spindle is determined, and the equal distribution of steam at each end of the cylinder ensured.

There are two ways of setting the valves·—

(1) By equalizing the "lead" when the crank is at the extreme end of each stroke.

(2) By equalizing the full opening of the valve for steam admission at each end of the travel of the valve, without taking into consideration the position of the piston.

The first of these methods, known technically as *setting the valves by the centre*, gives the most accurate results, but the second method is frequently used in running-shed practice, as it takes a shorter time, and appears to obtain the most correct average between forward and back-gear, when there is a slight difference in the length of the eccentric-rods. The method of setting the valves by the centre may be thus briefly described.

It is first necessary to get the exact position of each crank on the forward and back centre. The *forward centre* is when the crank is at its nearest point to the cylinder, the piston being at the extreme end of its stroke at the *front* end of the cylinder.

The *back centre* is when the crank is at its furthest point from the cylinder, the piston being at the extreme end of its stroke at the *back* end of the cylinder.

The following is the method by which the exact position of the crank on each centre is obtained—

The driving-wheel is set in the position for the crank to be *nearly at the end of its stroke*, and a vertical line is drawn with a sharp-pointed scriber upon one of the slide-bars and the slide-block next to it. A slight dent or centre dot is now punched at any convenient point on the engine frame, and this is the point from which the observations are taken by means of a trammel, which is a piece of thin steel rod in the shape of an **L**, having a sharp point at the end of each leg.

One of these points is placed in the centre dot on the framing, and with the other point a mark is made on the outer side of the tyre of the wheel. The wheel is then turned past the end of the stroke, and stopped when the marks on the slide-block and slide-bar again exactly correspond with each other.

It must be clearly understood that this mark is made as

the cross-head is on the *outward stroke ;* when the wheel is
turned the slide-block moves to the end of the stroke, and
then comes back again towards the mark on the bar, the
wheel being stopped when the marks again exactly correspond
on the *return stroke.*

Another mark is now made on the tyre of the wheel by
the trammel as before. The distance between the two
marks on the tyre is accurately divided by a pair of com-
passes, and a centre dot made on the dividing line.   When
the wheel is turned to the position in which the point of one
leg of the trammel is in the centre dot on the frame, and the
point of the other leg in the centre dot on the wheel, the
piston is at the extreme end of the stroke, and the engine is
said to be " on the centre."

The same operation is gone through to get the centre at
the opposite end of the stroke, and for the two centres of
the other crank.   There are therefore altogether four centres
to get ; each is marked in the same way on the tyre of the
wheel, and as the cranks are at right angles to each other,
the circumference of the wheel is thus divided into four
equal sections.

For the purpose of this description it will only be
necessary to refer to one side of the engine, each valve
being set in exactly the same way.

The crank is placed on the forward centre, one point of
the trammel in the centre dot on the frame, and the other
on the wheel.

The valve should then be open for the admission of
steam to give the lead. This opening is accurately measured,
and the crank then turned a half revolution, *i.e.* to the
opposite centre, which must also be gauged by the trammel.
The valve should now be open to give the lead at the
opposite end of the stroke.   This opening is also measured
and the two measurements compared.   If the eccentric-rod

and valve spindle are exactly the proper length, the two openings will be equal. If there is a difference the valve spindle must be lengthened or shortened as required until the lead is equalized.

Most of the Crewe engines are fitted with eccentric-rods made exactly to a standard length, and it is not the practice to alter them in setting the valves, the adjustment being obtained by means of the screw and nut shown at SN (Fig. 43). Sometimes the eccentric-rods are fitted with liners, where they are bolted to the eccentric-straps, and the adjustment is effected by altering the thickness of the liners. This is shown in the valve gear illustrated in Fig. 44, chap. iv.

If there is no means of adjustment provided, the eccentric-rods must be taken to the smith's shop and lengthened or shortened as required.

When each rod can be adjusted separately, each valve should be carefully set in forward and back gear, but when the adjustment is on the valve spindle it is best to get the valves right for forward gear, and overlook any small inaccuracy in the back gear movement, provided it is not of too glaring a description. With some kinds of link motion it is found advisable to give slightly more lead to the front port.

To enable the fitter to accurately measure the openings of the ports, an iron template or skeleton pattern of the ports is fixed to the outside of the steam-chest, and a similar pattern of the valve—attached to the front end of the valve spindle—is made to travel over the template of the ports as the wheel turns. The position of the valve and ports at each part of the stroke can thus be easily seen and measured.

When the valves are set "by the travel," the centres are not marked off on the driving-wheels. The engine is moved until the valve is found to be open to its fullest extent for the steam admission to one port. This opening is measured, and the engine moved on until the valve is opened to its fullest extent for the admission of steam to the opposite port, which is also measured.

The two measurements are then compared, and any difference there may be between them is adjusted by the screw and nut on the valve spindle.

With engines fitted with the Joy valve gear, that for the most part run chimney first, it is found in practice to be the best plan to set the valve accurately for forward gear, and not take back gear into consideration at all.

It may be observed that in setting any valve gear the driver's lever should be placed, not in full gear, but in the position it will normally occupy when the engine is running with an average load.

CHAPTER XI.

CLASSIFICATION OF ENGINES.

THE classification of engines in regard to the position of the cylinders and frames has already been explained. There are further important differences in classification which may now be touched upon.

A Tender Engine carries its supply of feed-water and fuel upon a separate vehicle called the tender. Such engines are used for long runs in which the opportunities for replenishing the tank are few and far between, and when the nature of the work entails the consumption of a large quantity of coal.

A Tank Engine carries these supplies upon the engine itself, the feed-water in convenient tanks and the coal in a receptacle, at the back of the foot-plate, called the "coal bunker." The classification of tank-engines may be thus further subdivided.

1. *Side-tank Engines*, which carry the feed-water in rectangular tanks, extending alongside the boiler at either side upon the side frames.

2. *Saddle-tank Engines*, which carry the water in a semi-circular tank, resting upon the top of the boiler and fire-box shell.

Tank-engines are used for short trips when water can be

frequently obtained, and the work is of such a nature that the mileage run only requires the engine to carry a comparatively small amount of fuel. These engines are very useful for branch-line work; they can run almost equally well in either direction, which is a great advantage when there is a difficulty in getting to and from a turn-table. The extra weight of the coal and water gives the driving-wheels a good grip on the rails.

A *Single Engine* has a pair of driving-wheels working entirely independently of all the other wheels. Such engines run more freely at high speeds than engines that have their wheels coupled together, but the adhesion to the rails with single driving-wheels is not so great as with coupled wheels. Single engines are therefore unsuitable for working heavy trains over lines with steep gradients, and when starting the wheels are apt to "slip," that is, to spin round upon the rails without moving the engine. These engines are used principally for light express passenger trains, and there is no doubt that when once a speed is attained, they compare favourably with coupled engines, both in the matter of economy and general satisfactory working.

The chief upholder of single wheel engines in modern times is Mr. Patrick Stirling of Doncaster, and he has built some very splendid engines of this class. The long, quick, and punctual running on the Great Northern Railway is well known to most people, and great credit is due to the large single engines working their express trains for obtaining for the Company the notoriety they undoubtedly possess in this respect. At the same time the maximum weight of their fastest trains is not so great as that of some other railways, and the road is exceptionally favourable in the matter of gradients.

A *Four-wheels Coupled Engine* has two pairs of wheels

coupled together by outside rods working on crank-pins on the wheels. The driving-wheels are acted upon by the piston and connecting-rod in the same way as a pair of single driving-wheels, and the wheels to which they are coupled are of the same diameter. By coupling the wheels together the adhesion to the rails is greatly increased, and thus a material advantage in starting the train from a state of rest is obtained. Generally speaking, the wheels are not of such large diameter as the single wheels of an express passenger engine, but 7 ft. wheels can be coupled together with excellent results, provided the machinery is powerful enough to drive them. The part of the engine not carried on the coupled wheels is usually supported on a bogie or a radial axle-box—which may be either at the leading or trailing end of the engine. The usual plan is to couple the driving (middle) wheels to the trailing-wheels, and to carry the leading end upon a bogie or radial axle-box, but this position is sometimes reversed, the trailing end being so carried, and the leading wheels under the smoke-box coupled to the driving-wheels. With four-wheels coupled engines the wheels not coupled are always much smaller than the driving-wheels.

Six-Wheels Coupled Engines are for working goods and mineral trains. The six wheels are of course all the same diameter, which should not exceed about 5 ft., as the wheel base of the three pairs of wheels is rigid, and the larger the wheels the longer this rigid wheel base. Occasionally engines are constructed with six wheels coupled and an additional pair of smaller wheels either at the leading or trailing end. Engines with six coupled wheels possess great advantage when starting a heavy load, as the steam acting upon the piston communicates its power to all the six wheels at once.

Mr. Webb has lately built at Crewe a very powerful

CLASSIFICATION OF LOCOMOTIVE ENGINES.

Position of Cylinders.	Description of Wheels, &c.			Typical Illustration.
	Leading end.	Centre of Engine.	Trailing end.	
	Express Passenger Engines.			
Outside	Bogie	Single driving-wheels	Ordinary axle-boxes	G. N. Ry. (Fig. 113)
,,	Ordinary axle-box	,, ,, ,,	,, ,, ,,	L. & N.-W. Ry. 7ft. 6in. (Fig. 27)
Inside	Bogie	Single driving-wheels	{ 4 Wheels coupled } Ordinary axle-box	L. & S.-W. Ry. (Fig. 124) Midland Ry. (Fig. 126)
,,	Ordinary axle-box	,, ,, ,,	,, ,, ,,	G. E. Ry. (Fig. 112)
,,	Bogie	,, ,, ,,	{ 4 Wheels coupled }	Midland Ry. (Fig. 127) L. & N.-W. Ry.(Fig. 104)
,,	Ordinary axle-box	,, ,, ,,		
Outside and Inside Compound	{ 4 Wheels coupled } Coupled	Coupled	Ordinary axle-box	L.B.& S.-C. Ry. (Fig.120)
	Radial axle-box	Single driving, from low-pressure cylinder	{ Single driving from high-press. cylinder }	L. & N.-W. Ry.(Fig.135)
Inside Compound	Bogie	Single driving-wheels	Ordinary axle-box	N.-E. Ry. (Fig. 138)
	Goods Engines.			
Inside	Coupled	Coupled	Coupled	L. & N.-W. Ry.(Fig.107)
	Side Tank Engines.			
Outside	Bogie	{ Coupled 2 Pairs of wheels coupld. }	{ Coupled Radial axle }	N. L. Ry. (Fig. 142) L.& N.-W. Ry.(Fig.105)
Inside	Ordinary axle			
,,	Coupled	Coupled	Coupled	G. E. Ry. (Fig. 111)
,,	{ 4 Wheels coupled }	coupled	Bogie	S.-E. Ry. (Fig. 131)
	Saddle Tank Engine.			
Inside	Coupled	Coupled	Coupled	G. W. Ry. (Fig. 117)

goods engine with *eight wheels coupled*, which will presently be described.

Engines may also be classified as "Simple" or "Compound," a distinction fully explained in chap. xvi.

The table on page 189 is a list of some of the more important combinations of these different classifications as illustrated by types of various modern locomotives running on different railway lines.

CHAPTER XII.

TENDERS.

THE present familiar form of tender which runs on six wheels is the development of a very much more primitive arrangement that carried the coal and water for the earlier types of locomotives.

The original plan was to carry the coal on a waggon, which also carried the feed-water in a barrel, and was attached in the usual way to the locomotive by a coupling-chain with intermediate buffers, leaving a gap over which the driver and fireman had frequently to step. The waggon gradually gave way to a four-wheeled tender, which carried the water in an iron tank fitted with a brake.

As weight and speed increased, it was found necessary to carry larger supplies of coal and water, and tenders are now invariably mounted on six wheels, and are constructed to carry a large tank for storing the feed-water for the boiler, as well as the coal for the engine furnace, and are fitted with a powerful brake acting upon all the wheels. The brake is operated by a hand-screw gear, worked by the fireman, but the power for working it may also be derived from any one of the following sources—

1. By steam from the boiler, as explained in chap. viii., p. 166.

2. By vacuum from a reservoir connected with the automatic brake apparatus, as explained in chap. xiii., p. 208.

3. By compressed air from a reservoir connected to the Westinghouse brake apparatus, as explained in chap. xiii., p. 217.

When any one of these three methods is employed, it invariably only supplements the hand-gear, which must always be kept in good working order, and available for use in case the other means of applying the brake fail to act from any special cause.

Tender wheels are usually about 3 ft. 9 in. to 4 ft. in diameter, and are made of steel or wrought-iron with steel tyres and axles, manufactured and put together in the same way as locomotive wheels.

The framework of the tender consists of plates, kept in position by cross-stays, and a foot-plate at the leading end which adjoins the foot-plate of the engine. The frames are fitted with horn-blocks for the reception of the axle-boxes, and the weight is carried by springs above the axle-boxes in the same manner as the spring, illustrated in Fig. 90, p. 158, carries the weight of a locomotive.

The tank for the feed-water rests directly on the framework of the tender. The sides and back of the tender are usually formed by the outer plates of the tank, the coal being stored in a recess between the two side portions of the tank and on the top of the back part of the tank. The tank is made of iron plates a quarter of an inch thick. Sometimes it has no recess or "well" in the centre, but extends across the whole width of the tender frame; it is then shallower, and the sides and back of the tender rise some distance above the top of the tank, *upon* which the coal is stacked.

The tender is secured to the engine by a single draw-bar,

which has a pin passing through it and the foot-plate of the

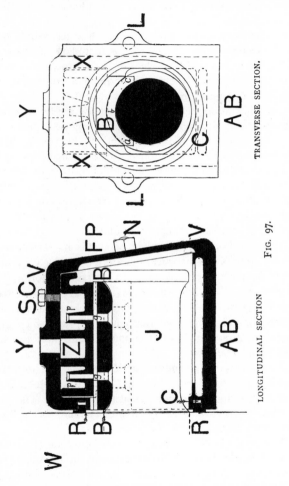

FIG. 97.

engine. There are short buffers between the engine and

tender, and these should be slightly in compression when the two are coupled together, so as to hold engine and tender firmly together and without any play between the buffers. Side chains are provided in case the draw-bar should break.

A sheet-iron plate hinged to the foot-plate of the tender is let down on to the foot-plate of the engine, thus covering the space between them and forming a continuous floor common to engine and tender.

An illustration of a modern form of tender axle-box is shown in Fig. 97, and may be thus briefly described—

J is the journal of the axle, and B the step or bearing made of brass, phosphor bronze, or gun-metal, beneath which the journal revolves. With this form of bearing, as is the case with other tender and rolling stock axles, the bearing surface only extends over about a third of the circumference of the axle, as shown at *a*, *b*, *c* (see transverse section). No other part of the axle-box touches the journal.

The axle-box itself is made of cast-iron. It fits in the tender horn-plates between the dotted lines (XX), and is kept in position by flanges. The portion forming the journal fits into the cast-iron axle-box (AB) immediately below the casting (Z), which forms a kind of tray from which the oil is guided through the passages (*p g*), by means of trimmings, on to the journal, and into the lower part of the axle-box.

The weight is transmitted at Y through the top of the axle-box casting (Z) and bearing (B) on to the journal by a spring fixed above the axle-box at the point Y. The spring is attached at either end by links or suitable means to the framework of the tender.

The front of the axle-box is a cast-iron plate (FP), which is held to the axle-box by studs fixed in the lugs (L) in the casting. These studs pass through corresponding lugs in the cover-plate (FP), which thus forms a close joint round the front edge of the axle-box, as shown in the section at VV, and constitutes one of the sides of the oil chamber. The oil is prevented from escaping at the other side of the axle-box by the ring (R), which abuts against the boss (W) of the wheel. This ring is kept in position by a spring in the groove (G) in the axle-box casting, into which the ring (R) is fitted. A completely oil-tight chamber in which the journal revolves is thus formed, and it should be always kept quite full. This can be done by unscrewing the set screw (SC), and pouring oil through the hole in the top of the casting. The oil finds its way through the passages (p p) on to the top of the axle, and through the groove (g) into the chamber.

These axle-boxes require very little attention compared to an ordinary trimmed bearing ; and so long as they are kept full of oil, they cause little or no trouble, and are not liable to heat and cause failure.

The usual weight of a modern main line tender in working order, with its maximum complement of coal and water, is from thirty to thirty-five tons, but this varies according to the class of work the engines are engaged upon. When long runs are made without stops, the tenders must be able to carry large supplies of coal and water, although this axiom does not apply in the matter of water to the London and North-Western and the Lancashire and Yorkshire tenders, as they are fitted with an apparatus for taking up water while running, and are therefore of lighter construction than those of other companies, who are dependent for their water supply upon the places where the trains stop.

A London and North-Western Railway tender in working order weighs 25 tons when it has on board 1800 gallons of water and four tons of coal. A Midland express passenger tender weighs 36 tons with only 3½ tons of coal, but then it has to carry a sufficient water supply to take it from start to stop on the longest runs made. Midland tenders, therefore, have a tank capacity of 3250 gallons, or nearly double that of a London and North-Western tender.

The following table gives some comparative figures dealing with the size and weight of the tenders of certain railway companies. The weight should as far as possible be adjusted so as to fall equally on each axle-box—

	1	2	3		
RAILWAY.	TANK CAPACITY.	AMOUNT OF COAL CARRIED FOR WEIGHT GIVEN IN COL. 3.	WEIGHT IN WORKING ORDER.		
	GALLONS.	T. C. Q.	T. C. Q.		
London, Brighton & South-Coast	2,250	2 0 0	27 7 0		
Midland	3,250	3 10 0	36 1 1		
Caledonian	2,850	—	33 9 0		
Great Northern	2,800	—	34 18 3		
Great Eastern	2,640	3 0 0	30 12 0		
Manchester, Sheffield & Linc. ...	3,080	4 0 0	35 0 0		
North-Eastern	3,940	4 0 0	40 1 0		
London, Chatham & Dover ...	2,600	4 15 0	34 3 0		
London & South-Western ...	3,000	—	32 0 0		
Great Western	3,000	2 10 0	32 0 0		
London & North-Western ...	1,800	4 0 0	25 0 0		

The difference in the weight of the London and North-Western tenders compared with those of other lines is very marked, and of course these light tenders mean a very appreciable diminution of the dead weight to be hauled, and consequent reduction in working expenses.

The troughs from which the water supply for London and North-Western engines running on the main line is obtained are about 500 yards in length, and are 17 in. wide by 6 in. deep. They are laid down between the rails in the centre of the 4 ft. 8½ in. gauge, and the normal depth of the water in them is 4 in., the supply to the

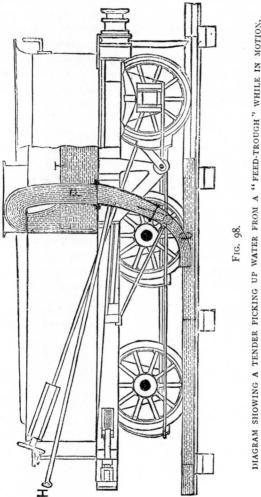

FIG. 98.

DIAGRAM SHOWING A TENDER PICKING UP WATER FROM A "FEED-TROUGH" WHILE IN MOTION.

troughs being kept up by valves which open automatically and refill the troughs when the normal depth is lowered.

Seventy yards from each end of the trough the bottom slopes upwards towards the end of the trough, at which point it is level with the top of the sides. The gradient of the line follows this slope, so that practically the bottom plate of the troughs is at all points, whether in or out of the water, the same distance below rail level. A section of a London and North-Western tender, fitted with the " pick-up apparatus," is shown in Fig. 98.[1]

By means of the handle (H) the scoop (C) is lowered, by the engine-man, into the trough, and the speed of the train forces the water through the scoop into the pipe (P), from whence it passes into the tank (T). When the tank is full the scoop is again put into the out-of-gear position in which it is above and clear of the troughs. Should the driver neglect to replace the scoop in its normal running position before the engine has passed over the troughs, the decreased pressure of water, owing to the slope of the trough, gradually allows a balance weight, fixed to the gear, to automatically move the scoop into its normal position.

----

[1] This illustration appears in *The Working and Management of an English Railway*, and is reproduced by kind permission of the executors of the late Sir Geo. Findlay.

CHAPTER XIII.

BRAKES.

WHEN railways were in their infancy, and indeed until comparatively recent times, the only brake power available for checking the speed and stopping trains, was the hand-brake on the engine—worked by the engine-man—assisted by the hand-brake in the van worked by the guard.

The earlier forms of hand-brake were of an inferior description. Those on the guards' vans were similar in construction to the present form of hand lever brake used on goods waggons. When the guard wished to apply the brake he had to get out of his van and stand on the lever.

This old-fashioned contrivance gradually gave way to improved forms of hand-brakes, in which the power was applied to the wheels by a screw acting upon levers.

For a long period, during which the weight and speed of trains continued steadily to increase, there was no corresponding increase in the brake-power under the control of the men in charge of the train, although there was an improvement in the hand-brakes, both on the locomotives and rolling stock.

As railways multiplied and the traffic increased on the different lines, serious accidents were of frequent occurrence, and it was seen that a large percentage of these accidents might have been avoided if the trains had been supplied with brakes capable of stopping them more quickly.

About the year 1873 the brake question came very prominently to the fore, and the expediency of fitting all passenger trains with a continuous brake acting upon every vehicle of the train became generally recognized. Subsequently it became apparent that such a brake ought to be under the immediate control of the driver and guard, either of whom should be able to apply it instantaneously to its fullest extent in case of emergency.

About this period there were a number of continuous brakes brought out. Among the most important were—

Clarke & Webb's chain brake.

Smith's vacuum brake.

The Westinghouse vacuum brake.

The Westinghouse air brake.

The London and North-Western Railway Company led the way in grappling with the continuous brake question. Having by many trials and experiments satisfied themselves upon the efficiency of the Clarke & Webb brake, they set to work to fit up their stock with it.

The principle upon which this brake was constructed was the utilization of the power developed by the momentum of the train to actuate the brake for stopping it.

A friction pulley fixed to the axle of the guard's van revolved with the axle. A loose pulley, to which a drum or windlass was attached, depended from the frame-work of the van. Connected to this drum was a chain extending underneath the carriages and attached to levers actuating the brake-blocks.

To apply the brake a lever in the van was lowered, and this brought the two friction pulleys together. The revolving pulley on the axle caused the loose pulley to revolve and so wind the chain on the drum, thus pulling on the brake levers under the carriages and applying the brake-blocks to the tyres. When the chain was wound tight the loose pulley stopped revolving, and was held in position by friction with the pulley on the axle, which continued to revolve so long as the train was in motion.

The chief argument against this brake was the liability of the chain to break and so render it useless, and in case of the train parting between the vehicles the brake-power was at once destroyed from the same cause.

To utilize the force developed by the train itself for the purpose of checking the speed of the train is certainly a good principle theoretically. The power developed by a train running at a high speed is enormous, and so long as it is required to keep the train moving, this power is doing good service and rendering assistance to the working of the engine ; but when a stop has to be made, the power derived from the impetus of the train not only ceases to be of service, but is counteracting the object in view, namely, the stoppage of the train.

Messrs. Clarke & Webb's chain brake therefore possesses the double advantage of putting this superfluous energy to good use, and of obviating the necessity of producing further power to act against and bring under control a force that is otherwise being entirely thrown away.

Trains fitted with this brake were divided into sections, each under control of one van. This was to prevent one set of friction pulleys acting on too long a length of chain, it being found that five or six vehicles coupled to one van gave the most satisfactory results. The driver had control over a section of the continuous brake by means of a cord passed over the top of the carriages from the brake lever in the van on to the foot-plate. After the London and North-Western Railway Company began to fit up their trains with the chain brake, they soon had more vehicles fitted with a continuous brake than any other line. It did not, however, act on the engine, and Mr. Webb at the same time fitted the engines and tenders with powerful steam brakes, which are still in use, and will be found fully described on p. 166.

The chain brake has done excellent service on the London and North-Western Railway, and the number of its failures reported to the Board of Trade compared very favourably with other contemporary forms of continuous brake.

As has been mentioned, the brake was not entirely automatic in its action, and in case of a break loose in the middle of a section, it became useless on that section, but the earlier forms of compressed air brake and vacuum brake were not automatic at all.

These two latter have since been greatly improved and made thoroughly automatic, and as they comply with the present requirements of the Board of Trade in this respect, the chain brake has now been practically abandoned, although it is still admitted to be one of the best forms of brake for short close-coupled trains. Indeed, it is only under pressure that the North London Railway Company have within the last year removed it from their stock and replaced it with the automatic vacuum brake.

The brake question has passed through various phases since the year 1873, and the final result has been that the automatic vacuum and the Westinghouse compressed air brakes are practically the only two left in the field. These at present divide the honours, both of them having staunch supporters among the leading railway companies throughout the civilized world.

It is a pity that there *should* be two brakes in the field, as with passenger rolling stock it is almost as important for the brake gear as for the gauges to be common to all companies. Where vehicles have to run over lines using different brakes, such vehicles have to be fitted both with the vacuum and the Westinghouse brake, an expense which would be avoided were all railway companies unanimous in the matter of continuous brakes.

The following are the most important qualifications that should be possessed by a continuous brake, and are claimed for the automatic vacuum and Westinghouse brakes—

1. To be practically instantaneous in its action, and to apply itself over the whole length of the train and on the engine at the same time.

2. To be capable of being worked upon trains of any length without difficulty; the guards and engine-driver each to have equal facility for instantaneously applying the brake.

3. To be automatically available on any detached portion of the train, although separated from the source from which its power is derived. That is to say, if the train breaks loose and the couplings between any portion become detached or broken, the brake to instantaneously apply itself on both portions.

4. To be absolutely certain in its action.

With both the Westinghouse and automatic vacuum brakes there is under each carriage a reservoir and a cylinder in which is a piston connected to the brake lever, and the brake is actuated by air pressing on this piston.

In the case of the Westinghouse brake, air at a pressure of 75 to 80 lbs. per square inch is pumped from the engine through a pipe extending throughout the train into each reservoir, and is maintained at this pressure both in reservoir and train-pipe while running. When the pressure is released from the train-pipe the reservoir is automatically cut off from the train-pipe and is placed in communication with the cylinder and made to act upon the piston, which it forces outwards and thus applies the brake.

With the vacuum brake the cylinder is usually placed vertically, and the air is exhausted from the train-pipe, reservoir, and cylinder above and below the piston to the extent of 20 in. of vacuum. To apply the brake, air is admitted into the train-pipe, and enters the cylinder below the piston. The admission of air to the train-pipe automatically cuts it off from the reservoir, and the portion of the cylinder above the piston, which is forced upwards by atmospheric pressure, and actuates the brake-blocks.

It will thus be seen that with the vacuum brake the pressure on the pipes is *external*, being the atmospheric pressure acting in obedience to the law that nature abhors a vacuum, and with the Westinghouse brake the pressure is *internal*, being that of compressed air acting against the normal atmospheric pressure outside the pipes.

The *pressure* in the one case is obtained by a small donkey pump, which is fixed on the engine, and *pumps* air into the train-pipe, cylinders, and reservoir.

The *vacuum* in the other case is created by an apparatus called the " *ejector*," which by the action of a jet of steam is made to *exhaust* the air from train-pipe, cylinders, and reservoir.

Of the two brakes the one most favoured in this country is the automatic vacuum, as will be seen by the following list showing the kind of brake used on all the railways in the United Kingdom. If we go outside our own domains we find, however, that in most other parts of the world the majority is considerably in favour of the Westinghouse brake, and it is remarkable to note that it entirely holds the field in North America. It may, however, at the same time be borne in mind that the Westinghouse brake is an American invention.

The following table is an abstract from the Board of Trade Returns, showing the number of engines fitted with various kinds of continuous brakes, and the class of brake used on different railways in the United Kingdom, for the six months ending June 30, 1892. Since that date the percentage of engines fitted has considerably increased.

Name of Brake.	Name of Railway Company.	Engines and Tenders.	
		Fitted with Brakes.	Fitted with Apparatus for working the Brakes.
Automatic Vacuum	Barry	5	—
	Brecon and Merthyr . .	8	—
	Cambrian . . .	13	7
	Cheshire Lines . . .	—	—
	Corris	1	—
	Furness	44	—
	Great Northern . . .	674	9
	Great Western . . .	—	1,886
	Hull, Barnsley, and W. Riding Junction.	16	—
	Lancashire and Yorkshire .	834	2
	London and North-Western .	975	355
	London and South-Western .	527	15
	Manchester and Milford .	3	83
	Manchester, Sheff., and Linc. .	515	
	Manchester South Junction and Altrincham.	11	—
	Maryport and Carlisle . .	14	—
	Mersey	7	9
	Midland	—	1,125
	Midland & South-Western Junc.	7	—
	Neath and Brecon . .	1	—
	North-Eastern . . .	6	23
	North London . . .	54	—
	North Staffordshire . .	36	—
	Pontypridd, Caerphilly, and Newport.	2	2
	Rhondda and Swansea Bay .	8	—
	Severn and Wye and Severn Bridge.	5	—
	Somerset Joint Committee .	—	58
	South-Eastern . . .	289	1
	Taff Vale	36	—
	Wirral	8	—

Name of Brake.	Name of Railway Company.	Engines and Tenders.	
		Fitted with Brakes.	Fitted with Apparatus for working the Brakes.
	Wrexham, Mold, & Connah's Quay.	8	—
	Glasgow and South-Western .	60	—
	Highland . . .	78	—
	Belfast and County Down .	16	—
	Belfast and Northern Counties	56	—
	Cavan, Leitrim, and Roscommon Light.	8	—
	Clogher Valley . . .	6	—
	Cork, Bandon, and South Coast	7	—
	Cork and Muskerry Light .	4	—
	Dundalk, Newry, & Greenore	5	—
	Great Northern of Ireland .	90	—
	Great Southern and Western	107	—
	Midland Great Western .	57	—
	Tralee and Dingle . .	5	—
	Waterford and Limerick .	20	—
	Waterford, Dungarvan, and Lismore.	1	—
	West Carbery . . .	4	—
	West Clare	7	—
Westinghouse Automatic	Colne Valley and Halstead .	3	—
	East and West Junction .	3	—
	Eastern and Midlands . .	19	—
	Great Eastern . . .	493	—
	Hull, Barnsley, and W. Riding Junction.	19	—
	Isle of Wight . . .	3	—
	Isle of Wight Central . .	4	—
	London, Brighton, & S. Coast	357	—
	London, Chatham, and Dover	196	—
	Londonderry . . .	3	—
	London, Tilbury, & Southend	35	—
	Metropolitan District . .	54	—
	Midland	29	—
	North-Eastern . . .	569	—
	N. Wales, Narrow Gauge .	2	—
	Rhymney	19	7
	West Lancashire . . .	9	—
	Caledonian	331	57
	Glasgow and South-Western .	98	—
	Great North of Scotland .	63	—
	North British . . .	201	45

Name of Brake.	Name of Railway Company.	Engines and Tenders.	
		Fitted with Brakes.	Fitted with Apparatus for working the Brakes.
	Castlederg and Victoria Bridge	3	—
Clarke & Webb's	North London [1] . . .	—	82
Smith's Vacuum	Metropolitan . . .	70	—
	South-Eastern . . .	4	—
	Belfast and Northern Counties	1	—
	Dublin, Wicklow, and Wexford	45	—
	Sligo, Leitrim, and Northern Counties	5	—
Vacuum	North Staffordshire . .	35	51
Totals		7,305	3,677
Total number of engines returned as FITTED with Continuous Brakes to 30th June, 1892.		7,305 or 65 %	3,677 or 33 per cent.
Number of engines FITTED with Continuous Brakes during the six months ending 30th June, 1892.		529 or 5 %	89 or 1 per cent.
Number of engines NOT FITTED with Continuous Brakes.		3,887 including 3,677 engines fitted with apparatus for working the continuous brake, or 35 per cent.	

The Westinghouse Brake Company contend that their brake is the least liable to failures that may lead to disaster, such as the refusal of the brake to work. It is, however, more complicated than the vacuum brake, and in the matter of minor failures, the reports rendered to the Board of Trade are said to show that the vacuum brake, while enjoying the same freedom from the responsibility for accidents, gives less trouble and causes fewer delays.

[1] The North London Railway Stock (engines and carriages) is now fitted throughout with the automatic vacuum brake.

The pressure of the external atmosphere against the internal vacuum in itself tends to keep the pipes together, whereas the outward pressure of compressed air in itself tends to rupture the pipes, and with the Westinghouse brake there have been a number of delays to trains through the accidental bursting of pipes, causing the brake to go on throughout the train. These delays have been greatly reduced by the stronger pipes now used, and it must be borne in mind that all mishaps of this description have erred on the side of safety.

Previous to the introduction of the present system, there were compressed air and vacuum brakes, which were non-automatic in their character. When an application of the brake was desired, the driver had to create the air-pressure or vacuum for the purpose. The means to do this were at his disposal alone, and the guard was unable to apply the brake, which was moreover useless on any part of the train detached from the engine.

We are, however, running rather wide of the mark in regard to the brake question, as applied to locomotives, and we will now proceed to give a brief description of these two brakes so far as they apply to the engine.

The automatic vacuum and Westinghouse brakes can both be fitted to the wheels of the engine and tender, the cylinder and brake gear being of the same description as that on the carriages.

The *automatic vacuum brake* may be thus briefly described.

The brake-blocks are applied to the wheels by a combination of levers acted upon by the brake-piston.

The engine, tender, and each vehicle on the train carries its own vacuum reservoir and brake cylinder, which are connected with the ejector by a pipe running from end to end of the train.

The *ejector* upon the engine exhausts the air from the

train-pipe, cylinder, and reservoir. When the vacuum is raised, all these three parts of the brake gear are in communication with each other, and the same vacuum in each.

The brake is applied by admitting air into the train-pipe at any point in its length. This may be done by the valves provided for the purpose on the engine, and in the guard's van, or from any accidental opening of the pipe.

Directly air is admitted into the train-pipe a small valve, at the juncture between reservoir and train-pipe, closes automatically, and cuts the reservoir off from the train-pipe. The air admitted to the latter does not therefore enter the reservoir in which the vacuum is still maintained.

The connection between the train-pipe and the top part of the cylinder above the piston is through the reservoir only.

The air admitted to the train-pipe therefore does not enter the top part of the cylinder, which remains exposed to the full force of the vacuum in the reservoir.

Not so the bottom part of the cylinder, which has direct communication with the train-pipe into which air has been admitted. This is therefore the state of affairs upon the admission of air into the train-pipe.

There is a vacuum in the brake cylinder above the piston. The atmospheric pressure in the train-pipe acts upon the bottom of the piston and forces it up.

The rod attached to the piston actuates a lever connected to an arrangement of pull-rods, and other levers which draw the brake-blocks tightly against the tyres of the wheels.

When the brake has to be released, the driver again produces the vacuum by means of his ejector, until the vacuum in the train-pipe is the same as that in the reservoir and at the top of the piston ; the small valve between reservoir and train-pipe then automatically opens, the piston and brake lever fall by their own weight assisted by spiral springs to the " off " position, and the blocks are released from the tyres.

The usual amount of vacuum maintained while running is 20 in. below the atmospheric pressure, and directly there is a failure to maintain the vacuum from any cause, the brake begins to go on.

The driver is able to regulate the action of the brake in accordance with the power required. If a sudden stop is wanted he opens the air-valve wide, and the vacuum in the train-pipe is altogether destroyed, causing the brake to go on to its fullest extent, the whole 20 in. of vacuum acting upon the piston, whose surface is about 314 sq. in., giving a pressure of about 10 lbs. per sq. in., or a pull of nearly a ton and a half on the brake-rod. If a partial application is desired, he reduces the vacuum in the train-pipe to 15, 10, or 5 in., as the case may be ; and the power of the vacuum acting upon the piston is equal to the difference of the amount in the reservoir and the amount in the train-pipe.

Thus, if, when running with 20 in. of vacuum, the driver allows it to drop down to 10 in. in the train-pipe, the power exerted by the brake is equal to 10 in. of vacuum, or about 5 lbs. to the square inch.

The principle of the ejector (which is invariably the means of *creating* the vacuum), as designed by Mr. Webb and used on the London and North-Western Railway, is shown in Fig. 99. The steam enters the ejector through the pipe (SP), and is admitted through the passage (P) to the steam-cone (SC).

It will be seen that this cone gradually diverges, and the expanding steam is so guided by this divergence as it passes through the cone that the jet discharged into the barrel exactly fills it up without the velocity of the steam being checked ; the steam therefore in passing through the barrel (B) of the ejector, draws the air from behind it, acting in the same way as a piston in the cylinder of an air-pump. This action lifts the valve (V), and air is drawn through from the chamber (X), which is in communication with the train-pipe. The air passes into the chamber (Z), round the steam-cone, and thence into the barrel (B), and out through the exhaust (E) with the steam. At the point D a small drip-valve is screwed into the ejector to get rid of any condensed steam which may drop from the mouth of the cone.

VC is the valve-cover screwed into the ejector-case. This cover also acts as a guide for the valve (V).

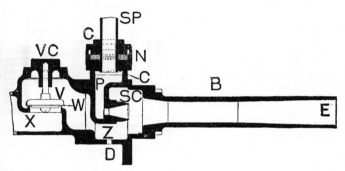

FIG. 99.

G is a gland screwed down by the nut (N) on to the packing, which presses on the cone (C), thus making a steam-tight joint.

So long as the steam is passing through the ejector, air is being drawn through from the train-pipe, cylinders, and reservoirs until the required amount of vacuum is attained.

This ejector is not used for *maintaining* the vacuum while running after the brake is once released, because of the great quantity of steam it uses. The vacuum is kept up after once being created either by a small ejector or an air-pump. A small ejector is capable of raising as strong a vacuum as a large one, but the passages being smaller, less steam is used, and it takes a longer time to exhaust the air from the train-pipe ; for this reason it is not suitable for creating the initial vacuum, although equally efficient for maintaining it when once created.

The London and North-Western, Great Western, and North Stafford Railway Companies use a pump for maintaining the vacuum while running. This is a simple form

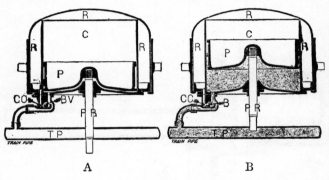

A   B

FIG. 100.

of air-pump worked off one of the cross-heads of the engine ; it gives very little trouble in its management, or expense in maintenance, and has the advantage over the small ejector of practically using no steam in keeping up the vacuum while running.

Fig. 100 shows the section of a vacuum brake cylinder, train-pipe, and connections. Diagram A shows the position of the piston at the bottom of the cylinder with the brake off. P is the piston, C the cylinder, and R the reservoir which surrounds the cylinder. TP is the train-pipe. The air has been exhausted from the train-pipe, reservoir, and cylinder. The ball valve (BV), having no pressure on either side of it, lies in the recess B, and the connection is opened between the train-pipe and reservoir.

Upon air being admitted to the train-pipe, the vacuum in the reservoir at once acts upon the ball (B), drawing it up against the seating of the connection (CO), and closing the passage between the reservoir and train-pipe, thus preserving the vacuum in the reservoir and at the top of the piston. The atmospheric pressure, which has access to the bottom of the piston, forces it up in the cylinder into the position shown in diagram B, and thus applies the brake by means of the piston-rod (PR) which is attached at its lower end to the lever actuating the brake-blocks. The shaded part represents the train-pipe and the part of the cylinder into which air has been admitted to apply the brake. The London and North-Western Railway Company, and several other lines, had fitted their engines with steam brakes long before the introduction of the automatic vacuum brake. By an ingenious arrangement, the steam brake is now made to work automatically with the vacuum brake. The admission of air into the train-pipe has always the effect of opening the steam valve to the cylinder of the steam brake, which is thus applied at the same time as the vacuum brake; but there are various forms of automatic gear for this purpose adopted by different locomotive engineers.

Fig. 101 shows the part of an engine to which the automatic brake (as arranged by Messrs. Gresham & Craven) is fitted, and the following is a description of the arrangement—

I. *Steam valve for turning steam from the boiler to the cylinder.*—This valve has two positions, "open" and "closed," and must always be full opened when running, and closed when the engine is in the shed, to avoid

condensations in the steam-pipe.   By its use the ejector
may be examined whilst the boiler is under steam.

II. *Combination ejector.*—This "ejector" consists of two
ejectors known as the "large" and "small," the latter being
placed inside the former. The small one is worked con-
tinuously, and is controlled by a small screw steam valve,
this valve being adjusted to give the required vacuum. The
large ejector is worked by the admission of steam through a

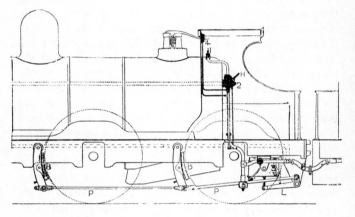

Fig. 101.

disc-valve placed underneath the air-valve, and upon the
same spindle, and is opened by the driver's handle being
placed in the position marked "Off."   The action of both
is the same, steam is admitted around the cones and passes
through the ejector barrel at a great velocity, withdrawing
the air from the train-pipe and cylinders, and carrying it
along the exhaust-pipe into the chimney of the locomotive.

To obtain the best vacuum the admission of steam to
the ejectors should be adjusted, the steam valves only

requiring to be slightly opened for the ordinary steam pressures.

The driver's handle (H) has three positions, " Off " being the position when it is required to release the brake quickly, and in which position steam is admitted to the large ejector. In " Running Position " the large ejector steam-valve and air-valves are both closed, and the brake is released slowly by the small ejector only, and the vacuum also maintained after the brake is released. " On " is the position for applying the brake fully ; the air-valve being open, the air passes through the holes in the disc, and applies the brake. The range of movement between " Running Position " and " On " is for regulating the brake, by letting in more or less air to apply or increase the power after application, or to withdraw the air to release or diminish the power on the blocks.

A small auxiliary pipe is carried from the ejector by the side of the train-pipe, and is connected only to the engine and tender vacuum chamber. This pipe is in communication with the small ejector when the driver's handle is in full " On " position, and thereby constantly maintains the vacuum on the top of the engine and tender pistons. At the top of this pipe is fixed a small valve, by opening which the brake can be released on the engine and tender after the steam to the ejector has been closed.

III. *Brake cylinder.*—This cylinder is self-contained in the vacuum chamber as applied to carriages, and is the only fitting required. The piston fits freely in the cylinder, and is packed with a rolling rubber ring, which, when the piston moves, rolls between it and the cylinder, making a perfect packing without friction. The piston-rod is coated with brass, and works through a brass bush, and a packing rubber prevents air passing the rod.

At the bottom of the cylinder is attached the *ball-valve*,

the branch of which is connected by a small hose-pipe to the train-pipe. This valve is of the most simple construction, as there is only one moving piece; and that being a small brass ball, having a rolling action in a horizontal position, has consequently no friction.

The spindle with release lever is added for the purpose of withdrawing the ball from its seat, when it is required to release the brake by hand. This spindle is made air-tight by a small diaphragm, the pressure on which, when a vacuum is created, pulls in the spindle, and allows the ball to go freely to its seat.

IV. *Driver's vacuum gauge.*—The driver's vacuum gauge has two pointers, one on the left marked "train-pipe," and one on the right "vacuum chamber," both indicating the vacuum carried. When the brake is applied, the pointer on the left indicates the amount of vacuum remaining in the train-pipe and below the pistons: the difference between it and the pointer to the right, which indicates the vacuum in the vacuum chamber or reservoir and above the pistons, is the amount of power applied on the underside of the brake pistons. For instance, if 10 in. is indicated in the train-pipe, and 20 in. in the vacuum chamber, the brake is applied with a power of 10 in., or about half its full power.

V. *Drip-trap.*—This trap is placed on the train-pipe at the bottom of the down-pipe from the ejector, so that any moisture will drain into it. It is fitted at the bottom with a self-acting ball-valve, which opens when all the vacuum in the train-pipe is destroyed, and allows the water which may have collected to run out. This valve should be occasionally examined and cleaned.

VI. *Universal hose couplings.* This coupling consists of a pair of castings exactly alike, with horns top and bottom, and it is impossible to couple them wrongly. To couple, they should be lifted up sufficiently high to enable the bottom

horn to be placed together, and then lowered, the top plug
of one being placed in the slot of the other.   To uncouple,
it is simply necessary to raise the couplings, when they will
separate.

The manner in which the lever (L) is made to act upon
the pull-rods (P) and brake-blocks (B) can be easily understood on referring to the illustration.

The following description of the *Westinghouse brake* is
extracted from the Company's official " General description
of the apparatus " —

Fig. 102 shows the brake complete on engine and tender,
and the following is a list of the different parts :

The triple valve (F), by means of which the instantaneous
automatic action is produced.

The small reservoir (G), in which is stored the compressed
air for applying the brakes.

The brake cylinder (H), with piston and rod.

The brake levers and blocks.

The steam-engine (A) *and pump* (B), which produce the
compressed air.

The main reservoir (C), for storing the air necessary for
releasing the brakes and charging the small reservoirs.

The driver's brake valve (D), which regulates the flow of
air from the main reservoir into the brake-pipe.

The brake-pipe (E), which extends throughout the length
of the train.

The pump being started by admitting steam to the
cylinder A, air is forced from the cylinder B into the
main reservoir (C), which is connected to the driver's brake
valve (D).

The compressed air stored in the main reservoir is turned
into the brake-pipe (E) by means of the driver's brake
valve.

It then fills the brake-pipe and flows through the branch

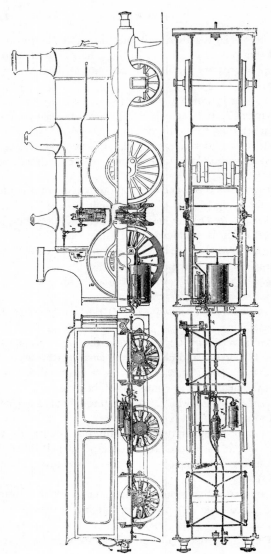

FIG. 102.

pipe on the tender and each vehicle to the triple-valve (F), through which it passes into the small reservoir (G), where it remains until the brake has to be applied, the pressure being uniform in both reservoirs and the triple-valve.

So long as this uniform pressure is maintained the brakes are off. Directly air escapes from the train-pipe the triple-valve moves automatically and admits the compressed air from the reservoir to the cylinder, forcing out the pistons and rods and thus applying the blocks to the wheels.

The brakes are released by re-charging the brake-pipe with compressed air, which causes the triple-valve to lift and cut off the reservoir from the cylinder, which it again places in communication with the atmosphere, thus releasing the compressed air from the back of the piston, which is then forced into the "Off" position by a spring and the blocks released from the wheels.

Turning now to Fig. 103, a section of the *double-acting air-pump* must first be studied. Steam from the boiler enters the chamber (G), the ports from which, to each end of the cylinder, are opened for supply and exhaust by the movement of the valve (1). The valve consists of two pistons (1 1) on the same stem, and as the upper piston is of greater diameter than the lower, the tendency of the pressure in the chamber (G) is always to raise the valve unless held down by the greater pressure of the large piston (2), which is supplied with steam from the chamber (*d*). In the position shown in the illustration steam is passing into the bottom of the cylinder (A), and forcing the main piston (3) upwards. As the main piston completes its upward stroke, the plate (4) pushes up the rod (5) working in the hollow piston-rod, and with it the slide valve (6). This closes the passage (*e*) from chamber (*d*) to the piston (2), and at the same time opens the exhaust passage (*f*) to the atmosphere through *g*, which relieves the pressure

on the top of the piston (2). The steam in the chamber
(G) then raises the main valve (1) and enters the top of the
cylinder above the main piston (3), and at the same time
the steam on the lower side is exhausted. On completing
its downward stroke the main piston again draws the rod
(5) and slide valve (6) to the position shown, thus reversing
the position of the main valve (1), and consequently of
the main piston (3).

No particular description of the bottom cylinder and
valves (b) is required. Each upward stroke admits air below
the piston and discharges air from above the piston into
the main reservoir (C), each downward stroke does the
reverse.

There are three principal positions for the *driver's handle*
in working the brake.

In the first position, a free communication is formed
through the large ports (a, a) in the valve (1) from the main
reservoir to the brake-pipe ; but

In the second position, the air must pass through the
small valve (3) and the hole (g), before it reaches the brake-
pipe.

This valve (3) is held on its seat by a spiral spring of a
strength corresponding to 10 lbs. per square inch, so that
when feeding in this *second position*, the pressure in the
brake-pipe is 10 lbs. less than that in the main reservoir.
This extra pressure is utilized when releasing the brakes.

A little further to the right the position is *neutral*.
There is then no communication between the main reservoir
and the brake-pipe, neither can air flow from the brake
pipe to the atmosphere ; turning the handle, however,
farther to the right has the effect of taking weight off the
valve (2), which is then lifted by the pressure in the brake-
pipe, and some of the air escapes from it into the atmosphere
at M.

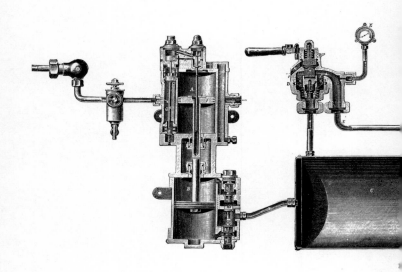

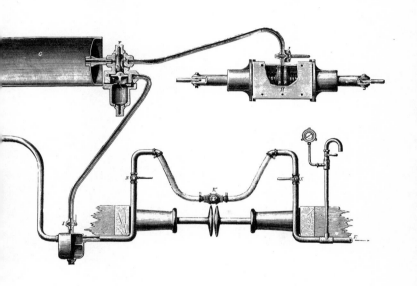

This escape of air applies the brakes with a force corresponding to the reduction of pressure shown by the brake-pipe gauge (L).

In the third position, all the weight is taken off the discharge valve (2), thus allowing air to escape rapidly, which applies the brakes with full force.

In the *first position* of the handle there is a leak through the hole (c) to remind the driver, after releasing the brakes, to bring the handle to the *second position, where it must remain whilst the train is running*.

Operation.—To apply the brakes in ordinary stops, the brake valve should be opened gently until the desired reduction of pressure is observed on the gauge, after which the handle should be moved back gently to prevent further escape of air.

If the driver's brake valve is operated in a rough way, serious inconvenience is caused to the passengers ; and it may even result in the rupture of the screw couplings.

To prevent the jerk which is often experienced with all kinds of brakes at the moment when the train comes to rest, it is sufficient for the driver to release the brakes at the last revolution of the wheels in order to give the carriages time to assume their normal position. When doing so the hand-brake on the tender may be put on to advantage, so as to hold the train at the platform.

The *triple valve* (F) is simply a small piston (1) carrying with it a slide valve (2) which can be moved up or down by *increasing or decreasing the pressure in the brake-pipe*.

As soon as the air from the main reservoir is turned into the brake-pipe (by means of the driver's valve), the piston (1) is pushed up into the position shown, and air is allowed to feed past it through a small groove (a) into the reservoir (G). At the same time the slide valve (2) covers the port (b) to the brake cylinder, and is in such a position that the air from the latter may exhaust into the atmosphere through *c*.

The piston (1) has now the same air pressure on both sides, but if the pressure in the brake-pipe is *decreased*, the piston and slide-valve are forced down, thereby uncovering the passage (*b*), through which air from the reservoir (G) flows through the pipe (*f'*) into the brake cylinder (H) between the pistons (P), thus applying the brakes. The brake-pipe is shut off as soon as the triple valve piston (1) passes the groove (*a*).

To release the brakes, the piston and slide-valve are again moved into the position shown, by the driver turning air from the main reservoir into the brake-pipe. The air in the brake cylinder escapes through *c*, and at the same time the reservoir is re-charged.

To release with more certainty the driver must be careful to maintain extra pressure in the main reservoir, by keeping the handle of his brake valve in the second or " feed " position, while the train is running.

The *couplings* (K) are exactly alike, and an air-tight joint is formed between them by means of the rubber packing ring in each, which being forced together by the air pressure behind them, the joint thus becomes tighter by increase of pressure.

These couplings are united by simply placing them face to face nearly at right angles, the stop-pins being on the under side, so that the projection of the one fits the corresponding groove of the other, and then turning the couplings straight.

No damage is done to the couplings if drawn apart forcibly by the separation of the train, as the rubber rings are forced into their respective couplings far enough to permit the projections to disengage from their grooves, and the brakes will then go full on.

The figure H represents the standard form of *brake cylinder* for a carriage. It contains two pistons, which are held in the position shown by the spiral springs within. When air is admitted, the two pistons are thrust outwards with equal force, and the brakes go on. When the air is allowed to exhaust, the springs expanding push back the pistons and release the brakes.

A leakage groove is provided to prevent the brakes from being applied when the air flows slowly from the triple-valve to the cylinder as the result of a leak in the brake-pipe. This groove permits air to pass the piston (p), unless it is admitted suddenly, in which case the piston moves past the groove. For this reason drivers should never discharge less than 5 lbs. air pressure to apply the brake.

The *coupling cocks* (N) are for cutting off the brake gear from the atmosphere, when vehicles that are charged are detached from a train. This cock must also be closed at the rear of the last vehicle on the train.

CHAPTER XIV.

MODERN LOCOMOTIVES.

Through the kindness of different locomotive superintendents in supplying photographs, the author is enabled
to introduce examples of some of the different types of
modern locomotives running on various lines in the United
Kingdom.

The general details of the structure of a locomotive have
already been briefly described, but it will be understood
that these details vary greatly in accordance with the ideas
of their designers, and the special class of work for which
an engine is constructed. The principal, however, is the
same in all cases, whatever may be the special form of
design ; and any further detailed description will not now
be attempted. The leading features of the engines illustrated will simply be mentioned, and it is hoped that the
reader will, by what he has read in the previous pages, be
able to gain some idea of their general structure.

It may be useful here to note the formula for finding the
tractive force of a locomotive, which is—

$$\frac{(\text{Diam. of cylinder in in.})^2 \times \text{stroke in in.}}{\text{Diameter of driving-wheel in inches.}} = \begin{cases} \text{Tractive force in lbs. for} \\ \text{each lb. of effective steam} \\ \text{pressure upon the piston.} \end{cases}$$

An engine having cylinders 17 in. in diameter and 24 in. stroke, and driving-wheels 4 ft. 3 in. in diameter, has therefore a tractive force amounting to

$$\frac{17 \times 17 \times 24}{51} = 155\cdot6 \text{ lbs. for each lb. of effective steam pressure per sq. inch on the piston.}$$

This is the tractive force exerted by a London and North-Western coal engine (Fig. 106), which has the foregoing dimensions.

The effective pressure of steam on the piston with different rates of expansion is thus given in Molesworth's formulæ, the boiler being assumed at 100 lbs. per square inch—

			EFFECTIVE PRESSURE.
Steam cut off at $\frac{3}{4}$ stroke	...		90 lbs.
,,	$\frac{5}{8}$,,	...	80 ,,
,,	$\frac{1}{2}$,,	...	69 ,,
,,	$\frac{3}{8}$,,	...	50 ,,
,,	$\frac{1}{4}$,,	...	40 ,,

The adhesive force per ton of load on the driving-wheels is—

			PER TON.
When the rails are very dry	...	...	600 lbs.
When the rails are very wet	...	...	550 ,,
In ordinary weather	...	...	450 ,,
In foggy weather, or when the rails are greasy			300 ,,
In frost or snow	...	...	200 ,,

In coupled engines the adhesive force may be taken as exerted by the load on all wheels coupled to the driving-wheels.

The adhesive power must be greater than the tractive force of an engine on the rails, otherwise the wheels will slip.

These formulæ applied to the particulars given of the

different engines illustrated will enable the reader to gain some idea of their hauling power.

The necessity of *balancing* locomotive engines may also be alluded to here ; it was discovered early in their history ; indeed, Stephenson refers to the matter in the year 1845.

If an engine is not balanced at all, or is improperly balanced, it is found that a very irregular motion takes place when it is run at any speed, and it has been shown by actual experiments that it is impossible to run an unbalanced engine at the same speed as one that is balanced, and that there is a great saving of fuel effected by the proper distribution of weight in the rotating parts.

Mr. D. K. Clarke, in 1856, balanced the engine "Canute" on the London and South-Western Railway, and found an estimated saving of 4 lbs. of coal per mile, or 20% on its previous consumption. Several goods engines, having four coupled wheels and outside cylinders, were also balanced about the same time, with the result that 4 lbs. of coal per mile were saved, which amounted to 11% of the total consumption.

Le Chatelier, in 1849, also balanced a six-coupled goods outside cylinder engine, and found it ran with complete steadiness at the rate of 30 miles an hour with a load. He then tried it with balance weights off, and found it impossible to attain a higher speed than 25 miles an hour, and that with violent oscillation and unsteadiness.

To balance an engine properly, the revolving and reciprocating parts—viz., the pistons, piston-rods, cross-heads, connecting-rods, and cranks—must be balanced by weights in the wheels. This can all be calculated, and the engine balanced theoretically, but it is still open to a certain minimum of error through the variation between the actual weight of the metal and the calculated weight, and perhaps through slight variations between the sizes of actual parts and their drawings.

It must also be noted that when an engine is balanced it is only correct for the speed at which it is usually required to run, and some authorities hold that, after theoretically balancing an engine, the best way is to sling it up and then set it in motion at its proper number of revolutions, and adjust the balance weights until there is no perceptible oscillation or irregular movement about the engine.

For engines with inside cylinders, it is usual to put a counter-weight in the wheels on each side of the engine, equal to about three-quarters of the gross disturbing weight ; and for outside cylinder engines, the balance weights should equal at least seven-eighths of the disturbing weight. As a matter of practice, it is best to distribute the balance weights over two or three spaces between the wheel spokes. The position of the balance weights between the spokes can be seen in many of the illustrations given.

The London and North-Western Railway Company's most modern express passenger engines are of the compound type, and will be described in a succeeding chapter. The engines which immediately preceded the compounds were likewise designed by Mr. Webb, and are known as the " 6 ft. 6 in. coupled " class. These are most useful engines, and have done splendid work on the line, and there are at present 166 of them running, chiefly employed in working express passenger trains. During the race to Scotland in 1888, an engine of this class worked the 10.0 a.m. *ex* Euston between Crewe and Carlisle, and on one trip covered the distance from Preston to Carlisle, 90 miles, in exactly 90 minutes, having a gradient of no less than 1 in 75 to climb between Tebay and Shap Summit. Assuming that the gradient was surmounted at the rate of 45 miles an hour, the engine must on this occasion have lifted the dead weight of the train *one foot per second*.　The 6 ft. 6 in. coupled engine is still a standard type of express passenger engine on the London and North-Western Railway, although not so powerful as the modern compound engines.

The particular engine of this class, illustrated in Fig. 104, is the " Charles Dickens," now a famous engine, and one that is well known to every habitual traveller between London and Manchester.　It is stabled at Manchester, and daily runs from that city to London and back, the total

FIG. 104.

distance being 366½ miles.　Except when stopped for repairs, the " Charles Dickens " has since February 1882 made this journey every day, working up the 8.30 a.m. from Manchester, and returning with the 4.0 p.m. from Euston. On September 12, 1891, it completed its 2651st trip, having accomplished the extraordinary feat of running 1,000,000 miles in 9 years 219 days.　No other engine in the world has run so many miles in a like period of time. Between these dates, in addition to the Manchester and

London trips, 92 other journeys were made, and altogether 12,515 tons of coal were consumed. At the end of February 1893, the total mileage run by the "Charles Dickens" was 1,138,557.

The London and North-Western 6 ft. 6 in. coupled engines are fitted with the straight link motion, illustrated in Fig. 42. The leading end of the engine is carried on a pair of 3 ft. 9 in. wheels with ordinary axle-boxes, and the weight is distributed as follows—

			TONS	CWT.
Leading-wheels	...	...	10	5
Driving-wheels	...	...	11	10
Trailing-wheels	...	...	11	0
Tender (1800 gals.) ...		...	25	0
	Total	...	57	15

The principal dimensions are—

Cylinders, 17 in. by 24 in.
Heating surface : tubes, 980·3 sq. ft. ; fire-box, 103·3—total sq. ft., 1083·6.

The wheels are made of steel, as is also the boiler, which carries a pressure of 150 lbs. per square inch.

The engine (in common with all other London and North-Western engines required to work passenger trains) is fitted with the steam brake, which works automatically with the vacuum brake on the train, upon admission of air into the train-pipe. The ejector creates the vacuum, which is maintained while running by an air-pump driven off the cross-head

An illustration of the latest type of London and North-Western Railway passenger tank engine is given in Fig. 105. This class of engine is doing very useful work on the line. The coupled wheels are 5 ft. 6 in. in diameter, so that the engine is capable of running at a high speed, and as the tanks hold 1347 gallons of water and the coal bunker 2½ tons of coal, it is serviceable, not only for local passenger trains, but also for main line passenger work, provided the runs between stations are not too long.

As these engines run equally well in either direction, they can be arranged with short margins at terminal stations, since the time taken by a tender engine in turning and getting to and from a turntable is saved. They are also powerful enough to work goods trains when required, and

FIG. 105.

are employed for mixed goods and passenger work on the Oxford, Cambridge, and other branches, where a saving in engine power can often be effected by an engine working a goods train in one direction and a passenger train in the other. Altogether, these engines are giving great satisfaction, and proving a very useful addition to the locomotive-stock of the London and North-Western Railway.

The principal dimensions are—

Cylinders, 17 in. in diameter by 24 in. stroke.
Diameter of coupled wheels, 5 ft. 8 in. (with new tyres).
Diameter of leading and trailing-wheels (the latter fitted with radial axle-boxes), 3 ft. 9 in.
Total wheel base, 22 ft. 5 in.
Heating surface: tubes, 960·2 sq. ft. ; fire-box, 94·6 sq. ft.— total sq. ft., 1054·8.

The boiler pressure is 150 lbs. per sq. in., and the weight is distributed as follows—

			TONS	CWT.
Leading-wheels	...	.	10	7
Driving-wheels	...	...	14	18
Intermediate wheels	...	...	14	0
Trailing-wheels	...	...	11	5
	Total	...	50	10

The total length over buffers is 33 ft. 9 in.

A standard type of London and North-Western goods engine, called the "DX" class, which has already been illustrated in Fig. 28, chap. ii., may be again noticed here. This class of engine is still working important goods trains on the line, although it is now thirty-four years since the company began to build them. There are at the present time 750 "DX" engines at work. During Mr. Webb's time they have been fitted with his steel boilers, which carry a pressure of 140 lbs. to the sq. in. The addition of the cab and the altered form of splashers has considerably metamorphosed their original appearance.

In chap. x. a description has been given of the erection of one of Mr. Webb's coal engines, designed for the heavy mineral traffic on the line. Fig. 106 is an illustration of an engine of this class.

It has six coupled wheels 4 ft. 3 in. in diameter, made of cast-iron, similar in construction to the wheel illustrated in

Fig. 88.　The boiler pressure is 140 lbs. to the sq. in., and the following are the principal dimensions—

> Cylinders, 17 in. by 24 in.
> Heating surface: tubes, 980 sq. ft. ; fire-box, 94·6 sq. ft.—total, sq. ft. 1074·6.
> Grate area, 17·1 sq. ft.

Weight—

			TONS	CWT.
Leading-wheels	...	...	10	6
Driving ,,	...	..	10	0
Trailing ,,	...	...	9	5
Tender	...	...	25	0
	Total	...	54	11

FIG. 106.

This engine is capable of drawing 35 loaded coal waggons, amounting to a gross weight of 541 tons, at an average speed of about 25 miles per hour, over the ordinary gradients of the main line at all seasons of the year.

In the summer-time, when the rails are usually in good

condition, this load is, in some instances, increased to 45 loaded coal waggons, making the total weight of the train, exclusive of engine and tender, about 640 tons. In such cases, the average timed speed of the trains is 15 miles per hour.

For simplicity of design and economy in first cost, combined with efficiency and cheap working, Mr. Webb's coal engines stand perhaps second to none.

FIG. 107.

A powerful engine, designed by Mr. Webb for working the most important through express goods trains on the London and North-Western Railway, is illustrated in Fig. 107. It has six coupled wheels 5 ft. in diameter, and is known as the 18 in. goods type; so called from the diameter of the cylinders, which was, at the time they were first built, larger than had previously been used with London and North-Western Railway engines. These engines are chiefly employed working express goods trains between London, Carlisle, Liverpool, and Manchester. They are capable of working heavy trains at a high speed, and are doing excellent work on the line. The wheels are made of steel, and the weight is distributed on them as under—

			TONS.	CWT.
Leading-wheels	...	...	11	14
Driving ,,	...	...	12	0
Trailing ,,	...	...	11	10
	Total	...	35	4
Weight of tender	...	...	25	0
	Total	...	60	4

The principal dimensions are—

> Total length over buffers, 46 ft. 7 in.
> Heating surface : tubes, 980 sq. ft. ; fire-box, 103·5 sq. ft.—total sq. ft. 1083·5.
> Grate area, 17·1 sq. ft.

The boiler pressure is 150 lbs. per sq. in., and the "Joy" valve gear is used to regulate the distribution of steam in the cylinders.

An example of an ordinary run from London to Liverpool with an express goods train worked by an engine of this class is given. The speeds include any signal slacks the train may have met with.

10.40 P.M. GOODS ex CAMDEN, FEB. 3RD, 1893.

MILES.	STATION.	TIME OF ARRIVAL.	TIME OF DEPARTURE.	SPEED PER HOUR.	NO. OF WAGGONS.
		A.M.	P.M.		
	Camden ...	—	10.52		
45¼	Bletchley ...	12.40	12.50	25·1	} 40
35⅞	Rugby ...	2.12	2.32	26·2	
50¾	Stafford ...	4.20	4.30	28·2	} 43
24½	Crewe ...	5.35	5.45	22·6	
28⅞	Ditton ...	6.50	7.0	26·6	} 35
9¼	Edge Hill ...	7.30	—	18·5	
194½	Average speed	—	—	25·7	

The standard London and North-Western Railway shunting engines are very handy engines for the purpose for which they were designed, and are capable of getting through a large quantity of work in a comparatively short space of time. They have six coupled cast-iron wheels 4 ft. 3 in. in diameter, and the feed-water is carried in a " saddle " tank on the top of the boiler. The cylinders are 17 in. in diameter, and have a 24 in. stroke, whilst the boiler pressure is 120 lbs. per sq. in. The tank holds 600 gallons, and the bunker 25 cwts. of coal.

The following are other particulars—

Length over buffers, 28 ft. 3 in.
Weight—

			TONS	CWT.
Leading-wheels	...	...	10	13
Driving ,,	...	...	12	0
Trailing ,,	...	...	10	14
	Total	...	33	12

Heating surface : tubes, 981 sq. ft. ; fire-box, 87·3—total sq. ft., 1068·3.

The " side tank coal engine," designed for working heavy mineral trains in the colliery districts, where great weights have to be hauled, has six coupled cast-iron wheels 4 ft. 3 in. in diameter ; the trailing end is carried on a pair of 3 ft. 9 in. wheels, running in a radial axle-box under the coal bunker and rear tank.

The weight is thus distributed—

			TONS	CWT.
Leading-wheels	...		11	5
Driving-wheels	...		12	0
Intermediate coupled wheels		...	10	6
Trailing-wheels	...	...	9	9
	Total	...	43	0

Heating surface : tubes, 960·2 sq. ft. ; fire-box, 94·6—total
    sq. ft., 1054·8.
Boiler pressure, 150 lbs. per square inch.

The cylinders are 17 in. in diameter, with a stroke of 24 in.

Some of these engines are fitted with the vacuum brake, which renders them serviceable for working local passenger trains when required.

The capacity of the tanks is 1150 gallons. There are three separate tanks, one on each side and one at the bunker end. These are, of course, all connected together, and the same level of water maintained in each.

The most recent type of coal engine designed by Mr. Webb, the first of which has just been turned out of the shops, is illustrated in Fig. 108. As will be seen, it has eight coupled wheels, which are made of cast-iron, and are 4 ft. 3 in. in diameter. The cylinders are 19½ in. in diameter with a 24 in. stroke, the steam-chests being placed above them.

The tractive force is therefore—

$$\frac{19\frac{1}{2} \times 19\frac{1}{2} \times 24}{51} = 179 \text{ lbs. for each effective lb. of steam pressure per sq. in. on the piston.}$$

This, combined with the adhesion obtained by the eight coupled wheels, renders the engine very powerful. The boiler is of the " Greater Britain " type, having a combustion chamber in the middle of the barrel (see p. 312).

It will be noticed that the leading and trailing ends of the engine considerably overhang the wheels. This is to secure as short a wheel base as is possible with four pairs of coupled wheels. That the wheel base is a very moderate one, considering the particular form of construction of this engine, the following diagram will show—

FIG. 108.

Length be-tween wheel-centres	Extreme front end of engine.	Centre of leading wheels.	Centre of driving wheels.	Centre of interme-diate whls.	Centre of trailing wheels.	Extreme end of footplate.
		←—5′9″—× 5′9″—× 5′9″—→				

Total length over buffers ← —————————31′ 5½″————————→

		T.	C.	T.	C.	T.	C.	T.	C.
Weight ...		12	5	12	5	12	5	12	8

Total weight, 49 tons 3 cwt.

Total weight of engine and tender, 74 tons 3 cwt.

The particulars of the heating surface are—

	SQ. FT.	SQ. FT.
Tubes	701·4 +	419·4
Fire-box	127	
Combustion chamber	39·1	
Total ...	1286·9	

Boiler pressure, 160 lbs. per sq. inch.

Capacity of tank, 2060 gals.

,,   ,,   coal space, 109 cub. ft.

Its general design and dimensions show that this is an exceedingly powerful engine, and there is no doubt it will be able to work heavier coal trains than railway companies have yet tried to run. By increasing the number of waggons taken, the number of trains will be decreased, and thus a saving in engine power and train mileage effected, as well as the liability to delays being lessened.

In order to give an idea of the engine stock possessed by a large railway company, the Table A (pp. 240, 241), which comprises a complete list of the different standard classes of London and North-Western Railway engines and the number of engines of each class, has been prepared.

Another Table, B (pp. 242—244), gives the numbers and names of all the passenger engines owned by this company, on the 30th Nov., 1893.

In speaking at the last annual dinner of past and present Crewe engineers, pupils and apprentices, in February last, Mr. Webb stated that the engines of the London and North-Western Railway Company run no less than 60,000,000 miles per annum, which is equivalent to a journey round the world every 3 hours and 50 minutes, or 122 miles every minute, or two miles every second. The water evaporated daily in doing this amounts to 25,000 tons, and the quantity of coal used to nearly 4000 tons.

Mr. Webb at the same time paid a tribute to the skill of the British mechanic, by whose labour such an enormous mileage is being obtained from the engines, with an almost perfect freedom from failure or disaster that could be attributed to defective workmanship.

The following statement, taken from actual practice, gives an idea of the number of miles run by London and North-Western Railway passenger engines between the times they are in the shops for general repairs—

NO. OF ENGINE.	CLASS.	ACTUAL MILEAGE RUN.	AVERAGE MILEAGE.
1309	7' Compound	86,579	87,379
1307	,, ,,	88,179	
2062	6' Compound	47,660	
2061	,, ,,	44,729	
513	,, ,,	45,246	
644	· ,, ,,	42,296	44,983
1666	4 W C 6' 6"	56,164	
1525	,, ,,	55,116	
749	,, ,,	65,981	
861	,, ,,	59,095	
1672	,, ,,	55,503	
1514	,, ,,	58,621	
2177	,, ,,	53,834	
480	,, ,,	55,181	57,437
838	4 W C 5' 6"	55,525	55,525

TABLE A.
PASSENGER ENGINES.

CLASS.		NO. OF EACH CLASS.	CYLINDERS. Diameter and Stroke.	WEIGHT. Leading. T. C.	Driving. T. C.	Intermediate. T. C.	Trailing. T. C.	TOTAL WEIGHT. T. C.	ENGINE AND TENDER LENGTH OVER BUFFERS.	REMARKS.
7′ Compound[1] Greater Britain	...	2	Low 30 × 24 / High 15 × 24	12 16	15 10	15 10	8 6	77 2	54′ 0½″	The standard tenders have a tank capacity of 1800 gallons, and weigh 25 tons in working order.
7′ Compound Teutonic Class	...	10	Low 30 × 24 / High 14 × 24	14 10	15 10	—	15 10	70 10	50′ 5¼″	
6′ 6″ Compound Experiment Class	...	30	Low 26 × 24 / High 13 × 24	10 8	14 4	—	13 3	62 15	46′ 9″	
6′ Compound Dreadnought Class	...	40	Low 30 × 24 / High 14 × 24	12 10	15 0	—	15 0	67 10	49′ 4″	
5′ 6″ Compound Side Tank	...	1	Low 26 × 24 / High 14 × 20	11 12	15 0	14 6	11 2	52 0	32′ 11½″	
4′ 6″ Compound Side Tank	...	1	Low 26 × 24 / High 14 × 18	11 14	15 10	15 12	8 1	50 17	33′ 6½″	
5′ Compound Side Tank	...	1	Low 30 × 24 / High 14 × 24	12 15	15 0	13 16	13 9	55 0	33′ 6¼″	
5′ 9″ Metropolitan Side Tank Compound	...	1	Low 26 × 24 / High 13 × 24	11 7	18 1	—	17 9	46 17	32′ 1″	
5′ 9″ Metropolitan Tank	...	10	17 × 24	10 6	18 12	—	18 4	47 2	32′ 1½″	
5′ 6″ 4 w. c. Side Tank (8 wheels)		90	17 × 24	10 7	14 18	14 0	11 5	50 10	33′ 9″	
4′ 6″ 4 w. c. Side Tank (8 wheels)		180	17 × 20	10 1	13 10	13 6	9 1	45 18	34′ 0½″	

	No.	Cylinders										Total length
4' 6" 4 w. c. Side Tank (6 wheels)	50	17×20	9	16	13	12	—	14	16	38	4		29' 0"
7' 6" Express Single Drivers ...	60	16×24	10	16	11	10	—	7	0	54	6		44' 8"
6' 6" (New Type) 4 w. c. ...	166	17×24	10	5	11	10	—	11	0	57	15		46' 6"
6' (New Type) 4 w. c. ...	60	17×24	10	7	11	10	—	11	7	58	4		45' 11"
6' (Old Type) 4 w. c. ...	30	16×20	8	8	10	0	—	7	14	51	2		44' 10"
5' 6" 4 w. c. ...	20	17×24	10	8	10	10	—	10	10	56	8		46' 6"

GOODS ENGINES.

	No.	Cylinders										Total length
5' 6 w. c. DX. ...	406	17×24	10	10	10	10	—	10	0	56	0		45' 5"
5' 6 w. c. Special DX. ...	418	17×24	10	10	10	0	—	8	10	54	0		45' 5"
5' 6 w. c. 18" cylinder ...	40	18×24	11	14	12	0	—	11	10	60	4		46' 7"
4' 3" 6 w. c. Coal Engine ...	500	17×24	10	6	10	0	—	9	5	54	11		45' 8"
4' 3" 8 w. c.	1	19½×24	12	5	12	5	12 5	12	8	74	3		51' 9¾"
4' 3" 8 w. c. Compound Coal Engine ...	1	Low (1) 30×24 / High (2) 15×24	12	10	14	8	12 14	9	13	74	5		51' 9¾"
4' 3" 6 w. c. Special Tanks ...	260	17×24	10	18	12	0	—	10	14	32	12		28' 3"
4' 3" 6 w. c. Side Tanks ...	280	17×24	11	5	12	0	10 6	9	9	43	0		39' 9½"
4' 4 w. c. Shunters (Tank) ...	52	14×20	10	17	—	—	—	11	18	22	15		22' 5½"
2' 6" 4 w. c. Small Shunters ...	10	9×12	7	11	—	—	—	7	12	15	3		19' 0½"
Odd classes	22												
Total ...	2742												

1 Left-hand figures denote diameter of driving-wheels ; W, wheels ; C, coupled.

TABLE B.

PASSENGER ENGINES.

NO.	NAME.	NO.	NAME.	NO.	NAME.
	8′ 6″ SINGLE WHEEL.		6′ COMPOUNDS.		7′ 6″ SINGLE WHEEL (*continued*).
		2	City of Carlisle		
3020	Cornwall	173	City of Manchester		
		410	City of Liverpool	97	Atalanta
	7′ COMPOUND (8 wheels).	437	City of Chester	111	Russell
		503	Dreadnought	117	Tiger
2053	Greater Britain	504	Thunderer	127	Peel
	Queen Empress	507	Marchioness of Stafford	134	Owl
				139	Cygnet
	7′ COMPOUNDS.	508	Titan	165	Star
1301	Teutonic	509	Ajax	184	Problem
1302	Oceanic	510	Leviathan	196	Leander
1303	Pacific	511	Achilles	218	Wellington
1304	Jeanie Deans	513	Mammoth	222	Lily
1305	Doric	515	Niagara	229	Watt
1306	Ionic	545	Tamerlane	230	Monarch
1307	Coptic	637	City of New York	234	Mazeppa
1309	Adriatic	638	City of Paris	279	Stephenson
1311	Celtic	639	City of London	291	Prince of Wales
1312	Gaelic	640	City of Dublin	531	Lady of the Lake
		641	City of Lichfield	561	Prince Oscar
	5′ 6″ COMPOUNDS.	643	Raven	562	Palmerston
66	Experiment	644	Vesuvius	563	Combermere
300	Compound	645	Alchymist	564	Majestic
301	Economist	647	Ambassador	565	Napoleon
302	Velocipede	648	Swiftsure	610	Princess Royal
303	Hydra	659	Rowland Hill	612	Princess Alice
305	Trentham	685	Himalaya	618	Princess Alexandra
306	Knowsley	1353	City of Edinburgh	622	Prince Alfred
307	Victor	1370	City of Glasgow	665	Lord of the Isles
310	Sarmatian	1379	Stork	667	Marmion
311	Richard Francis Roberts	1395	Archimedes	675	Ivanhoe
		2055	Dunrobin	719	Outram
315	Alaska	2056	Argus	723	Clive
321	Servia	2057	Euphrates	754	Ethelred
323	Britannic	2058	Medusa	762	Locke
333	Germanic	2059	Greyhound	802	Red Gauntlet
353	Oregon	2060	Vandal	803	Tornado
363	Aurania	2061	Harpy	804	Soult
365	America	2062	Herald	806	Waverley
366	City of Chicago	2063	Huskisson	818	Havelock
372	Empress	2064	Autocrat	827	Victoria
374	Emperor		7′ 6″ SINGLE WHEEL.	833	Clyde
519	Shooting Star			834	Elgin
520	Express	1	Saracen	837	Faerie Queen
1102	Cyclops	7	Scorpion	1427	Edith
1104	Sunbeam	28	Prometheus	1428	Eleanor
1111	Messenger	33	Erebus	1429	Alfred Paget
1113	Hecate	44	Harlequin	1430	Pandora
1115	Snake	60	Tantalus	1431	Psyche
1116	Friar	61	Phosphorus	1432	Panopea
1117	Penguin	77	Mersey	1433	Daphne
1120	Apollo			1434	Eunomia

TABLE B (continued).

PASSENGER ENGINES.

NO.	NAME.	NO.	NAME.	NO.	NAME.
	7′ 6″ SINGLE WHEEL (continued).		6′ 6″ 4 W. C. (continued).		6′ 6″ 4 W. C. (continued).
1435	Fortuna	863	Meteor	1489	Brindley
1436	Egeria	864	Pilot	1513	Shakespeare
	6′ 6″ 4 W. C.	865	Envoy	1514	Scott
		866	Courier	1515	Milton
193	Rocket	867	Disraeli	1516	Byron
253	President Garfield	868	Condor	1517	Princess Helena
254	President Lincoln	869	Llewellyn	1518	Countess
256	President Washington	870	Fairbairn	1519	Duchess
		871	Proserpine	1520	Franklin
257	Duke of Albany	872	Wizard	1521	Gladstone
260	Duke of Connaught	883	Phantom	1522	Pitt
262	Wheatstone	890	Sir Hardman Earle	1523	Marlborough
264	Buckland			1524	Wolfe
265	Thomas Carlyle	919	Nasmyth	1525	Abercrombie
271	Minotaur	941	Blenkinsop	1526	Drake
275	Vulcan	942	Shah of Persia	1527	Raleigh
276	Pluto	945	Humphrey Davy	1528	Frobisher
295	Penmaenmawr	955	Charles Dickens	1529	Cook
304	Hector	974	Richard Cobden	1530	Columbus
308	Booth	1020	Wordsworth	1531	Cromwell
364	Henry Pease	1105	Hercules	1532	Hampden
379	Sedgwick	1132	North-Western	1666	Ariadne
380	Quernmore	1141	S. R. Graves	1667	Corunna
381	Patterdale	1170	General	1668	Dagmar
382	Buckingham	1173	The Auditor	1669	Ilion
393	Brougham	1177	Princess Louise	1670	Ganymede
394	Eamont	1183	Plynlimmon	1671	Shamrock
395	Scotia	1187	Chandos	1672	Talavera
396	Tennyson	1189	Stewart	1673	Lucknow
403	Isabella	1193	Joshua Radcliffe	1674	Delhi
477	Caractacus	1194	Miranda	1675	Vimiera
478	Commodore	1211	John Ramsbottom	1676	The Nile
480	Duchess of Lancaster	1212	Pioneer	1677	Badajos
		1213	The Queen	1678	Airey
482	Pegasus	1214	Prince Albert	1679	Bunsen
506	Sir Alexander Cockburn	1215	Albion	1680	Livingstone
		1216	Premier	1681	Minerva
512	Lazonby	1217	Florence	1682	Novelty
514	Lawrence	1218	Phaeton	1683	Sisyphus
517	Marathon	1219	Lightning	1684	Speke
619	Mabel	1220	Belted Will	1685	Gladiator
696	Director	1480	Newton	1744	Magdala
749	Mercury	1481	The Duke of Edinburgh	1745	John Bright
787	Clarendon			1746	Bevere
789	Breadalbane	1482	Herschel	1747	John Mayall
790	Hardwicke	1483	Newcomen	1748	Britannia
857	Prince Leopold	1484	Telford	1749	Hibernia
858	Sir Sala Jung	1485	Smeaton	2001	Henry Crosfield
860	Merrie Carlisle	1486	Dalton	2002	Madge
861	Amazon	1487	Faraday	2003	Alecto
862	Balmoral	1488	Murdock	2004	Witch

TABLE B (continued).

PASSENGER ENGINES.

NO.	NAME.	NO.	NAME.	NO.	NAME.
	6′ 6″ 4 w. c. (continued).		6′ 4 w. c. (continued).		6′ 4 w. c. (Old Type continued).
2005	Lynx	642	Bee		
2006	Princess	724	Eden	773	Centaur
2175	Precedent	731	Croxteth	793	Martin
2176	Robert Benson	733	Chimera	794	Woodlark
2177	Edward Tootal	735	Charon	852	Kestrel
2178	Pluck	736	Memnon	885	Vampire
2179	Patience	738	Terrier	995	Medea
2180	Perseverance	739	Sutherland	1163	John O'Gaunt
2181	Buffalo	742	Spitfire	1164	Odin
2182	Giraffe	748	Waterloo	1166	Wyre
2183	Antelope	752	Glowworm	1168	Cuckoo
2184	Reynard	757	Banshee	2151	Baltic
2185	Alma	758	Hardman	2152	Sybil
2186	Lowther	763	Violet	2154	Loadstone
2187	Penrith Beacon	764	Shap	2155	Liver
2188	Chillington	792	Theorem	2156	Sphinx
2189	Avon	795	Falstaff	2157	Unicorn
2190	Princess Beatrice	805	Caliban	2158	Serpent
2191	Snowdon	814	Henrietta	2159	Shark
2192	Caradoc	817	Constance		
2193	Salopian	819	Puck		(These engines are being gradually rebuilt and converted into 6′ 4 w. c. new type.)
2194	Cambrian	821	Diomed		
		824	Adelaide		
	6′ 4 w. c. (New Type).	828	Tubal		
		829	Turk		5′ 6″ 4 w. c.
35	Talisman	830	Trent	255	Eglinton
36	Thalaba	832	Sanspareil	408	Simoom
81	Greystoke	901	Hero	426	Warrior
124	Marquis Douro	902	Onyx	427	Fame
231	Firefly	934	North Star	626	Emerald
285	Phalaris	935	Planet	680	Giffard
418	Zygia	1045	Whitworth	697	Harrowby
419	Zillah	1162	Saddleback	838	Henry Cort
434	St. Patrick	2150	Atlas	847	Cedric
444	Pyphon	2153	Isis	1143	Marquis
445	Ixion			1145	Cossack
446	Siren		6′ 4 w. c. (Old Type).	1147	John Rennie
468	Wildfire			1148	Boadicea
469	St. George	90	Luck of Edenhall	1149	Helvellyn
479	Mastodon	209	Petrel	1151	Lapwing
485	Euxine	263	Pheasant	1153	Sirocco
486	Skiddaw	401	Zeno	1155	Dragon
604	Narcissus	404	Zopyrus	1180	Pearl
609	The Earl of Chester	414	Prospero	2145	Precursor
628	Tartarus	424	Sirius	2147	Champion
632	Ostrich	487	John O'Groat		
633	Samson	631	Hotspur		(There were originally 40 of these engines; 20 have been converted into side tanks.)
634	Ellesmere	732	Hecla		
635	Zamiel	737	Roberts		
636	Eclipse	746	Castor		

CHAPTER XV.

MODERN LOCOMOTIVES (*continued*).

TAKING the other large railway companies in alphabetical order we now come to

The Great Eastern Railway.

This company's most recent type of express passenger

FIG. 109.

engine, designed by Mr. Holden, the locomotive superintendent, is shown in Fig. 109, and it is an interesting engine, because it is the first passenger engine in this country to which the principle of burning liquid fuel has been permanently applied.

As will be seen from the illustration, the driving and trailing-wheels are coupled, the weight in front being supported on a single pair of wheels.

The following are the principal dimensions—

		FT.	IN.
Diameter of driving and trailing-wheels ...		7	0
,, leading-wheels		4	0
,, cylinders		1	6
Length of stroke		2	0
Heating surface, 1230·6 sq. ft.			
Grate area, 17·9 sq. ft.			

	TONS	CWT.	QRS.
Weight of engine in working order ...	42	0	0
,, tender ,, ,, ...	32	5	3
Total ...	74	5	3

The liquid fuel is carried on the tender in a tank, the capacity of which is 500 gallons, and some details of the apparatus for consuming it are given in chap. xviii. Mr. Holden's experiments in the burning of liquid fuel have been very successful, and the results he has obtained doubtless mark an epoch in locomotive history. The engine "Petrolea" is doing its work very well, and is taking some of the heaviest and most important trains on the Great Eastern Railway.

The engine illustrated in Fig. 110 was designed by Mr. Holden for working the excursion traffic to seaside places in the summer, and for fast cattle and fish trains in the winter-time. It has cylinders 17½ in. in diameter with a stroke of 24 in., and 5 ft. 8 in. coupled wheels. The engine is fitted with the Westinghouse brake, and also with an ejector and vacuum pipes for working the automatic vacuum brake when attached to other companies' trains. The two cylinders are cast in one piece with the valve-chests below them. The valve motion has the ordinary shifting link, and the cross-heads work on heavy single guide bars. The boiler is of steel, butt-jointed. The leading end is carried on one pair of wheels, 4 ft. in diameter, the journals of which run in two outside and two inside axle-boxes, so constructed as to allow considerable lateral play.

FIG. 110.

The following is the heating surface—

Tubes	...	...	1107·4 sq. ft.
Fire-box	...	...	100·9 ,,
Total	...	1208·3 sq. ft.
Grate area	...	...	18 ,,

The weight is thus distributed—

			TONS	CWT.	QRS.
Leading-wheels	...	...	14	2	3
Driving ,,	...	...	13	13	0
Trailing ,,	...	...	12	10	1
		Total ...	40	6	0

Mr. Holden has also constructed at Stratford a very useful class of six wheels coupled, tank engine, for running local goods and passenger service, which is illustrated in Fig. 111. This engine has inside cylinders, 16½ in. by 22 in., and driving-wheels 4 ft. in diameter. The heating surface is

FIG. 111.

959·24 sq. ft., and the grate area 12·4 sq. ft. Its total weight in working order is 40 tons.

The goods engines on the Great Eastern Railway are of the usual six wheels coupled type. The wheels are 4 ft. 11 in. in diameter, and the cylinders 17½ in. by 24 in. The weight of the engine in working order is 38 tons 4 cwt. 2 qrs., and the tender 30 tons 12 cwt. 2 qrs.

The Great Eastern single-wheeled express engines, of

which Fig. 112 is an illustration, have the following dimensions—

Driving-wheels, diameter, 7 ft.
Leading and trailing wheels, diameter, 4 ft.
Cylinders, diameter, 18 in. ; stroke 24 in.
Heating surface, 1230·46 sq. ft.
Grate area, 17·9 sq. ft.

	TONS	CWT.	QRS.
Weight of engine in working order ...	40	3	2
,, tender ,, ,, ...	32	7	0

FIG. 112.

The boilers, cylinders, motion, etc., of this engine are identical with those of the four coupled express engines, the mixed traffic engines, the six wheels coupled engines, and also a new main line passenger tank engine, now being built at Stratford. In this way the interchangeability of parts, which effects so great an economy both in first cost and in subsequent repairs, is ensured.

Great Northern Railway.

A type of express passenger engine, which never fails to excite universal interest and admiration, is Mr. Patrick Stirling's outside cylinder express passenger engine with 8 ft. single driving-wheels.

Mr. Stirling first commenced building engines of this type about 25 years ago, and excepting certain trivial alterations in the design of various parts, no important change has been made ; and they are still making the magnificent express runs for which the Great Northern Railway is so justly celebrated.

These engines were expressly devised to run at exceptionally high speeds, and are still enabling the Great Northern Railway to hold its own in the matter of speed with any other railway company in the world, while continuing to adhere to what must now be called an old-fashioned design of locomotive.

The important relation which the speed and weight of a train bear to each other is not usually understood by the ordinary travelling public. The fact of a locomotive being capable of running at the speed attained by any trains of the present day was demonstrated many years ago, and the aim of locomotive superintendents has not been to increase that speed, but to build engines capable of maintaining the same standard, notwithstanding the enormously increased weight of trains.

Although perhaps they can hardly be expected to grapple with what is considered a really heavy load in these days, the Great Northern single-wheeled engines are still doing excellent service on the main line trains, and performing, even at the present time, some of the fastest runs that are being done in the world. Only lately an average speed of upwards of 77 miles per hour was recorded over a distance of 12 miles with the 2 p.m. express from Manchester to London. Some exceptionally high speeds were attained during the famous East and West Coast race in August 1888 ; but although the public were at that time much impressed by the extraordinary speed at which the trains on both the competing lines ran, it must be borne in mind that to run a light train of five or six coaches at an average speed of from 55 to 60 or even 65 miles an hour, is not nearly such a hard task for a locomotive as to run a heavy train of 15 or 16 main line coaches at from 45 to 50 miles an hour. All honour is due to the single-wheeled engines, which still find themselves able to cope with the Great Northern express trains of the present day ; but it is but fair to remember that the locomotives running on this line have the advantage over their competitors in the Scotch traffic, as far as gradients and weight of trains are concerned.

An example of a Great Northern 8 ft. passenger engine is given in Fig. 113, and the following are its principal dimensions—

	FT.	IN.
Diameter of cylinders	0	18
Length of stroke	0	28
Wheels, bogie, diameter	3	10
,, driving ,, ...	8	0
,, trailing ,, ...	4	6

Heating surface : tubes (174), 936 sq. ft. ;
    fire-box, 109—total sq. ft., 1045.
Grate area, $17\frac{3}{4}$ sq. ft.

Weight in working order—

	TONS	CWT.
Bogie	17	11
Driving-wheels	17	0
Trailing ,, ...	10	12
Total ...	45	3

The engine is extremely simple in design, everything being

well-proportioned, and there is not one superfluous part to cause any extra complications.

Mr. Stirling's 4 wheels coupled inside cylinder engines with 5 ft. 6 in. driving-wheels, coupled in front (the trailing end

FIG. 113.

being carried on one pair of wheels) are powerful, useful engines, capable of working both goods and passenger trains.

The following are the principal dimensions of this class of engine—

	FT.	IN.
Diameter of cylinders	0	18½
Length of stroke	0	26
Wheels, leading, diameter	5	6
,, driving ,, ...	5	6
,, trailing ,, ...	4	0

Heating surface : tubes, 823·6 sq. ft. ; fire-box, 92·4 sq. ft.—total sq. ft., 916·0. Grate area, 16¼ sq. ft.

Weight in working order—

				TONS	CWT.
Leading-wheels	...	...	...	12	16
Driving ,, ...	...	...	...	14	0
Trailing ,, ...	...	...	...	8	6
			Total ...	35	2

Total weight of tender loaded, 34 tons, 18 cwt., 3 qrs.
Capacity of tank, 2800 gallons.

The following is a list of the other principal classes of engines on the Great Northern Railway—

7 ft. 6 in. single driving wheels express passenger engine, cylinders 18 in. by 26 in.

Goods engine, 6 wheels coupled, 5 ft. in diameter, cylinders $17\frac{1}{2}$ in. by 26 in.

4-wheels 6 ft. 6 in. coupled passenger engine, driving and trailing-wheels coupled. Cylinders $17\frac{1}{2}$ in. by 26 in.

4 coupled bogie, side tank, 5 ft. 6 in. wheels, leading and driving-wheels coupled, with bunker carried on bogie.

The Great Northern Railway Company possess altogether 948 locomotives.

Great Western Railway.

Mr. W. Dean, the locomotive superintendent of the Great Western Line, has lately designed and constructed at the Company's works at Swindon some very fine engines for working the express passenger service to the West of England. The abolition of the broad gauge has necessitated putting on the line a number of new narrow gauge engines, and the long-established fame of the "Flying Dutchman" is not likely to suffer in consequence of the change. In his most recent type of express passenger engine Mr. Dean goes in for cylinders no less than 20 in. in diameter and 7 ft. 8 in.

single driving-wheels. The length of the stroke is 24 inches, and the weight on the driving-wheels 19 tons. As the boiler develops a pressure of 160 lbs. to the square inch, it is obvious that this engine is both capable of working heavy trains and of running at a high speed.

Fig. 114 is an illustration of an engine of this class, from which it will be seen that Mr. Dean has reverted to the

FIG. 114.

system adopted by McConnell and other earlier locomotive engineers, of constructing the fire-box shell of larger vertical diameter than the barrel of the boiler. The latter is telescopic, with a mean internal diameter of 4 ft. $1\frac{11}{16}$th in. The tubes are of iron, ground at the ends to ensure a good bearing surface in the holes of the tube-plates. At the fire-box end they are expanded, beaded over, and further secured by ferrules.

Chief particulars—

Length of boiler between tube plates, 11 ft. 9¼ in.
Number of tubes, 249.
Diameter of tubes (outside), 1¾ in.
Heating surface : tubes, 1342·85 sq. ft. ; fire-box, 123·88 sq. ft.
——total sq. ft., 1466·73.
Area of fire-grate, 20·8 sq. ft.
Length of wheel base, 18 ft. 6 in.

Weight of engine in working order—

				TONS	CWT.
Leading-wheels	...	...	...	13	4
Driving ,, ...	...	...	...	19	0
Trailing ,, ...	...	...	...	11	18
		Total	...	44	2
Weight of tender (full) with 50 cwt. coal ...				32	0
Total weight of engine and tender in working order				76	2

The tender runs on six wheels, and has a coal capacity of
four tons, and the tank holds 3000 gallons of water.

The line from Paddington to Swindon rises 260 ft., but on
the whole the Great Western main line as far as Bristol is
exceptionally favoured in the matter of gradients, and the
new single-wheeled engines are in every respect admirably
fitted for the work which they have to perform.

Fig. 115 illustrates another form of Great Western coupled
engine employed on parts of the line where steep gradients
and heavy trains are to be contended with.

Chief dimensions—

				FT.	IN.
Diameter of leading-wheels	...	...		4	0
,, driving ,,	...	...		6	6
,, trailing ,,	...	...		6	6
Diameter of cylinders ...	...	...		0	17½
Length of stroke	...	...	...	0	24

Heating surface : tubes, 1262 sq. ft. ; fire-
box, 102—total sq. ft., 1364.

The weight is thus distributed—

				TONS	CWT.
On leading-wheels	...	...	...	12	0
,, driving ,,	..	...	...	14	0
,, trailing ,,	...	...	...	12	6
	Total	...	...	38	6

The boiler is of steel with iron tubes, and carries a pressure of 150 lbs. to the square inch.

Mr. Dean has also built at Swindon some powerful coupled engines for working the express passenger service on other parts of the line where the gradients are heavier,

FIG. 115.

and the following are particulars of the type of coupled engines, of which Fig. 116 is an illustration.

		FT.	IN.
Diameter of leading-wheels		4	0
,, driving ,, } Coupled ...		6	0
,, trailing ,,		6	0
Diameter of cylinders		0	18
Length of stroke		0	24

Boiler pressure, 150 lbs. per sq. in.
Heating surface : tubes, 1352 sq. ft. ; fire-box, 116 sq. ft.—total sq. ft., 1468·8.
Grate area, 19 sq. ft.
Total weight, 42 tons.

This is a very good specimen of a double-framed engine. It has inside and outside axle-boxes on the driving-wheels and outside cranks, upon which the connecting-rods work. It will be seen that the weight is carried on laminated springs underneath each wheel.

The Great Western trains between London and Birmingham are very heavy and fast. The Corridor train leaving Paddington at 1·30 p.m., when empty, weighs about 200

FIG. 116.

tons exclusive of engine and tender, and is timed at an average speed of over 47 miles per hour. Some of the trains on the London and Birmingham service load to upwards of twenty vehicles.

Many of the passenger trains on the Great Western Railway are worked by side-tank engines. Some of those running in the London district and working the residential trains between Paddington and Slough are doing a large mileage daily. Excellent results are still obtained from them in contending with the heavier traffic of to-day, although they are of a distinctly old-fashioned type.

The following are the chief dimensions of these engines—

					FT.	IN.
Diameter of leading-wheels	...	...			3	6
,,	driving	,,	}Coupled	...	5	0
,,	trailing	,,		...	5	0
,,	cylinder	,,	...	...	0	16
Length of stroke		...	...		0	24

Heating surface : tubes, 1209 sq. ft. ; fire-box, 99 sq. ft.—total sq. ft., 1308.

Weight—

					TONS	CWT.
Leading-wheels	...	...	...		11	12
Driving	,,	...	...	...	14	0
Trailing	,,	(with 20 cwt. of coal)	...		14	0
		Total	...		39	12

The boiler pressure is 150 lbs. to the square inch.

The Great Western Company have also some very powerful saddle-tank engines, which are used chiefly for the heavy local coal trains in the South Wales district, and also for local goods and passenger trains on other parts of the line where the gradients are heavy. Fig. 117 illustrates an engine of this type. It has cylinders 17 in. in diameter with a stroke of 24 in. The tank has a capacity of 1100 galls., and the total weight in working order is $45\frac{1}{2}$ tons. This, combined with the six coupled wheels $4\frac{1}{2}$ ft. in diameter, gives the engine great tractive force.

With the exception of a few shunting engines, the Great Western Railway Company's engines are *all* fitted with air-pumps for maintaining the vacuum for working the brake ; practically every engine on the system is therefore

available to work passenger trains if required to do so in
case of emergency.   The goods engines are of the usual

FIG. 117.

six wheels coupled type.   The majority have double frames,
but the present standard goods engines have single frames.

Lancashire and Yorkshire Railway.

The bogie passenger engine, illustrated in Fig. 118, was
constructed by Mr. Aspinall, locomotive superintendent of
the line, for working the express traffic between Manchester
and Liverpool, York and Southport, Blackpool and Manchester.   Some of these trains are very heavy and fast, and
it was necessary to construct a powerful engine to work
them satisfactorily.

It will be seen from the illustration that the driving and
trailing-wheels are coupled, the leading end of the engine
being carried on a bogie.

The cylinders are 18 in. in diameter by 26 in. stroke, and

therefore the engine possesses great tractive force and is altogether suitable for the special purpose for which it was designed.

The leading particulars are—

	FT.	IN.
Diameter of driving and trailing-wheels	7	3
Diameter of bogie ,, ,, ...	3	0½

Heating surface: tubes (220), 1¾ in. diameter, 1108·73 sq. ft.; fire-box, 107·68 sq. ft.—total sq. ft., 1216·41.

Fire-grate area, 18¾ sq. ft.

FIG. 118.

Weight in working order—

	TONS	CWT.	QRS.
On bogie-wheels	13	16	0
,, driving ,, ...	16	10	0
,, trailing ,, ...	14	10	0
Total ...	44	16	0
Weight of tender loaded	26	2	2

Capacity of tank, 1800 gallons.

The Lancashire and Yorkshire goods engine, illustrated in Fig. 119, was designed to work the heavy fast goods on the line. The loads taken vary considerably, ranging from 15 to 60 waggons, according to the gradients over which

FIG. 119.

they have to travel, which at some parts of the line are as steep as 1 in 27.

The following are the leading particulars of this engine—

				FT.	IN.
Diameter of leading, driving, and trailing-wheels ...				5	1

Heating surface: tubes, 1102·26 sq. ft.; fire-box, 107·68 sq. ft.—total sq. ft., 1209·94.

Fire-grate area, 18¾ sq. ft.

Weight in working order—

				TONS	CWT.	QRS.
On leading-wheels ...	...	...		13	16	2
,, driving ,, ...	...	...		15	0	0
,, trailing ,, ...	...	...		13	0	2
Total	...	...		41	17	0
Weight of tender, loaded	...	...		26	2	2

Capacity of tank, 1800 gallons.

A powerful tank engine has also been designed by Mr. Aspinall for working the heavy passenger traffic on the main lines, on which there are some very heavy gradients, especially between Manchester and Oldham, Rochdale and Blackburn. The gradients between Manchester, Oldham, and Rochdale are 1 in 27, 1 in 63, and 1 in 80.

Between Manchester and Blackburn, a distance of about $24\frac{1}{2}$ miles, 13 miles are on rising gradients, 1 in 72, 1 in 74, etc., with about six miles of falling gradients. The number of coaches taken by these engines is 13. The approximate weight of engine and coaches is 250 tons. The engines are fitted with the arrangement for taking up water when running, which is raised and lowered by the vacuum for actuating the brake, and can be used when the engine is working either backward or forward.

The following are the leading particulars—

Diameter of cylinders, 18 in. by 26 in. stroke.
   ,,   leading-wheels (radial axle-boxes), 3 ft. $7\frac{3}{4}$ in.
   ,,   driving and trailing-wheels, 5 ft. 8 in.
Heating surface : tubes, 1108·73 sq. ft. ; fire-box, 107·68
    sq. ft.—total sq. ft., 1216·41.
Fire-grate area, $18\frac{3}{4}$ sq. ft.

Weight in working order—

					TONS	CWT.
On leading wheels (radial axle-box)	...		...		13	10
,, driving	,,	...	...	...	16	12
,, trailing	,,	...	...	...	15	2
			Total	...	45	4
Capacity of tank, 1340 galls. ; ditto, coal bunker					2	0

London, Brighton, and South-Coast Railway.

The line south of the Thames, which has hitherto enjoyed the best reputation for punctuality, is perhaps the London, Brighton, and South-Coast, and there is no doubt that the splendid runs of the London and Brighton trains, and their general punctual working, is to be attributed to the engineering skill and enterprise of the late Mr. William Stroudley, locomotive superintendent of the line. Mr. Stroudley was certainly one of the most go-ahead locomotive men in the country, and the engines he built at the Company's works at Brighton have proved themselves capable of working perhaps heavier and faster trains than any others running between London and the south coast of England.

The most important train running from Brighton to London is the 8.45 a.m., which is allowed one hour and ten minutes, the distance being 50½ miles. The return train leaves London Bridge at 5 p.m., and arrives at Brighton at 6.5 p.m., thus covering the distance in one hour and five minutes, the average speed being 46·5 miles an hour.

The weight of these trains when loaded with passengers is estimated at 245 tons, the total moving weight therefore being—

		TONS	CWT.
Weight of engine and tender		66	0
Weight of train		245	0
Total ...		311	0

The line between London and Brighton rises at either end from the starting-point. For a distance of 2½ miles out of London, the gradient is 1 in 100, the ruling gradient throughout being about 1 in 264, with three summits between London and Brighton, viz. Merstham Tunnel, Balcombe Tunnel, and Clayton Tunnel.

In 1882 Mr. Stroudley constructed a powerful express engine, designed specially for this service, of which the "Gladstone" (Fig. 120) is an illustration. It will be noted that the leading and driving-wheels are coupled together, and the trailing end carried on a smaller pair of wheels.

The chief particulars of this engine are—

Diameter of cylinders, 18¼ in.
Length of stroke, 26 in.
Diameter of coupled wheels, 6 ft. 6 in.
Total heating surface, 1485 sq. ft.

	TONS	CWT.
Weight of engine in working order ...	38	14
Weight of tender ,, ,, ...	27	7
Total ...	66	1

Fig. 120.

Engines of the "Gladstone" type are fitted with the Howe curved link motion, illustrated in Fig. 43, and the reversing gear is, by an invention of Mr. Stroudley's, actuated by the compressed air in the Westinghouse brake reservoir. This is an arrangement which has found great favour among the drivers, as it greatly reduces the manual labour necessary with ordinary reversing gears, and gives them a means of operating the machinery instantaneously should emergency arise.

The valves are placed underneath the steam-chest with the idea that when steam is shut off the valves fall off the faces of the ports, and therefore friction is avoided.

All the London, Brighton, and South-Coast trains and engines are fitted with the Westinghouse brake, which is applied, on the engine illustrated, by two cast-iron blocks to each of the coupled wheels.

Mr. Stroudley used to feed his boilers entirely with hot water, heated by exhaust steam turned into the tender. The ordinary form of feed-pump was alone used on these engines, and there is no doubt that this was a very economical arrangement. It is, however, stated that there were a considerable number of failures with the pumps, and Mr. Billinton, Mr. Stroudley's successor, is reverting to the usual system of injectors.

The London, Brighton, and South-Coast Railway Company have some small tank-engines running local passenger trains between London Bridge, Croydon, etc., which are doing excellent service, and working very economically. The goods engines on this line are of the usual six wheels coupled type.

London, Chatham, and Dover Railway.

The most important traffic for which the London, Chatham, and Dover Company have to provide is the fast mail and continental traffic to and from London ; and the engines employed upon this service were designed by Mr. Kirtley, the locomotive superintendent, and built at the Company's works at Longhedge. These are powerful engines, with inside cylinders, 6 ft. 6 in. coupled wheels, and a bogie at the leading end. The following are the principal particulars of an engine of this type, illustrated in Fig. 121.

Diameter of cylinders, 18 in.
Length of stroke, 26 in.
Diameter of coupled wheels, 6 ft. 6 in.
Boiler pressure, 150 lbs. per square inch.

			TONS	CWT.	QRS.
Weight on bogie wheels	...	...	13	11	0
Weight on driving-wheels	...	...	15	13	3
Weight on trailing-wheels	...	...	13	4	1
Total weight in working order	...		42	9	0

Heating surface : tubes 1010 sq. ft. ; fire-box, 110 sq. ft.—total
sq. ft., 1120.
Grate area, 17 sq. ft.

FIG. 121.

The standard brake on the London, Chatham, and Dover
stock is the Westinghouse, but they have some vehicles
fitted with the automatic vacuum, and engines fitted with
the apparatus necessary for working both brakes.

Fig. 122 is an illustration of a London, Chatham, and
Dover tank-engine used for Metropolitan tunnel and main
line work. This is a powerful engine, and starts away with

a train very readily, an important advantage for a local passenger engine.

The driving and leading-wheels are coupled, the trailing end being carried on a bogie; the rigid wheel base between the coupled wheels is 7 ft. 6 in.

When the engine is working in the Metropolitan tunnels, the exhaust steam, instead of passing away through the chimney, is carried by a large pipe at the side of the boiler

FIG. 122.

into the tank and there condensed; an arrangement adopted on all engines that have to run on the London underground railways, to whatever company they may belong.

Chief particulars—

		FT.	IN.
Diameter of coupled wheels		5	6
,, bogie ,, ...		3	0
,, cylinders		0	17½
Length of stroke		0	26
Total length over buffers		32	6

Heating surface : tubes, 995 sq. ft. ; fire-box, 100 sq. ft.—total sq. ft., 1095. Grate area, 16·5 sq. ft.

Capacity of tank, 970 galls. ; ditto, coal bunker, 2 tons.

The London, Chatham, and Dover Company have also another class of side tank engine, built on the same lines, but with smaller cylinders and boiler.

The London, Chatham, and Dover goods engines are of

FIG. 123.

the usual six wheels coupled type, and are well-designed engines, neat in appearance, and of powerful construction. Fig. 123 is an illustration of an engine of this class, and the following are the principal particulars—

	FT.	IN.
Diameter of cylinders ...	0	18
Length of stroke ...	0	26
Diameter of wheels ...	5	0

Heating surface : tubes, 1000·4 sq. ft. ; fire-box, 102·0 sq. ft.— total sq. ft., 1102·4.

Grate area, 17 sq. ft.

Boiler pressure, 150 lbs. per sq. in.

Weight—

				TONS	CWT.	QRS.
On leading-wheels	...	...	...	13	2	0
,, driving ,,	...	...	...	15	4	2
,, trailing ,,	...	...	...	10	19	2
Total weight in working order	...	...	39	6	0
Weight of tender	...	...	...	34	3	1
Total weight of engine and tender in working order				73	9	1

Fig. 124.

London and South-Western Railway.

A very fine specimen of a modern simple express passenger engine is Mr. Adams' outside cylinder 7 ft. 1 in. coupled engine, illustrated in Fig. 124. This powerful engine has cylinders 19 in. in diameter with a 26 in. stroke. The driving and trailing-wheels are coupled, the leading end being carried on a bogie, whose wheels are 3 ft. 9¾ in. in diameter.

The tractive force exerted for each pound of effective steam pressure on the piston is therefore

$$\frac{19 \times 19 \times 26}{85} = 107\cdot4 \text{ lbs.}$$

These engines work such trains as the 12.30 p.m. Bournemouth express, running from Waterloo to Southampton without a stop, a distance of $79\frac{1}{4}$ miles, at the rate of $47\cdot55$ miles per hour ; the express from Bournemouth, which runs from Southampton to Vauxhall (78 miles) without a stop, at the rate of 50 miles an hour ; the 2.15 p.m. Waterloo to Christchurch, 104 miles without a stop, at the rate of 46 miles an hour ; the 11 a.m. Waterloo to Salisbury ($83\frac{1}{2}$ miles) at the rate of $43\cdot5$ miles an hour; and the 3 p.m. Waterloo to Basingstoke, 48 miles, in exactly one hour.

These runs have very often to be accomplished with loads of as much as ten six-wheeled vehicles weighing 15 tons each, and four bogie carriages of about 20 tons each, giving a gross train load (including engine and tender) of about 310 tons.

The following are further leading particulars of the engine—

Heating surface : tubes, 1245·6 sq. ft. ; fire-box, 122·16 sq. ft.— total sq. ft., 1367·76

Grate area, 18 sq. ft.

Boiler pressure, 175 lbs. per square inch.

Weight in working order—

				TONS	CWT.	QRS.
On bogie-wheels	...	...	...	18	7	2
,, driving ,,	...	...	...	15	9	0
,, trailing ,,	...	...	...	14	17	0
		Total	...	48	13	2
Weight of tender	...	...	...	33	4	0
Total weight of engine and tender in working order				81	17	2

Capacity of tank 3300 gallons.

The engine is fitted with a steam brake, which works automatically with the vacuum brake on the train. A special feature of the South-Western engines is Adams' vortex blast-pipe, which is illustrated and described in chap. viii., fig. 92.

A London and South-Western tank-engine, used for working local passenger trains, is illustrated in Fig. 125.

FIG. 125.

It has driving-wheels 4 ft. 10 in. in diameter, coupled to the leading-wheels, while the trailing. or bunker end of the engine is carried on a bogie with 3 ft. wheels. Further particulars of this engine are—

Cylinders, diameter, 17 in.; stroke, 24 in.
Heating surface: tubes, 897·76 sq. ft. ; fire-box, 89·75 sq. ft.— total sq. ft., 987·51. Grate area, 13·83.

Weight in working order—

				TONS	CWT.	QRS.
On leading wheels	...	...	...	14	10	2
,, driving ,,	...	...	...	15	0	0
,, bogie ,,	...	...	...	15	1	0
			Total ...	44	11	2

Capacity of tank, 800 gallons.

These are exceedingly useful engines for working the important local services, of which there are many on the South-Western Railway. They have also comfortable and roomy foot-plates, and are a very favourite class of engine with the drivers. The position of the injector, just under the tank and near the foot-plate, renders it easy to get at for examination, which is further facilitated by the construction of the injector itself, as it is put together in two longitudinal sections. By unscrewing four bolts, half the injector can be taken down, and all the cones, etc., thoroughly examined in a very short time.

The following is a list of the standard types of the most important South-Western engines—

DESCRIPTION OF ENGINES.	DIMENSION OF CYLINDERS.	TOTAL LENGTH OVER BUFFERS.		WEIGHT IN WORKING ORDER.		
	IN. IN.	FT.	IN.	T.	C.	Q.
7 ft. 1 in. four wheels coupled— Bogie at leading end ; outside cylinders (Fig. 124)	19 × 26	53	8¾	48	13	0
6 ft. 7 in. four wheels coupled— Bogie at leading end ; outside cylinders	19 × 26	54	2⅜	48	11	0
6 ft. leading and driving-wheels coupled—one pair of trailing-wheels	18 × 26	50	8⅜	43	8	0
5 ft. 7 in. four wheels coupled— Bogie side-tank engine, leading and driving-wheels coupled— Bogie at trailing end ; inside cylinders	18 × 26	35	1½	53	0	0
4 ft. 10 in. four wheels coupled— Bogie side-tank engine, leading and driving-wheels coupled— Bogie at trailing ends ; inside cylinders (Fig. 125)	17 × 24	30	8½	44	11	2
Shunting four wheels tank-engine, 3 ft. 9½ in. coupled wheels ...	16 × 22	24	10½	32	8	2

Midland Railway.

Fig. 126 is an illustration of the most recent type of Midland main line express passenger engine, designed by Mr. S. W. Johnson, the locomotive superintendent of the line.

This engine has single driving-wheels, 7 ft. 6 in. in

FIG. 126.

diameter. The leading end is carried on in a bogie similar in detail to that illustrated in Fig. 87.

Engine No. 1853 was exhibited at the Paris Exhibition in 1889, and obtained the Grand Prix. The trains worked by this class of engine are the most important on the Midland Railway, and many of them are timed at speeds averaging upwards of fifty miles an hour, with loads varying from nine to thirteen coaches.

These engines are fitted with the automatic steam and vacuum brake, and also with a steam-sanding apparatus and sight-feed lubricator.

The following are chief particulars of the engine—

Diameter of cylinders, 18½ in.

Length of stroke, 26 in.

Total length over buffers, 52 ft.

Boiler pressure, 160 lbs. per square inch ; tubes (242), diameter, 1⅝ in.

Heating surface : tubes, 1123 sq. ft. ; fire-box, 117—total sq. ft., 1240.

Grate area, 19½ sq. ft.

		TONS.
Total weight of engine in working order	...	43
,, ,, tender ,, ,,	...	35
Total	...	78

Water capacity of tender, 3250 galls.

Coal   ,,   ,,   ,,   3½ tons.

Fig. 127.

Fig. 127 is an example of a Midland four-wheels coupled express passenger engine, designed by Mr. Johnson in 1876, which has cylinders 18 in. in diameter, with a stroke of 26 in. The coupled wheels are 7 ft. in diameter, and the boiler pressure 160 lbs. to the square inch, so it will be seen that these are very powerful engines ; in fact, they are now employed in running the heaviest passenger trains between London, Leicester, and Leeds, and taking loads varying from twelve to twenty vehicles at a speed which frequently reaches fifty miles an hour.

An engine of this class obtained a gold medal at Saltaire in 1887.

Principal particulars of the engine—

Diameter of coupled wheels, 7 ft.
Total heating surface, 1261 sq. ft.

	TONS	CWT.	QRS.
Weight on bogie wheels	14	12	1
,, driving ,, ...	15	0	0
,, trailing ,, ...	13	2	2
	42	14	3
Weight of tender in working order ...	36	1	1
Total ...	78	16	0

Fig. 128 is an illustration of an engine with four coupled wheels, a bogie and tank. In this case, the bogie is at the trailing end of the engine, underneath the foot-plate, and the leading and driving-wheels are coupled. The coupled wheels are 5 ft. 3 in. in diameter, and the cylinders 18 in. by 24 in. stroke. The capacity of the tank is 950 gallons, and that of the coal bunker 1½ tons.

These engines work branch line and suburban passenger trains, and also the Midland Company's trains working on the Metropolitan Railway. Those employed on the latter service are fitted with a condenser apparatus for turning the exhaust steam into the tanks.

The Midland Railway goods engines have six wheels coupled, with cylinders 18 in. in diameter, a stroke of 26 in., and wheels 5 ft. 2½ in. in diameter. The engines designed for mineral traffic are of a similar description, but the wheels are only 4 ft. 10 in. in diameter.

A powerful side-tank engine with six coupled wheels, 4 ft. 6 in. in diameter, is used for working heavy mineral branch line traffic and shunting purposes. These have inside cylinders 17 in. in diameter by 24 in. stroke.

Until 1885 Mr. Johnson used a maximum boiler pressure

FIG. 128.

of 140 lbs. to the square inch, but in that year he commenced to build steel boilers, carrying a pressure of 160 lbs. per square inch.

The standard *North-Eastern Railway Engines* will be described in the chapter on Compound Locomotives.

It may here be noticed that the latest design of North-Eastern compound, with tender attached, is the heaviest complete engine and tender running in this country, the total weight amounting to no less than 86 tons 14 cwt. 2 qrs. It has an arrangement of foot-plate and cab designed by Mr. Worsdell, which is perhaps more comfortable than that of any other English locomotive.

The North-Eastern engines run through from Newcastle to Edinburgh, a distance of $124\frac{1}{2}$ miles, without a stop, which is the longest run made in this country.

Manchester, Sheffield, and Lincolnshire Railway.

The Manchester, Sheffield, and Lincolnshire Company has come very much to the front lately in connection with Sir Edward Watkin's new grand trunk railway between the north and south of England.

This line already forms a very important connection with the Great Northern Railway at Retford, and it is over its permanent way that these Companies run their competing trains between London and Manchester; the Manchester, Sheffield, and Lincolnshire engines working the trains between Manchester and Grantham, and the Great Northern engines between Grantham and London. The gradients on the Manchester, Sheffield, and Lincolnshire line are exceptionally heavy, and in the first 22 miles on the up journey from Manchester, vary from 1 in 97 to 1 in 200. There are also some very heavy gradients after leaving Sheffield on the down journey, and engines working express trains have to face these gradients after running 56 miles from Grantham to Sheffield.

One of the most recent Manchester, Sheffield, and Lincolnshire engines, constructed at the Company's works at Gorton, from the design of Mr. Thomas Parker, the late locomotive superintendent, is shown in Fig. 129.

As will be seen, the driving and trailing-wheels are coupled, and the leading end of the engine is carried on a bogie.

Principal particulars—

		FT.	IN.
Diameter of coupled wheels	... ...	6	9
Diameter of cylinder	... ...	0	18
Length of stroke	... ...	0	26

Total heating surface, 1128 sq. ft. Grate area, 18·85.

			TONS	CWT.
Weight on bogie	...	...	13	19
Weight on driving-wheels	...	...	16	10
Weight on trailing-wheels	...	...	15	11
Total	...	...	46	0
Total weight of engine and tender in working order	...	...	81	0

FIG. 129.

There is little doubt that in a short time, the Manchester, Sheffield, and Lincolnshire Company's engines will be running between London and the north on the new line, which is now in course of construction.

South-Eastern Railway.

An express passenger engine constructed at the South-Eastern Locomotive Works, Ashford, Kent, from the designs of Mr. James Stirling, is illustrated in Fig. 130.

This represents the South-Eastern standard modern express engine, of the same type as that exhibited at the Paris Exhibition in 1889. It has now for some years done excellent service on the line, working the heavy express and mail continental trains between London and Dover, which are made up to loads varying from 15 to 25 vehicles. The gross weight of such trains is from 180 to 300 tons, and

FIG. 130.

they are run at high speeds. The gradients on some parts of the South-Eastern system are very heavy, especially on the line to Hastings.

It will be seen that the engine has eight wheels—two pairs coupled, with a bogie at the leading end. The weight on the driving and trailing-wheels is 28 tons 2 cwt.

The particulars of the heating surface are—

			SQ. FT.
Tubes	...	...	917
Fire-box	...	...	103·5
	Total	...	1020·5

The coupled wheels are 7 ft. in diameter, and the cylinders are 19 in. in diameter by 26[1] in. stroke.

The engine is fitted with Mr. Stirling's steam reversing gear, which consists of a vertical steam cylinder, in which is a piston fixed on a rod passing through to a second cylinder 5 in. in diameter, which is filled with water or oil. The lower end of the piston-rod is coupled to the reversing lever.

To operate the gear two handles are used, one to determine the direction of the motion, and the other to control the steam supply to the top cylinder, and to regulate the passage of water from one side of the piston to the other in the water cylinder. The steam forces the piston to any required position for forward or back gear or expansive working, and the water keeps the piston stationary in the position to which it is moved. This gear is much appreciated by the engine-men, who by its means have at their hand a quick-acting gear which can be instantly brought into play with practically no manual exertion at all.

The boiler is of steel, with a copper fire-box and brass tubes. There is no dome; the steam is conveyed to the cylinders through a long pipe perforated with 260 half-inch holes. This pipe is fixed inside the top of the barrel, through which it extends from end to end. The weight is distributed as shown below—

				TONS	CWT.
Bogie-wheels	...	...	...	13	8
Driving-wheels	...	...	...	15	5
Trailing-wheels	...	...	...	12	17
		Total	...	41	10

Both engine and tender are fitted with the automatic vacuum brake.

Another South-Eastern engine, constructed by Messrs. Neilson and Company of Glasgow, from the designs of Mr. James Stirling, is illustrated in Fig. 131. This is a side-

[1] Mr. J. Stirling was one of the first, if not the first, locomotive engineer to introduce the 26 in. stroke with inside cylinder engines.

tank engine, with coupled leading and driving-wheels 5 ft. 6 in. in diameter. The bunker or trailing end of the engine is carried on a bogie. The cylinders are 18 in. by 26 in., and from this and the general design of the engine it will be noted that it is a powerful and useful engine. It is fitted with the automatic vacuum brake.[1] The vacuum cylinder is underneath the side tank and just in front of

FIG. 131.

the tank are the cylinders of Mr. Stirling's steam reversing-gear.

The South-Eastern Railway standard goods engines are of the usual six wheels coupled type, and were built by Messrs. Sharp, Stewart, and Company from Mr. Stirling's designs.

With the exception of compound engines, which will be dealt with in another chapter, we have now noticed one or more of the representative locomotives running on all the most important English railways. It will not be possible

[1] Several of the South-Eastern Railway engines are also fitted with the Westinghouse brake, for the benefit of foreign rolling stock.

to mention the engines owned by the smaller lines, but it will be understood that, taking them as a whole, they are a counterpart of those types already illustrated.

There is, however—closely connected with the London and North-Western system—a smaller railway, one of whose engines is illustrated in Fig. 132. This is a

North London Railway

tank engine, designed by Mr. J. C. Park, the late locomotive superintendent of the line. Although a small line, the North London Railway Company manufactures its own engines, which have to work a very important suburban traffic over a crowded line, upon which there are some very heavy gradients. The engine illustrated has coupled driving and trailing-wheels 5 ft. 6 inches in diameter, the leading end being carried on a bogie. The boiler is of steel, with copper fire-box and steel tubes. The cylinders are 17 inches by 24 inches, and the heating surface is—

Tubes (186 in number)	...	...	860	sq. ft.
Fire-box	...	...	91	,,
	Total	...	951	,,
	Grate area	...	16·62	,,

The weight is thus distributed—

Bogie ...	...	...	14	tons
Driving-wheels	...	...	16	,,
Trailing-wheels	...	...	16	,,
	Total	...	46	,,

These engines are doing good service on the line, and are in every way suited for the purpose for which they were constructed. They start away from stations very quickly when working passenger trains, and are strong enough to be utilized for working goods trains when required. They are fitted with Messrs. Gresham and Craven's gear for working the automatic vacuum brake.

Scotch Locomotives.

The two principal Scotch railways are the Caledonian, which runs in connection with the London and North-Western Railway and forms a part of the West Coast route to the North, and the North British Railway, which forms a portion of the East Coast route.

Through the kindness of Mr. Lambie, the locomotive

FIG. 133.

superintendent of the Caledonian Railway, and Mr. Holmes of the North British Railway, the author is enabled to give illustrations of the standard express passenger engines running on each of these important lines.

Fig. 133 is an illustration of Mr. Holmes's express bogie passenger engine, of which the following are the principal dimensions—

				FT.	IN.
Diameter of bogie-wheels	...	...	... ·	3	6
,, coupled wheels	...	..	...	6	6
,, cylinders	...	...	...	1	6
Stroke of cylinders	...	...	...	2	2
Centre of bogie to centre of driving-wheel			...	9	10
Centre to centre of bogie-wheels	...	...	6	6
,, ,, coupled wheels	...	...	9	0
Wheel base of engine	...	...	...	22	1
Boiler, length of barrel	...	...	...	10	3½
,, diameter ,,	...	...	...	4	5½
Length of fire-box (outside)	...	...	...	6	3

Heating surface : fire-box, 118 sq. ft. ; tubes, 1148 sq. ft.—total sq. ft., 1266. Fire-grate area, 20 sq. ft.

Number of tubes, 238 ; diameter, 1¾ in.

Working-pressure, 140 lbs. per square inch.

Weight of engine in working order—

				TONS	CWT.
Bogie	...	...	...	15	9
Driving-wheels	...	...	...	15	12
Trailing ,,	...	...	...	15	9
		Total	...	46	10

Tender—Diameter of wheels, 4 ft. ; wheel base, 12 ft.

Capacity of tank, 2500 galls.

Weight in working order, 32 tons.

The trains on the North British Railway are heavy and fast, and there are some stiff gradients on the line. Powerful engines are therefore required for working the main line service, and the general design and dimensions of the engine illustrated show that it is in every way suitable for the work upon which it is engaged.

The Caledonian Railway has several long and heavy gradients on its main line between Carlisle and Aberdeen, much the same kind of road as the London and North-Western Railway between Preston and Carlisle.

The London and North-Western compound engines bring some very heavy trains into Carlisle, to be there handed over to the Caledonian Railway Company, and they require a powerful class of engine to work them forward over the Scotch line.

Fig. 134 is an illustration of the most recent type of locomotive, designed by Mr. Drummond, the late locomotive superintendent of the line, and first built by Messrs. Dubs and Company of Glasgow.

The engine has two pairs of coupled wheels, 6 ft. 6 in. in

FIG. 134.

diameter, and a bogie in front, whose wheels are 3 ft. 6 in. in diameter.

The cylinders are placed between the frames, and are 18 in. in diameter, with a stroke of 26 in., the valves being on the top. The slide bars are of cast-iron of the box pattern, which protects the bearing-surfaces from dust. The first engine of this class was fitted by Mr. Drummond with the Bryce Douglas valve motion, illustrated in Fig. 47.[1] They

[1] This gear was afterwards removed, and the ordinary link motion substituted.

are also fitted with the Westinghouse brake, the air-pump being placed on the right side and the reservoir underneath the foot-plate. The engine tyres are of crucible and. the tender tyres of Bessemer steel, whereas the engine frames are of Yorkshire iron and the tender frames of steel.

The other chief particulars of the engine are—

			FT.	IN.
Length of boiler over all	...	...	16	$5\frac{7}{8}$
,, ,, barrel	...	...	10	$3\frac{1}{2}$
Diameter of barrel ...	...	...	4	4
Length of fire-box casing	...	...	6	$2\frac{3}{8}$
Width at top	...	...	4	$7\frac{1}{2}$
,, bottom ...	...	...	4	$0\frac{1}{2}$
Thickness of plates—				
Fire-box casing ...	...	...		$\frac{5}{8}$
Boiler barrel ...	...	...		$\frac{9}{16}$
Smoke-box, tube-plate	...	...		$\frac{3}{4}$
Fire-box plates ...	...	...		$\frac{9}{16}$
Tube-plate ...	...	...		$\frac{7}{8}$

Heating surface: tubes (226 in number), 1088·7 sq. ft.; fire-box, 122·0 sq. ft.—total sq. ft., 1210·7.

Grate area, 19·5 sq. ft.

Boiler pressure, 150 lbs. per square inch.

Weight in working order—

				TONS	CWT.
Bogie	...	...	...	14	12
Driving-wheels	...	...	...	15	5
Trailing ,,	...	...	...	15	3
		Total	...	45	0
Tender	...	...	...	30	0
	Total, engine and tender		...	75	0

This is altogether a good example of a powerful, modern express passenger engine, and its workmanship and design are both of the highest order.

Irish Locomotives.

This work, published under the title of *British Locomotives*, would be incomplete without some reference to those running on the railway lines of the sister isle.

The London and North-Western Railway, in whose service the author is engaged, and whose locomotive practice plays the most prominent part in all the descriptive matter in this book, is not only the high-road to Ireland as far as Holyhead, but its large fleet of steamships are exclusively employed in conveying traffic to and from Irish ports, and run in connection with Irish trains; nay, more than this, a part of the London and North-Western permanent way is actually laid on Irish soil, and is worked over by Crewe locomotives. It is therefore difficult for a London and North-Western man to consider Ireland as anything but a part of his own country, and his Irish fellow railway-servants as any but his own countrymen.

One of the most important lines in Ireland is the Great Southern and Western Railway, the locomotive department of which is engineered and superintended by Mr. Henry A. Ivatt, who—like his predecessor, Mr. Aspinall, now locomotive superintendent of the Lancashire and Yorkshire Railway—received his professional training on the London and North-Western Railway. Both of these gentlemen have done much to raise the locomotive department of the lines with which they are associated to a very high standard of efficiency.

Fig. 135 is an illustration of the standard express passenger engine running on the Great Southern and Western Railway, and the following are its principal dimensions—

> Cylinders, 18 in. diameter, 24 in. stroke.
> Wheels: bogie, 3 ft. diameter; driving and trailing, 6 ft. 6 in. coupled.
> Wheel-base: bogie, 5 ft. 3 in.; bogie to driving-wheel, 9 ft. 6⅝ in.; driving to trailing-wheel, 8 ft. 3 in.
> Boiler, 4 ft. 3 in. diameter, by 9 ft. 9 in. long, with 204 brass tubes, 1¾ in. outside diameter.
> Fire-box, 4 ft. 10 in. long, 3 ft. 11 in. wide, 5 ft. 9 in. high.

Heating surface : fire-box, 112 sq. ft. ; tubes, 938 sq. ft. ;
    grate area, 18¾ sq. ft.
Weight, 39 tons 4 cwt. ; steam pressure, 150 lbs.
Tender : Capacity of tank, 2,700 gallons ; carrying 3 tons of coal.

The boiler and frame-plates are of steel, and the cylinders are cast in one piece, the back covers being a portion
of the main casting. The engine is fitted with the automatic
vacuum brake.

The maximum load taken is eighteen six-wheeled coaches,

Fig. 135.

and the fastest run is with the American mail from Dublin
to Queenstown, 177 miles, in four hours. This train has
two stops of five minutes, the longest run without a stop
being 70 miles. The same engine works through from
Dublin to Queenstown.

With an average load of nine vehicles, the consumption
of coal is 28 lbs. per mile, and of oil 23 pints per 1000

miles.　The average miles run between shop repairs is 63,500.

The standard goods engines have six coupled cast-iron wheels of practically the same description as those illustrated in Fig. 88. Indeed, these engines, although they have larger wheels, are in outside appearance altogether very like the London and North-Western coal engine, illustrated in Fig. 106. The following are various details of their construction and working—

> Cylinders, 18 in. diameter, 24 in. stroke.
> Wheels, 5 ft. diameter, 6 coupled.
> Wheel base : leading to driving-wheel, 7 ft. 3 in. ; driving to trailing-wheels, 8 ft. 3 in.
> Boiler, 4 ft. diameter, 9 ft. 10 in. long ; 185 brass tubes, $1\frac{3}{4}$ in. outside diameter.
> Fire-box, 4 ft. 6 in. long, 3 ft. 11 in. wide, 5 ft. 4 in. high.
> Heating surface : fire-box, 101 sq. ft. ; tubes, 856 sq. ft. ; grate area, $17\frac{1}{2}$ sq. ft.
> Weight, 31 tons ; steam pressure, 150 lbs.
> Fitted with automatic vacuum brake.

Limit of load for main line, 45 loaded waggons or 55 empty.

Gradients (except terminal inclines), three miles of 1 in 128; four miles of 1 in 151; five miles of 1 in 140, etc.

Consumption of best South Wales coal, with an average load of 27·2 waggons, equal to 30 lbs. per mile.

Oil used, including cylinder oil, 21 pints per 1000 miles.

The Great Southern and Western side-tank engines used for working branch passenger trains have the following dimensions—

> Wheels : driving coupled, 5 ft. 6 in. diameter ; trailing and leading, 3 ft. 9 in. diameter (radial axle-boxes).
> Wheel base, 19 ft. 11 in.
> Cylinders, 16 in. diameter, 20 in. stroke.

Water-tank, capacity 1250 gallons.
Coal bunker, 50 cwt.
Boiler, 3 ft. 10 in. diameter, 9 ft. 4 in. long ; 174 tubes.
Heating surface : fire-box, 88·5 sq. ft. ; tubes, 770 sq. ft.
Fire-grate area, 16 sq. ft.
Weight of engine, 42 tons 16 cwt.
Steam pressure, 150 lbs.
Fitted with automatic vacuum brake.

In connection with the Great Southern and Western Railway main line, there are light railways worked by engines with the following dimensions—

Wheels, 3 ft. 8 in. diameter, 6 coupled ; wheel base, 10 ft. 11 in.
Cylinders, 10 in. diameter by 18 in. stroke.
Capacity of tank, 550 gallons ; carrying 12 cwt. of coal.
Boiler, 2 ft. 9 in. diameter, by 7 ft. 9 in. long ; 102 tubes.
Heating surface : tubes, 310 sq. ft. ; fire-box, 52 sq. ft ; grate area, 10 sq. ft.
Weight, 23 tons 7 cwt.

These engines are also fitted with the automatic vacuum brake, which acts upon all the wheels. The weight on any one pair of wheels is limited to eight tons, and they work over gradients of 1 in 60.

It may be of interest to some of our readers to close this chapter with a list of all the railway companies in the United Kingdom, showing the length of each line, the name of the locomotive superintendent, and the number of engines owned by each company at the beginning of the year 1893.

ENGLISH RAILWAYS.

RAILWAY.	MILES IN LGTH.	LOCOMOTIVE SUPERINTENDENT.	NO. OF ENGINES OWNED.	REMARKS.
Great Eastern	1145¾	J. Holden	928	
Great Northern	646	P. Stirling	948	
Great Western	2481	W. Dean	2049	
Lancashire & Yorkshire	527	J. A. F. Aspinall	1171	
London & North-Western	1887½	F. W. Webb	2722	
London & South-Western	857½	W. Adams	598	
London, Brighton & S.C.	476¾	R. J. Billinton	426	
London, Chatham & Dover	185¼	W. Kirtley	210	
Manchester, Sheffield & L.	247	T. Parker	720	
Midland	1300¼	S. W. Johnson	2296	
North-Eastern	1554¼	Wilson Wordsdell	1799	
South-Eastern	369	J. Stirling	378	
Barry	29	J. H. Hosgood	67	
Bishops Castle	9¾		2	
Cambrian	237	W. Aston	59	
Brecon & Merthyr Tydfil Junction	61½	G. C. Owen	30	
Cheshire Lines Committee	137	T. Parker	—	Worked by M. S. & L.
City & South London ...	3¼		16	Electric
Cleator & Workington Junction	28½	J. Taylor	5	
Colne Valley & Halstead	19		4	
Cockermouth, Keswick & Penrith	31½		—	Worked by L.& N.-W. or N.-E. Co.'s engines
Corris	11	J. R. Dix	3	
Eastern & Midlands ...	114	W. Marriott	39	
East & West, & Stratford- on-Avon, Towcester & Midland Junction	52	J. F. Burke	10	
Festiniog	14½	W. Williams	9	
Freshwater, Yarmouth, & Newport	12		—	Worked by Isle of Wight Central
Furness	139	R. Mason	123	
Garstang & Knot End ...	7	J. Starzaker	2	
Golden Valley Railway	19		—	
Gwendraeth Valleys ...	3½		—	
Hull, Barnsley & West Riding Railway & Dock Company	65	M. Stirling	69	
Isle of Man	27	J. Sproat	7	
Isle of Wight	12	H. Brent	8	
Isle of Wight (Central) ...	21¾		8	
Total ...	12,731½		14,706	

ENGLISH RAILWAYS (*continued*).

RAILWAY.	MILES IN LGTH	LOCOMOTIVE SUPERINTENDENT.	NO. OF ENGINES OWNED.	REMARKS.
	12,731½		14,706	
Liskeard & Caradon ...	10		3	
Liverpool, Southport & Preston Junction ...	7½		—	Worked by L. & Y. Co.
London & India Docks	2		25	
London, Tilbury, & South End	75	T. Whitelegg	36	
Manchester & Milford ...	41	J. W. Szlumper	5	
Manchester South Junction & Altrincham	9	T. Parker	—	Worked by M. S. & L.
Manx Northern ...	16½		4	
Maryport & Carlisle ...	41¼	W. Robinson	30	
Mawddwy	6¾		2	
Mersey	4		18	
Metropolitan	51⅜	J. J. Hanbury	70	
Metropolitan District ...	13	G. Estall	54	
Midland & South-Western Junction	56		7	
Neath & Brecon ...	40		6	
North London	12	J. Pryce	103	
North Staffordshire ...	201	L. Longbottom	139	
Northampton & Banbury Junction	15		—	
North Wales Narrow Gauge	12¼		—	
Oldham, Ashton-under-Lyne & Guide Bridge	6		3	Worked by L. & N.-W. Railway.
Pembroke & Tenby ...	27½	L. R. Wood	7	Jointly by L.
Ravenglass & Eskdale ...	7¼		2	& N.-W. & M. S. & L. lines
Rhondda and Swansea Bay	16		9	
Rhymney	45¾	C. Lundie	72	
Severn & Wye, & Severn Bridge	37		12	
Southwold	9		3	
Swansea & Mumbles ...	6		5	
Taff Vale	113	T. H. Riches	208	
Van	6		2	
West Lancashire ...	17		15	
Wigan Junction	11		—	Worked by M. S. & L. Raily.
Wirral	10½	E. G. Barker	8	
Wrexham, Mold & Connah Quay	26	F. Willans	16	
Total ...	13,683½		15,570	

SCOTCH RAILWAYS.

RAILWAY.	MILES IN LGTH.	LOCOMOTIVE SUPERINTENDENT.	NO. OF ENGINES OWNED.	REMARKS.
Caledonian	794½	J. Lambie	702	Includ. canals
Glasgow & South-West.	384	J. Manson	—	
North British	1247½	M. Holmes	325	Includ. leased
			692	lines and canals
City of Glasgow Union ...	6¼		—	Worked by N. B. & G. & S.-W. engines
Great North of Scotland	312¼	J. Johnson	77	
Highland	434¼	D. Jones	103	
Total ...	3178¾		1899	

IRISH RAILWAYS.

RAILWAY.	MILES IN LGTH.	LOCOMOTIVE SUPERINTENDENT.	NO. OF ENGINES OWNED.	REMARKS.
Ballycastle	16¼	G. Bradshaw	3	
Belfast & County Down	76	R. G. Miller	26	
Belfast and Northern Counties	202	B. Malcolm	65	
Cork, Bandon & South Coast	85¾	J. W. Johnstone	16	
Cork & Macroom Direct	24½	M. J. Reen	4	
Cork, Blackrock & Passage	6	C. E. Elwood	3	
Donegal	32		9	
Dublin, Wicklow & Wexford	144	W. Wakefield	51	
Great Northern (Ireland)	487	J. C. Park	145	
Great Southern & Western	530	H. A. Ivatt	178	
Londonderry & Lough Swilly	14½	T. Turner	6	
Midland Great Western	461	M. Atcock	114	
Sligo, Leitrim & Northern Counties	49	S. Murphy	1	
Waterford & Central Ireland	67	D. McDowell	10	
Waterford, Dungarvan & Lismore	43		7	
Waterford & Limerick ...	278¾	J. G. Robinson	46	
Waterford & Tramore ...	7¼	H. Waugh	4	
West Clare	27	G. Hopkins	7	
Total ...	2551		695	

GRAND TOTALS.

		MILES.	ENGINES.
English Railways		$13,683\frac{1}{2}$	15,570
Irish ,, ...		2,551	695
Scotch ,, ...		$3,178\frac{3}{4}$	1,899
	Total ...	$19,413\frac{1}{4}$	18,164

CHAPTER XVI.

COMPOUND LOCOMOTIVES.

THE compounding of locomotives has perhaps raised more discussion during recent years than any other question connected with this branch of engineering.

The subject is a very wide one, and the arguments for and against the system have been very forcibly contended, with perhaps this general result, that the disputants on each side retain their previous opinions.

The difference between a "Simple" and a "Compound" engine may be thus briefly stated : With the former, high-pressure cylinders only are employed, and the steam passes direct from the cylinder into the blast-pipe and thence into the atmosphere. With the latter, high and low-pressure cylinders are used, and the steam is exhausted from the high-pressure cylinder into another cylinder of larger diameter, where it again acts upon a piston and is further expanded before it is discharged through the blast-pipe.

The man whose name is most associated with compound locomotives in this country, and indeed among railway men in all parts of the world, is Mr. Webb, and the principle of which he is so staunch an advocate was also upheld, although in a different form, by Mr. T. W. Worsdell, late locomotive superintendent of the North-Eastern Railway.

It will therefore be recognized that "Compounds" have two very powerful champions, both eminently practical men, and one of them an active and distinguished locomotive engineer of present times.

Although but recently brought so prominently forward, the idea is not altogether a new one; and so far back as the year **1850**, John Nicholson, an engine-driver on the Eastern Counties Railway (now the Great Eastern), introduced a plan of continuous expansion to the notice of Mr. James Samuel, the then locomotive superintendent of the line.

In the year **1852**, Mr. Samuel applied the compound principle on Nicholson's system to a goods and a passenger locomotive, with results which he considered highly satisfactory.

Mr. Samuel's compound engines had two cylinders with piston areas approximately as one to two. The steam from the small cylinder was not actually exhausted into the large one, but was by means of a valve allowed to pass from the small to the large cylinder at a certain point of the stroke, and expansion went on in both cylinders at the same time. It should be understood that the steam was discharged from the *steam-side* of small cylinder piston into the large cylinder, not from the exhaust side, as with modern compounds.

Mr. Samuel's experiments in this direction do not seem to have been followed up, and until the year **1876** the question of the application of the compound principle to locomotive engines appears to have remained in abeyance.

In the latter year, M. Mallet designed three compound engines, which were built by MM. Schneider & Co., of Creusot, for the Bayonne and Biarritz Railway. These engines, which had two outside cylinders, respectively $9\frac{1}{2}$ and $15\frac{3}{4}$ in. in diameter, were brought into use in July **1876** and did good work.

In **1878** Mr. Webb converted one of the old single-wheel engines, built by Trevithick, into a compound on M. Mallet's system, and this engine worked some five years on the Ashby and Nuneaton branch of the London and North-Western Railway.

The results obtained were so encouraging that Mr. Webb was led to go more fully into the question of compounding modern locomotive engines ; and in the year **1881-2**, he built at Crewe an engine on this principle of an entirely new and original type.

Mr. Webb's idea in applying the compound principle

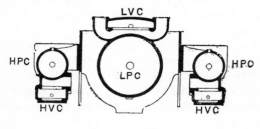

Fig. 136.

was not only to economize fuel, but also to gain increased power and various other advantages, to which reference will presently be made.

This engine (which was named the "Experiment") had two outside high-pressure cylinders, $11\frac{1}{2}$ in. in diameter, and one inside low-pressure cylinder 26 in. in diameter. The driving-wheels were 6 ft. 6 in. in diameter, and Joy's valve gear was used for the distribution of steam in the cylinders.

Fig. 136 is a cross section showing the positions of the three cylinders. The high and low-pressure engines work independently of each other, the middle and trailing-wheels not being coupled together. By this means coupling-rods are dispensed with, and the engine has the same freedom of running as a single-wheel engine, combined with the same adhesion to the rails as a coupled engine.

This system is now universally adopted in the Webb compounds, the high-pressure cylinders (HPC) driving the rear, or trailing-wheels, while the low-pressure cylinder (LPC) actuates the ordinary driving-wheels. The high-pressure valve-chests (HVC) are fixed below the cylinders, and the low-pressure valve-chest (LVC) in the smoke-box above the low-pressure cylinder.

The chief advantages claimed for the three cylinder compound engines are here enumerated—

1. Greater power.

2. Economy in consumption of fuel.

3. The whole of the available power of the steam is used.

4. A more even distribution of the strains upon the working parts, and larger bearing surfaces for the axles.

5. The same freedom of running as with a single engine, with the same adhesion to the rails as a coupled engine.

Clauses 3, 4, and 5 relate more to technical points in connection with the working of locomotives, but the first two considerations are eminently practical, and are most important from a commercial point of view. With regard to No. 1, the old adage that "the proof of the pudding is in the eating," may be applied as a convincing argument, for the author is in a position to state that the most recent types of compound express passenger engines on the London and North-Western Railway are at the present time working some of the heaviest and fastest express passenger trains in the world, and running them without assistance and without loss of time.

One of these engines (No. 1309, " Adriatic ") has now for several years been running the most important main line trains between London and Crewe, and the driver has never yet taken a "hooker-on" or "pilot" engine, except between Euston and Willesden, and yet not a minute of lost time has ever been recorded against this engine.

The 7 ft. compound engine "Coptic," No. 1307, which at the time of writing is in the shops for repairs, has run no less than 88,179 miles since it was last overhauled.

With regard to the question of economy, it is a very difficult matter to get at a fair comparative statement of the performances of engines on different railway lines, because the construction of the engines and the conditions under which they work differ so widely and in so many respects.

During the first few years after the introduction of compound engines on the London and North-Western Railway, some very accurate observations were made to compare their working with ordinary simple engines doing the same work on the line. In a discussion which took place before the Institution of Civil Engineers in January 1889, Mr. Webb made the following statement relative to the comparative working of compound and non-compound engines, based on observations extending over a considerable period of time—

"It might be taken that the smaller compound engines had burnt 26 lbs. per mile, and the large engines, which had run with heavy trains from London to Carlisle, 29 and 30 lbs. per mile for the actual work done. These engines, which had been in constant use, varied very little in their consumption of coal, including all the charges he had mentioned. He had the consumption of all the seventy-four engines reduced to train miles. The consumption of the smaller ones was 30·2 lbs. of coal per mile, including the 1·2 lb. for lighting up; and for the large engines between London and Carlisle, 36·6 lbs. per mile. He did not know what the engineers of other lines, doing a similar class of work at the same speed, could accomplish ; but he should be glad, with the consent of the directors of the respective companies, if they would bring their best engines for a trial, and he would suggest that Mr. William Anderson, of Erith, should be the referee. Each engine might come to Lowgill Junction or Tebay, and he would clear the way himself with twenty carriages or more up to Shap, to see what load could be drawn. If any engines could do better than his own, he would undertake to copy the engine that proved to be the best. The relative saving was a very difficult question, as the work was now much heavier, and the assistance almost nil. But in one case, a compound and a non-compound engine had been doing exactly the same amount of work for the whole of the time ; the compound engine had run with 23·2 lbs. of coal per mile, and the non-compound with 31 lbs. per mile, taken over a period of four years, the compound engine in question having been converted from one of the non-compounds, and the working pressure increased from 130 lbs. to 150 lbs. on the square inch. The working expenses and the shop expenses had been considerably reduced, and seeing that the capital account was closed, no one could say he took advantage of capital to get at these results."

A standard type of London and North-Western Railway three cylinder compound engine is illustrated in Fig. 137. These engines, which have 6 ft. driving-wheels, were first built and put to work on the line in **1884** and have done good service ever since. The following is a very graphic description of an engine of this class given by Mr. E. Worthington in a paper read by him before the Institution of Civil Engineers on the occasion to which reference has just been made—

"This engine weighs 42 tons 10 cwt. It comprises two outside high-pressure cylinders, 14 in. in diameter and

24 in. stroke, and one inside low-pressure cylinder, 30 in. in diameter and 24 in. stroke. There are thus three distinct engines, each actuated by Joy's valve gear. The two high-pressure engines have their slide-valves placed underneath the cylinders. The latter are attached to the outside frame-plates immediately below the side foot-plates, and midway between the smoke-box and the middle wheels, and act through their piston-rods and connecting-rods upon the trailing-wheels. The single low-pressure cylinder has its

FIG. 137.

slide-valve on the top, and is placed midway between the frames immediately below the smoke-box. Its connecting-rod takes hold of a single-throw crank on the axle of the middle pair of wheels. The boiler is worked at 175 lbs. per square inch, and the steam is conducted from an equilibrium regulator in the dome to a brass T pipe fixed to the smoke-box tube-plate, and thence by two copper steam-pipes, 3¾ in. in diameter, running first parallel with

the tube-plate, then through the back-plate which carries
the low-pressure cylinder, and between the inside and outside engine frames to the steam-chests of the high-pressure
cylinders.   The exhaust steam from each of these cylinders
is returned in a copper pipe, 5 in. in diameter, running
horizontally beneath the high-pressure pipe into the smoke-
box.   Each pipe then passes through the hot gases round
the smoke-box to the opposite side, and enters the steam-
chest of the low-pressure cylinder.   Thus the high-pressure
exhaust steam, at a pressure restricted by means of a safety-
valve to 80 lbs. per square inch, becomes superheated and
dried in these pipes by the waste gases of the smoke-box,
while the large capacity of the pipes obviates the necessity
for a separate steam-receiver.   The final exhaust escapes
through the back of the low-pressure slide-valve and steam-
chest cover into the blast-pipe, and thence to the chimney
in the usual way, the only difference being that the number
of exhaust beats for urging the fire is reduced to half, compared with an ordinary engine.   One of the pipes forming
the receiver in the smoke-box is fitted with a valve similar
in construction to the regulator, and opening direct into
the blast-pipe, which allows the driver to turn the exhaust
steam directly from the high-pressure cylinders into the
chimney, a course which may be useful in starting, should
the low-pressure crank stand on a dead centre.

"An ordinary screw-valve placed on the side of the smoke-
box enables the driver to admit a small amount of boiler
high-pressure steam into the receiver to start the low-
pressure crank when it is not on a dead point.

" These two starting valves are ingeniously arranged to
work with two distinct motions of one handle, the arrangement being such that the first may be locked open to the
chimney while the second remains shut.   Balanced side-
valves are used in all three engines.   The low-pressure

cylinder cocks are fitted with safety-valves to prevent the pressure rising above 80 lbs. per square inch ; and an automatic air-valve is placed in the receiver to open when the engine is running without steam in order to destroy the vacuum which would otherwise form in the receiver and act as a retarding force in the large cylinder.

"The reversing-gear consists of a hand-wheel and screw connected to the middle of a short lever, the ends of which are joined by long, stiff rods to the high-pressure and low-pressure reversing-shaft. Thus the two high-pressure and the one low-pressure engines can be reversed together, or by a simple means of locking either high-pressure or low-pressure, the other gear can be adjusted by the hand reversing wheel to the required amount of 'notching up' or steam cut-off required."

The foregoing description applies to present practice, except that Mr. Webb has discarded Joy's valve gear for the inside low-pressure motion, and now uses the shifting eccentric, illustrated in Fig. 48, and the pipes conveying the steam from the high to the low-pressure cylinders are fixed in the position shown in Plate II.

The following records of some of the earlier performances of these engines may be interesting—

On May 19, **1885**, an engine of this class worked the 10. a.m. from Euston to Carlisle ; the train weighed 207 tons, and the average speed, including stoppages, was 44·7 miles per hour, the coal consumed being 29·2 lbs. per mile. The section of this run from Tebay to Shap is on a rising gradient of 1 in 75, which was ascended at the rate of 33 miles per hour, the horse-power developed being 810.

On March 27 of the same year, a similar engine took a train from Liverpool to Crewe, which weighed 292 tons 15 cwt., at the rate of 43·4 miles an hour.

The "Marchioness of Stafford," an engine of this type,

was exhibited at the Inventions Exhibition in 1885, and was awarded a gold medal. The following are some of the principal dimensions of this engine—

Heating surface of fire-box	...	...	159·1 sq. ft.
Heating surface of tubes	...	...	1242·4 ,,
	Total	...	1401·5 ,,

Area of fire-grate, 20·5 sq. ft.
Diameter of driving-wheels, 6 ft. 3 in.
Diameter of leading-wheels, 3 ft. 9 in.
Cylinders (high-pressure), 14 in. by 24 in. stroke.
Do. (low-pressure), 30 in. by 24 in. stroke.
Steam pressure, 175 lbs. per sq. in.

Weight of engine in working order—

			TONS	CWT.
On leading-wheels	...	...	12	10
On low-pressure driving-wheels		...	15	0
On high-pressure driving-wheels		...	15	0
	Total	...	42	10
Weight of tender (empty)	...	...	12	1

In 1890, Mr. Webb—still adhering to the same general design—commenced to build larger engines, and Plate II. is a longitudinal section giving details of the various parts of one of these later compound locomotives, which have 7 ft. driving-wheels.

By comparing this plate with the index given on p. 306, the reader should be able to gain a fair idea of the design and structure of a London and North-Western Railway modern three-cylinder engine.

INDEX TO PLATE II.

7 FT. COMPOUND ENGINE.

Boiler and Fittings.

SV	Safety valves.
CB	Injector clack-box.
ISV	,, ,, steam valve.
W	Whistle.
FD	Fire-door.
RH	Regulator valve handle.
RR	,, ,, rod.
R	,, ,, ,,
D	Steam dome.
S	Longitudinal stay.
TT	Tubes.
M	Man-hole.
SP	Steam-pipe which passes from the dome through smoke-box and between the frames to the high-pressure cylinders.
SB	Smoke-box.
SD	,, ,, door.
SH	,, ,, ,, handle.
C	Chimney.
CE	Chimney extension piece.
D	Damper rod.

Cylinders and Connections.

LC	Low-pressure cylinder in section.
LVC	,, ,, valve chest and valve.
HPC	High-pressure cylinder in elevation.
SP	High-pressure steam-pipe.
HPE	,, ,, exhaust-pipe to low-pressure cylinder.
RV	Release valve on high-pressure exhaust-pipe, operated from foot-plate, to turn high-pressure exhaust into blast-pipe when starting.
EV	Relief-valve for low-pressure steam-chest, loaded to 80 lbs. per square inch.
BP	Blast-pipe.
P	Low-pressure piston.
SG	,, ,, ,, stuffing-box and gland.
FSG	Low-pressure guide-box and gland for front piston-rod, the object of which is to carry the weight of the piston and prevent friction on low-pressure cylinder.
GPR	Low-pressure piston guide-rod.
PR	,, ,, piston-rod.
VSG	,, ,, valve spindle stuffing-box gland.
DG	Low-pressure dummy gland.
OC	,, ,, cylinder oil-cup.
DCL	,, ,, drain-cocks from cylinder and valve chest.

DCG	Low and high-pressure valve and cylinder drain-cock gearing.
DCR	Cylinder drain-cock gear-rod, operated from foot-plate.

Frames.

MF	Main or outside frames.
IF	Inside frame.

Wheels.

LW	Leading.
DW	Low-pressure driving.
TW	High ,, ,,

Springs.

LS	Leading laminated springs.
SS	High and low-pressure driving-wheels, spiral springs.

Axle-boxes.

RA	Radial axle-box.
A	High-pressure axle-box.

Connecting-rod.

CR	Low-pressure connecting-rod.
BE	,, ,, ,, ,, big end.

Valve motions and reversing gear.

HPVM	High-pressure valve motion (Joy's gear).
HPRS	,, ,, ,, ,, reversing shaft.
HPR	High-pressure valve motion reversing rod.
LE	Loose eccentric (low-pressure).
ER	,, ,, rod, ,,
RS	Rocking shaft.
VL	Low-pressure valve link.

Brake gear, etc.

E	Large ejector.
AP	Air-pump.
PO	,, ,, lubricator.
SBC	Steam brake cylinder.
BG	Brake gear, described in Fig. 93.
TBP	Tender brake pull-rod.
VP	Vacuum pipes.
HC	Hose coupling.

Injector.

IN	Injector.
ISV	,, steam valve.
ISP	,, ,, pipe.
FP	,, feed-pipe.

Sundries.

HSA	Steam sanding arrangement.
B	Buffers.
DB	Draw-bar.
FP	Foot-plate.

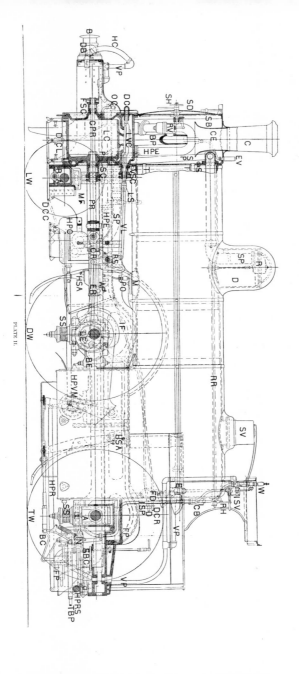

PLATE II.

PRINCIPAL DIMENSIONS OF 7 FT. COMPOUND ENGINE.

PLATE II.

		FT.	IN.
Distance from rail to top of chimney		13	$1\frac{1}{2}$
,, ,, ,, centre of boiler		7	$10\frac{1}{2}$
,, ,, ,, ,, buffers [1]		3	$4\frac{3}{4}$

BOILER.

		FT.	IN.
Length of boiler barrel ,...		11	0
Diameter of boiler barrel (inside)		4	1
Thickness of boiler plates			$\frac{1}{2}$
Diameter of tubes (external)			$1\frac{7}{8}$
Number of tubes	225		
Heating surface of tubes	1242·42 sq. ft.		
,, ,, ,, fire-box	159·10 ,,		
	1401·52 ,,		
Grate area	20·5 ,,		

CYLINDERS.

		FT.	IN.
High-pressure cylinders, centre to centre		6	6
,, ,, ,, diameter		1	2
,, ,, ,, stroke		2	0
,, ,, ,, travel of valve			$3\frac{3}{4}$
,, ,, ,, lap ,, ...			$\frac{7}{8}$
,, ,, ,, lead ,, ...			$\frac{1}{8}$
Low-pressure cylinder, diameter		2	6
,, ,, ,, stroke		2	0
,, ,, ,, travel of valve			$5\frac{1}{2}$
,, ,, ,, lap ,, ...			1
,, ,, ,, lead ,, ...			$\frac{1}{2}$

FRAMES.

		FT.	IN.
Distance between outside or main frame plates		4	0
Thickness of outside or main frame plates			$\frac{7}{8}$
,, ,, inside frame plates			$\frac{3}{4}$

[1] This is the standard of all railway buffers from rail level.

WHEELS.

| | DIAMETER. | | | | | | WEIGHT. | | |
	FT.	IN.					T.	C.	Q.
Leading-wheels ...	4	1½	with 3-inch tyres carrying				14	10	0
Low-pressure wheels	7	1	,,	,,	,,	,,	15	10	0
High ,, ,,	7	1	,,	,,	,,	,,	15	10	0
Total weight in working order							45	10	0

GENERAL.

	DIAMETER.	LENGTH.		FT.	IN.
Radial journals	6¾ in.	... 12 in.			
Low and high-pressure journals	7 ,,	... 13½ ,,			
Wheel base, high-pressure to low-pressure journals ...				9	8
,, low ,, leading or radial journals ...				8	5
Total wheel base ...				18	1
Length of low-pressure connecting-rod, centre to centre ...				6	3
,, ,, high ,, ,, ,, ,, ,, ...				8	3
Diameter of air-pump					5
Stroke of air-pump				2	0

SPRINGS.

				FT.	IN.
Leading springs, length				2	8
,, ,, thickness of plates					⅜
,, ,, width of plates					4½
Driving and trailing coiled springs—					
Length of outer spring					9⅞
Diameter of outer spring					4
Number of coils, 9, of square steel ...					$\frac{7}{16}$
Length of inner spring					9⅞
Diameter of inner spring					2½
Number of coils, 13½, of square steel ...					$\frac{7}{16}$

Outer spring coiled right, and inner left hand.

It may be here mentioned that Mr. Webb's compounds, although nominally single-framed engines, have practically a double framing for the low-pressure wheels; as two additional inside frame-plates extend from the back of the low-pressure cylinder to the cross-stay at the front of the fire-box, and the low-pressure driving-axle boxes are fitted between the inside frame and the main frame of the engine.

This particular form of construction, combined with the single crank on the low-pressure axle, enables a very wide bearing surface to be used for the low-pressure axle, the journals being 1 ft. 1½ in. long. The bearings of the rear driving axle are the same length, which is effected by extending the axle-box guides across between the main frames. They thus form a double cross-stay, connecting and strengthening the frames behind the fire-box. The leading end

Fig. 138.

of the engine is supported on ordinary plate-springs above the radial axle-boxes, whereas the middle and trailing-wheels have each four spiral springs underneath the axle-boxes.

The 7 ft. compound engine "Jeanie Deans," illustrated in Fig. 138, is at the present time working daily the down Scotch express leaving Euston at 2 p.m. and returning with the up Scotch express leaving Crewe at 7.38 p.m. These are both very heavy and fast trains, especially the down train, which frequently consists of fifteen or sixteen of the heaviest coaches running on the line. The "Jeanie

Deans" invariably takes this load without an assistant engine, and unless the traffic delays are exceptional, brings the train to a stand at Crewe station (158 miles away from the starting-point) punctual to the moment, not deigning to indulge in a late arrival on the plea of two or three permanent way slacks, which would afford an ordinary engine a satisfactory excuse for being five minutes behind time.

The following are particulars of a run from Crewe to London made on January 24, by the 7 ft. compound engine, No. 1309, with the 3.30 p.m. Scotch express from Crewe—

STATIONS.		MILES.	TIME.	SPEED PER HOUR.	REMARKS.
Crewe (*depart*)	...	—	3.55	—	25 minutes late
Betley Road	(*pass*)	$4\frac{7}{8}$	4.3	36·5	
Madeley	,,	$3\frac{1}{8}$	4.7	46·8	
Whitmore	,,	$2\frac{1}{2}$	4.10	50·0	
Standon Bridge	,,	$4\frac{1}{4}$	4.14	63·7	
Norton Bridge	,,	$4\frac{3}{8}$	4.19	52·5	
Great Bridgeford	,,	$2\frac{1}{4}$	4.21	67·5	
Stafford	,,	$3\frac{1}{8}$	4.25	46·8	
Brockton	,,	4	4.30	48·0	
Colwich	,,	$2\frac{3}{8}$	4.32	71·2	
Rugeley	,,	$2\frac{7}{8}$	4.35	57·5	
Armitage	,,	$3\frac{1}{4}$	4.38	65·0	
Lichfield	,,	$4\frac{3}{4}$	4.43	57·0	
Tamworth	,,	$6\frac{1}{4}$	4.50	53·5	
Polesworth	,,	$3\frac{1}{2}$	4.53	70·0	
Atherstone	,,	$4\frac{1}{8}$	4.58	49·5	
Nuneaton	,,	$4\frac{1}{8}$	5.3	49·5	
Bulkington	,,	$2\frac{5}{8}$	5.9	39·3	
Shilton	,,	$2\frac{1}{8}$	5.9	63·7	
Brinklow	,,	$3\frac{1}{4}$	5.13	48·7	
Rugby (*arrive*)	...	$5\frac{1}{2}$	5.20	47·1	23 minutes late
Rugby (*depart*)	...	—	5.26	—	24 minutes late
Welton	(*pass*)	$7\frac{1}{4}$	5.36	43·5	
Weedon	,,	$5\frac{5}{8}$	5.43	48·2	
Blisworth	,,	$6\frac{3}{4}$	5.50	57·8	
Roade Junction	,,	$2\frac{7}{8}$	5.53	57·5	
Wolverton	,,	$7\frac{1}{2}$	6.0	64·3	
Bletchley	,,	$5\frac{7}{8}$	6.7	50·3	

STATIONS.		MILES.	TIME.	SPEED PER HOUR.	REMARKS.
Leighton	,,	6⅜	6.15	47·8	
Cheddington	,,	4⅛	6.20	49·5	
Tring	,,	4⅜	6.25	52·5	
Berkhamsted	,,	3¾	6.29	56·2	
Boxmoor	,,	3½	6.32	70·0	
Kings Langley	,,	3½	6.35	70·0	
Watford	,,	3½	6.38	70·0	
Harrow	,,	6	6.44	60·0	
Willesden (*arrive*)	...	6	6.51	51·4	
Willesden (*depart*)	...	—	6.54	—	
Euston (*arrive*)	...	5½	7.3	36·6	18 minutes late

	157¾		52·9	average speed

2 hrs. 59 minutes actual running time

On this occasion the coal with which the engine happened to be supplied was of an inferior character not usually put on engines when about to work important express passenger trains. In consequence of this, the maximum steam pressure was not maintained, and yet eight minutes was made up in running.

The weight and composition of the train is here given—

				TONS	CWT.	QRS.
Engine and tender	...	...	...	70	0	0
Brake-van ...	...	...	...	12	14	2
Caledonian vehicle	...	...	...	18	0	0
Third-class carriage	...	...	...	21	9	2
Composite ,,	...	...	...	21	15	2
,, ,,	...	...	...	21	15	2
,, brake	...	...	...	18	13	0
,, carriage	...	...	...	21	15	2
,, ,,	...	...	...	21	15	2
Brake-van ...	...	...	...	12	14	2
		Total	...	240	13	2

One more instance of a run from Crewe to Rugby, with the same train and engine, on February 7, is given, as showing some exceptional speeds.

3.30 P.M. FROM CREWE.

STATIONS.	MILES.	TIME.	SPEED PER HOUR.	REMARKS.
Crewe (*depart*)	—	3.37	—	7 minutes late
Betley Road	4⅞	3.45	36·6	
Madeley	3⅛	3.49	46·9	
Whitmore	2½	3.52	50·0	
Standon Bridge	4¼	3.56	63·7	
Norton Bridge	4⅜	3.59	87·5	
Stafford	5⅜	4.4	64·5	
Colwich	6⅜	4.11	54·6	
Rugeley	2⅜	4.14	57·5	
Armitage	3¼	4.17	65·0	
Lichfield	4¾	4.21	63·3	
Tamworth	6¼	4.28	57·7	
Polesworth	3½	4.31	70·0	
Atherstone	4⅛	4.35	61·8	
Nuneaton	4⅛	4.41	41·2	
Bulkington	3⅝	4.45	54·3	
Shilton	2⅛	4.47	63·7	
Brinklow	3¼	4.50	65·0	
Rugby (*arrive*)	5½	4.57	47·1	right time
	Average speed	...	56·2	

These figures dispose of any question as to the ability of compound engines to run at high speeds.

The most recent type of compound is illustrated by the engine "Greater Britain" (Fig. 139). This is a sister engine to the "Queen Empress," exhibited at the Chicago Exhibition. Its special feature is Mr. Webb's patent boiler, the barrel of which is divided into two lengths, each having a separate row of tubes with a combustion chamber between them. This has the effect of arresting the gases as they pass from the fire-box, thus securing more perfect combustion, and causing all the heat developed to be fully utilized

for the generation of steam.   The engine is mounted on
eight wheels, the two pairs of driving-wheels, 7 ft. in
diameter, being in front of the fire-box.   The leading
wheels under the smoke-box are fitted with radial axle-
boxes, whilst the trailing-wheels under the foot-plate have
ordinary axle-boxes, which are allowed one inch side play

Fig. 139.

to further relieve the strain when travelling round curves.
The total weight of the engine is 52 tons, but this is so
distributed that no one pair of wheels carries more
than 15 tons 10 cwt.   The following are the chief
dimensions—

Heating surface of fire-box	...	120·6 sq. ft.
,, ,, ,, combustion chamber		39·1 ,,
,, ,, ,, tubes (front)	...	853·0 ,,
,, ,, ,, ,, (back)	...	493·0 ,,
Total heating surface	...	1505·7 ,,

	TONS	CWT.	QRS.
Weight on leading-wheels	12	16	o
,, ,, low-pressure driving-wheels ...	15	10	o
,, ,, high-pressure driving-wheels ...	15	10	o
,, ,, trailing-wheels	8	6	o
Total weight of engine in working order ...	52	2	o
,, ,, ,, tender ,, ,, ,, ...	25	0	o
,, ,, ,, engine and tender ...	77	2	o

The steam is distributed in the high pressure cylinders by the link motion, the shifting eccentric being used for the low pressure.

North-Eastern Railway Compound Engines.

Mr. Worsdell's compound engines have two inside cylinders, one high and the other low-pressure. They both act upon one crank axle in the same way as a pair of ordinary high-pressure cylinders. The position of the

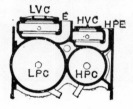

FIG. 140.

cylinders of a Worsdell compound is shown in the cross section (Fig. 140). HPC is the high-pressure cylinder from which the steam is exhausted into the low-pressure cylinder (LPC).

The valve-chests are in the smoke-box above the cylinders. The steam exhaust from the high-pressure cylinder is shown at HPE, from whence it is carried round the smoke-box to the low-pressure valve-chest (LVC), and is finally exhausted at E.

For a description of one of Mr. Worsdell's compound goods engines, of which Fig. 141 is an illustration, Mr. Worthington is again quoted. He says—" In outside appearance this engine is neat, simple, and substantial. It weighs 40 tons 7 cwt., and has six coupled wheels, 5 ft. 1¼ in. in diameter. The cylinders, which are 18 in. and 26 in. in diameter and 24 in. stroke, are placed as in the passenger compound engines beneath the slide valves, and inside the frames.

"The chief features of this goods engine to be observed are the starting and intercepting valves, which enable the engine-driver to start the engine by admitting sufficient high-pressure steam to the large cylinder, without interfering with the small cylinder, in case the latter is not in a position to start the train alone.

FIG. 141.

"The two valves are operated by steam and controlled by one handle. If the engine does not start when the regulator is opened, which will occur when the high-pressure valve covers both its steam ports, the driver pulls the additional small handle, which closes the passage from the receiver to the low-pressure cylinder, and also admits a small amount of steam to the low-pressure steam-chest, so that the two cylinders together develop additional starting power.

"After one or two strokes of the engine, the exhaust

steam from the high-pressure cylinder automatically forces the two valves back to their normal position, and the engine proceeds working compound."

An illustration of one of Mr. Worsdell's compound express passenger engines, designed in the year **1886** for main line traffic, is given in Fig. 142. The following are the principal dimensions—

High-pressure cylinder, 18 in. diameter, 24 in. stroke.
Low-pressure cylinder, 26 in. diameter, 24 in. stroke.
Diameter of driving-wheels, 6 ft. 8¼ in.
Number of tubes, 242, 1¾ in. outside diameter, and 10 ft. long.

Heating surface of tubes	...	...	1211·3 sq. ft.
,, ,, ,, fire-box	...	...	112·0 ,,
		Total heating surface ...	1323·3 ,,

Fire-grate area, 17·33 sq. ft.
Working pressure, 175 lbs. per sq. in.

FIG. 142.

These engines are still working on the North-Eastern main line, and it was with one of this class that the fastest run was performed when the race between the East and West Coast routes took place during the summer of **1888**.

The down Scotch express cleared the distance of $80\frac{1}{2}$ miles from York to Newcastle in eighty-two minutes, and that of 125 miles from Newcastle to Edinburgh in 128 minutes, completing the total journey in one hour and four minutes less than the time now allowed.

These engines have also been found exceedingly useful in working main line express meat and provision goods trains,

FIG. 143.

the work being performed with great economy, both in fuel consumption and repairs.

The large compound engines, having 7 ft. 6 in. single driving-wheels, and cylinders 20 in. and 28 in. in diameter by 24 in. stroke, shown in Fig. 143, were built at the Gateshead Works in the year **1890** to work the main line heavy passenger trains between Newcastle and Edinburgh.

Mr. Wilson Worsdell, the present locomotive superintendent

of the North-Eastern Railway, says they are now doing this work at an average consumption of 28 lbs. of coal per mile, which is very low for the heavy traffic and high rate of speed at which the trains have to travel; in fact, it is about 2 lbs. lower than the average of any other class of engine now running upon this line.

On one occasion the horse-power indicated when running at a speed of 86 miles per hour upon a level road with a train of eighteen carriages was 1068, the total weight of the train being 310 tons.

It is with this class of engine that the train leaving King's Cross at 8.30 p.m. runs the 125 miles from Newcastle to Edinburgh in two hours and forty-six minutes without a stop, this being one of the longest runs made by an engine without stopping to take water.

One of these engines was exhibited in the Edinburgh Exhibition in the year **1890**.

The following are particulars of comparative trials made between the working of compound and non-compound engines on the Great Eastern Railway in January and February, **1888**.

	COMPOUND.	NON-COMPOUND.
Number of vehicles	20	20
Weight of ,,	160 tons	160 tons
,, engine and tender	81 tons 7 cwt.	71 tons 14 cwt.
Total weight of train	241 tons 7 cwt.	231 tons 14 cwt.
Quantity of coal used in pounds	25,254	32,104
Number of pounds of coal used per engine mile	26·3	33·7
Number of pounds of coal used per train mile	28·3	35·9
Quantity of water used in gallons	19,383	24,155
Quantity of water evaporated per pound of coal	8·25	8

	COMPOUND.	NON-COMPOUND.
Total engine mileage	980	952
,, train ,,	892½	892½
,, time occupied in running	27 hrs. 38 min.	27 hrs. 36 min.
Average time per trip	1 hr. 58 min.	1 hr. 58 min.
Conditions of weather	Very rough and boisterous wind, with much snow.	Heavy wind.

The actual results of the comparative working of the engines may be thus summarized—

Ten non-compounds ran 186,890 miles, and consumed 68,228 cwt. coal = 40·9 lbs. per mile.

Ten compounds ran 185,091 miles, and consumed 57,720 cwt. of coal = 34·9 lbs. per mile.

Difference in favour of compounds = 6 lbs. per mile = 14½ per cent.

CHAPTER XVII.

LUBRICATION AND PACKING.

LUBRICATION is a subject to which locomotive engineers have during the last few years given considerable attention. The amount of oil and grease used in the course of a year by the locomotives and rolling-stock of a great railway company in itself represents a very large item, and the indirect expenditure that may be caused by damage to the machinery through neglect in using the means of lubrication provided, or by defective lubricants, adds considerably to this expense. To effect a saving in this direction it is therefore necessary—

1. To provide economical and efficient lubricants;
2. To fit up proper apparatus for distributing a sufficient supply of the lubricant to the different parts without waste;
3. To exercise such supervision over the drivers as will ensure their being on their guard against extravagance and waste; and at the same time make them feel that any damage caused by neglect or insufficient lubrication will not be overlooked.

The object of lubrication is to reduce friction, and thus prevent the development of heat. If a bearing is neglected it soon becomes hot, and when heat is generated, damage to the wearing parts ensues. This frequently results in the failure and stoppage of the engine, and consequent expense in repairing the part damaged.

For locomotive purposes the following lubricants are most generally used—

1. For the cylinders and valves : A thick mineral oil. Sometimes tallow or tallow and rape-oil mixed.

2. For the axles of the wheels : Rape-oil generally, supplemented by tallow in the tops of the axle-boxes, which melts and finds access to the journals when any heat is developed.

3. For the connecting-rod bearings, slide-bars, horn-blocks, coupling-rods and glands, also valve motion, small pins, etc. : Rape-oil.

4. For an axle running hot : Tallow or yellow grease.

5. For the air-pump used with the vacuum brake : Rape-oil and paraffin mixed.

Mr. Reddrop, the chief of the laboratory at Crewe, has kindly furnished the author with the following notes upon the various lubricants used—

" The principal oils and fats employed in the lubrication of the locomotive are mineral oil and rape-oil. Tallow was formerly employed in the lubrication of the cylinders, but has been largely dispensed with, owing to its corrosive action upon iron in the presence of high-pressure steam.

" The mineral oils or petroleums are the fluid or semi-solid bituminous oils, obtained from different localities, but all having a similar mineral origin and common characteristics. The oil is usually obtained by boring or drilling artesian wells, when it often spouts from the newly-opened well in enormous quantities, amounting to several thousand barrels a day in some cases. Pennsylvania now supplies a large proportion of the petroleum of commerce. These oils are all compounds, consisting of carbon and hydrogen, and belong to the series of hydro-carbons known to chemists as the paraffin or $C_n H_{2n} + _2$ series. The first members of this series are gaseous, and the final ones solid at the ordinary temperature; the intermediate ones, being liquid, are those adopted for lubrication. These oils are of incalculable value in the lubrication of the cylinders, in that they have no corrosive action upon the metal, and by their cheapness and improved qualities are becoming the most generally used of all the lubricants for this purpose. Their lubricating power may be increased by the addition of a small proportion of rape-oil where the piston speed is very great, as in locomotive cylinders, but even this cannot be done without a corresponding increase in the corrosive action upon the metal.

" Rape-oil is expressed from the seeds of several kinds of *Brassica*, of which *Brassica napus* and *Brassica rapae* are the principal. The crude oil requires purification before use. Purified rape-seed oil is of light yellow colour, and is extensively used for lubrication. The English seed is said to yield the best oil. Its specific gravity is usually 0·913 to 0·917.

"Nearly all vegetable and animal oils are compounds of glycerine with fatty acids, and in this respect essentially differ from the mineral oils. When kept for a long period decomposition takes place, acid is set free, and the oil becomes rancid. This rancid oil will attack and injure machinery. All animal oils further contain more or less gummy matter, which accumulates when exposed to the action of the atmosphere and retards the motion of machinery. Mineral oils do not absorb oxygen or thicken when exposed alone, or in contact with cotton wool, and consequently do not take fire spontaneously as vegetable and animal oils do. The consumption of mineral oils is largely increasing, and will to a great extent, if not entirely, supersede the use of animal and vegetable oils for lubricating purposes in the future.

" Railway grease is a mixture of a more or less perfectly formed soap, water, and neutral fat, and is largely used on the axles of railway carriages. It is usually made from tallow, palm-oil, soap, and water, which are heated together in a large iron vessel, and then run out and allowed to cool. The composition has to be slightly varied according to the season of the year—being made harder in summer than in winter, on account of the higher temperature to which it is exposed. It usually contains from 40 to 50 per cent. water, which materially aids in preventing the axles from getting hot, and renders it perhaps the most effective of all lubricants for this purpose."

In earlier days lubricators were unknown, and the machinery was treated to intermittent doses of oil from the oil can or feeder, some of which oil found its way to the part which required it, but a great proportion of which was wasted.

We will first consider the

Lubrication of Cylinders,

which has a most important effect upon the general working of an engine. In former times the same oil was used for this purpose as for the other parts of the machinery, but it became gradually recognized that the surface of cylinders and pistons working under intense heat and subjected continually to the moisture of the steam required a different treatment to those parts exposed to the ordinary temperature of the atmosphere. Tallow is still said by many engineers to answer very well for this purpose, but it is generally conceded that there are disadvantages in its use, such as the formation of deposit, its tendency to corrode pistons and other wearing parts, and the consequent involving of time and money for repairs. Some of the mineral oils now sold for cylinder lubrication are much cheaper than tallow, and are undoubtedly superior as cylinder lubricants.

In a paper read before the Association of Employers, Foremen, and Draughtsmen at Manchester in March 1883, Mr. J. Veitch Wilson observes—

"On the question of cylinder lubrication, engineers may be divided into three groups—

" 1. Those who continue to use tallow or suet, because, while it suits them as a lubricant, they find no harm arising from its use.

" 2. Those who, recognizing the objections to tallow, are still constrained to use it, having failed to find an efficient substitute.

" 3. Those who recognize the damage done by tallow, and have adopted hydro-carbon oils or preparations of these instead.

"Let me now state, upon the authority of every chemist who has ever given attention to this subject, that hydro-carbon oils (which include the oils made in this country from coal or shale), oils obtained from American petroleum, oils from the bituminous deposits of Russia and Trinidad, in fact all the oils to which the generic term 'mineral' is applied, are absolutely free from all tendency to oxidize. They are, therefore, in whatever other respects they may be suitable or unsuitable for the lubrication of cylinders, in this respect admirably adapted for the purpose. They can at any rate do no harm. But much more than this merely negative advantage can be claimed for these oils. When account is taken of the many different sources from which these oils are derived, the many different methods of manufacture and preparation, little wonder need be expressed at the great differences which are found in their quality and at the conflicting reports which we hear of their work. If it be true that 'all that glitters is not gold,' it is equally true that

all black oils are not adapted for cylinders. Some are little
better than the tarry residuum from oil stills, others so
volatile that they are little better than gas when they come
into contact with steam at even moderate pressures, others
so deficient in body as to be absolutely worthless as lubricants ; but from a mass of evidence on the subject I am
convinced that if care be exercised in the selection of the oil,
and equal care in its preparation, and in its application and
use, hydro-carbon oil will be found thoroughly efficient as a
lubricant, absolutely
harmless, and much
more economical than
tallow."

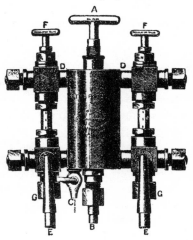

FIG. 144.

The lubricant used
in the cylinders of
London and North-
Western Railway
engines is thick, black
mineral oil, introduced
into the steam-chest
by a sight-feed lubri-
cator (Fig. 144), of
which the following is
a description—

The middle part of
the lubricator is a
plain chamber, which
is fitted at the top with an ordinary plug-tap (A), by means
of which the lubricator is filled with oil. This plug is
removed when filling, and closes against a steam-tight
valve seat when replaced.

B is the pipe by which steam is admitted from the boiler
into the lubricator. The steam inlet at the bottom of
the chamber is fitted with a check valve with rose openings,

to break up the steam into small particles and so cause instant condensation.

C is the drain-cock for drawing off the condensed water when the lubricator is re-filled. The condensed water in the chamber causes the oil to rise, and it overflows through the top outlets (D), passes through the glass and away to the cylinders through the lower outlets (E), each of which is connected by a small pipe to one cylinder.

The amount of oil passing through the glass is controlled by the conical or pencil valves (F), by means of which the required number of drops per minute can be regulated.

The object of the glass is to enable the driver to see that the lubricator is working properly, and keeping the cylinders supplied with oil.

The cocks (G), with lever handles, serve the purpose of closing the connection between the lubricator and the cylinders, thus enabling the glass to be replaced without closing the regulator.

Lubrication of Bearings.

The hollow space at the top of the axle-box is filled with a mixture of oil and tallow, which syphons through a worsted trimming on to the axle. So long as the axle is running cool, only the oil finds its way to the journal; if heat is developed, the tallow also gets to the axle. Tallow is a capital thing to bring an axle round if it "takes to bad ways," but is not to be recommended as a primary lubricant, as it only begins to work when heat is generated, and if everything is going on right, there should not be sufficient heat to melt the tallow.

Sometimes, when an axle is running very badly, a good dose of yellow fat, as railway grease is called, is the best thing to bring it round. Occasionally a small quantity of black-lead or a mixture of sulphur and black-lead is used for the same purpose.

The smaller bearings of all other parts of a locomotive are lubricated with rape-oil. The slide-bars, connecting-rods, coupling-rod bearings, and eccentrics are fitted with small cups, of which Fig. 145 is an illustration. The oil is drawn up through the worsted trimming (WT), and trickles through the pipe (P) on to the bearing to be lubricated. The oil-cup shown is of the pattern used for slide-bars and other places where they can be fixed on some stationary part of the mechanism. The cups used on the big ends, eccentrics, and other moving parts are fitted with a button fixed below the top opening, against which it is made to press by a spiral spring underneath it, thus closing the hole and preventing the oil from being thrown out.

Sometimes when a slide-block is running hot, through friction with the slide-bar, from lack of lubrication, a good lump of railway grease placed on each bar has the effect of getting them to run satisfactorily again.

FIG. 145.

The pins in the motion, not fitted with oil cups, and other parts where only a small quantity of lubrication is required, are simply oiled by putting a few drops on them with the oil-feeder when necessary.

The vacuum pump on a London and North-Western engine runs with a mixture of oil and paraffin. When rape-oil only is used, it has been found that the oil mixes with dust, congeals, and blocks up the air-passages. Indeed, excellent results have been obtained by the use of paraffin only, for lubricating the pump, and while complete freedom from blockage of parts by congealed oil has thus been obtained, a careful use of paraffin has not resulted in any damage to the bearing surfaces.

To give an idea of the amount of lubrication used by the different parts of a locomotive, the following quantity of oil, tallow, etc., has, according to accurate measurement, been used in one week by an engine running daily from London to Manchester and back, working a passenger train—

The distance run during week, 2227 miles.

CLASS OF OIL.	TOTAL USED FOR 2227 MILES.		TOTAL OUNCES USED PER MILE.
	lbs.	ozs.	
Non-corrosive (cylinders) ...	23	15	·0172
Rape (axle-boxes) ...	15	12	·0113
,, (rods and motion) ...	17	14	·0124
,, (other parts) ...	21	0	·015
,, (lamp)	2	4	·0016
Paraffin (pump)	3	10	·0026
Tallow	18	6	·0132

The average consumption of oil and grease by London and North-Western engines working from the Rugby Locomotive Station for a winter and a summer month is as follows—

CLASS OF WORK.	RAPE OIL. Qrts. per 100 mls.		CYLINDER OIL. Qrts. per 100 mls.		GREASE. Lbs. per 100 mls.	
	June 1892.	Nov. 1891.	June 1892.	Nov. 1891.	June 1892.	Nov. 1891.
Heavy express passenger trains	2·1	2·0	·9	1·0	1·3	1·2
Lighter, ditto	1·5	1·4	·7	·6	·8	·7
Slow passenger trains ...	1·6	1·6	·6	·9	·8	1·3
Express goods	1·6	1·5	·9	·8	·9	·7
Slow ,,	1·9	2·2	1·0	1·3	·6	·8
Mineral trains	1·5	1·5	·8	·8	·9	·7
Shunting engines, estimated at 5 miles per hour	1·4	2·0	·5	1·1	·1	·3

Packing.

As has been already explained, the piston-rods and valve-spindles are made to work "steam-tight" through the ends of the cylinders and valve-chests by means of packing placed in the stuffing-box and kept in position by the gland.

Increased pressures of steam now demand a much more durable and stronger packing than was formerly found to answer. The pressure necessitates the gland being screwed down tightly on to the packing to compress it firmly into the stuffing-box and against the piston-rod, otherwise the steam blows through. The high speed of the piston-rod generates heat, and the material must be of such a nature that it can withstand this heat, and at the same time exert a considerable pressure on the rod to keep it steam-tight, without causing damage through friction. Hemp saturated with tallow was a packing frequently used, but it is not found to answer under a high steam pressure, and with a high speed piston-rod. Packing of various forms and different materials and composition have lately been brought out. A series of rings of soft white metal placed in the stuffing-box in segments have been found to answer very well for piston-rods, but it is necessary to supplement the metal rings with some ordinary form of packing.

The following table (p. 330) shows the various amounts of different kinds of packing used for different purposes—

PURPOSE.	LENGTH OF PACKING REQUIRED TO FILL THE STUFFING BOX.		CLASS OF PACKING USED.
	FT.	IN.	
Compound Engines—			
High-pressure valve spindles ...	3	0	Cresswell's plaited
,, ,, piston-rods ...	3	6	greased packing in
Low ,, valve spindle ...	4	0	square or round sec-
,, ,, piston-rods ...	5	6	tion.
Ordinary Passenger Engines—			
Piston-rods (with metallic rings in			Grass packing.
stuffing-box)	1	4	
Valve spindles	0	11	
Goods Engines—			
Piston-rod	4	10	Grass packing.
Valve-spindle	2	0	
General—			
Regulator gland	2	0	Tuck's elastic packing, or asbestos packing.
Brake-piston	7	0	Soapstone packing.
Ejector steam-pipe expansion gland	0	5½	Tuck's elastic packing.

CHAPTER XVIII.

COMBUSTION AND CONSUMPTION OF FUEL.

WHEREVER coal is obtainable, it is still the fuel almost invariably used for locomotives, and the best kind for the purpose, in this country, is the anthracite or blind coal found in South Wales.

Coal, as everybody knows, is the product of a partial decomposition in vegetable matter. It is composed of carbon, hydrogen, nitrogen, oxygen, and a small percentage of sulphur, frequently mixed with other substances which constitute impurities from which many coals are entirely free. Carbon and hydrogen are the chief heat-giving ingredients, and their percentage varies greatly in different coals.

The Table on p. 332, given by Mr. Hutton,[1] shows the average composition of several kinds of coal.

The process of chemical combination, called combustion, which produces heat, is the uniting of carbon, hydrogen, and oxygen. The carbon is combustible partly in its solid state, and partly with the hydrogen in gaseous compounds, whereas the supporting element of combustion is oxygen, which must be admitted to the fire-box of a locomotive in proportion to the amount and character of fuel it contains.

[1] Hutton's *Practical Engineers' Handbook*, Table XV. p. 57.

CONSTITUENTS, ETC.	ANTHRACITE COAL.	ABERDARE COAL.	WELSH COAL.	NEWCASTLE COAL.	LANCASHIRE COAL.	DERBYSHIRE COAL.	YORKSHIRE COAL.	SCOTCH COAL.
Carbon, per cent. ...	92·00	88·28	86·26	83·60	80·70	80·00	79·90	79·50
Hydrogen „ ...	3·80	4·24	4·66	5·28	5·50	4·85	4·83	5·58
Oxygen „ ...	1·00	1·65	2·60	4·65	8·48	9·90	10·10	8·33
Nitrogen „ ...	1·00	1·66	1·45	1·22	1·12	1·35	1·40	1·14
Sulphur „ ...	·70	·91	1·77	1·25	1·50	1·10	1·00	1·45
Ash „ ...	1·50	3·26	3·26	4·00	2·70	2·30	2.77	4·00
Specific gravity ...	1·37	1·32	1·31	1·25	1·27	1·30	1·29	1·26
Weight of a cubic foot in lbs. in solid state	85·60	82·50	81·90	78·10	79·40	81·20	80·60	78·70
Weight of a cubic yard in tons in solid state	1·031	·994	·987	·941	·957	·978	·972	·948
Average bulk of 1 ton heaped in cubic feet	41	42	43	46	45	44	44·5	45·5
How it burns ...	With difficulty	Slowly	Slowly	Quickly	Quickly	Quickly	Quickly, and cakes	Quickly
Draught required ...	Quick	Quick	Quick	Ordinary	Ordinary	Ordinary	Brisk	Ordinary
Quantity of smoke ...	None	Scarcely any	Very little	Large	Large	Large	Large	Very large

When a sufficient supply of air is not provided, the fuel is not properly consumed, and large quantities of gas, instead of igniting in the fire-box and producing heat, escape away through the chimney mixed with smoke. Such volumes of smoke represent an entire waste of so much fuel, which is being discharged into the atmosphere without being utilized to produce heat and generate steam.

If the coal used is of good quality with a high percentage of carbon and the supply of air correctly regulated, there will be perfect combustion, and no smoke will be seen to issue from the chimney.

Air can be heated almost instantaneously, and the intense heat in the fire-box causes air admitted in due proportion to rise to the same temperature as the hot gases arising from the coal. The hot gases then unite with the heated oxygen of the air, and produce perfect combustion and intense heat.

When too great a volume of air is admitted into the fire-box, or when its admission is not properly regulated, it does not at once rise to the same temperature as the gases from the fire, and consequently the temperature in the fire-box is lowered, causing a strain on the plates and a loss of steam from reduced temperature.

Thirteen and a half pounds of atmospheric air are necessary for the combustion of one pound of coal, but more than this is required in locomotive practice, because the blast draws the air through the tubes before it has time to thoroughly unite with the furnace gases.

The principal amount of air is admitted by the damper through the fire-bars, and it thus becomes heated as it passes through the incandescent coal before mixing with the gases.

To promote perfect combustion with the most economical results, it is however necessary to admit a small quantity of

air *above* the fire, and this is done through the fire-hole.
Air so admitted, however, does not pass direct across the
fire-box to the tube-plate, but is arrested by the deflector-
plate, and its course directed down on the fire, so that it
becomes heated in the centre of the fire-box before reaching
the plates. The strong draught from the blast urges the
burning coals to a fierce heat, and they rapidly throw off
the inflammable gases, but if these gases pass away through
the tubes to the chimney without being properly consumed,
there is dense smoke, which means imperfect combustion
and great waste.

With the old style of fire-boxes there was an unlimited
supply of air below the fire-bars, and there were no deflector-
plates or brick arches; the gases were drawn off through
the chimney without any check, and for that reason coke
was the fuel always used for locomotives. However, by the
action of the damper, brick arch, and deflector-plate, the
admission of air to the fire-box is so regulated, and the
movement of the gases in the fire-box so controlled, that
almost perfect combustion is effected, and the superiority
of coal as a locomotive fuel is now fully established.

Many and various are the devices that have been tried,
to effect perfect combustion in a locomotive fire-box, and
the result of experiments has been the almost universal
adoption of a simple form of brick arch and deflector or
baffle-plate.

Mr. Webb has, as already explained, perfected an ingenious arrangement whereby the fire-hole door and
deflector-plate are combined, and in the boiler of his
engine, " Greater Britain," a chamber in the barrel of the
boiler further promotes the combustion of the gases before
they finally leave the heating surface of the tubes.

Coal from which the gases have been expelled, but which
is maintained at the temperature of incandescence, burns

with a red, yellow, or white flame without smoke, when sufficient oxygen is supplied.

The presence of water or its constituents in fuel promotes the formation of smoke, or of the luminous low temperature flame, which is ignited smoke.

Clinker is a glassy material which forms by the fusion of the ashes. It cakes in a hard substance on the bars, stops up the air spaces, and tends to choke the grate. The more mineral substances there are in coal the greater the amount of clinker formed.

The difference in the chemical composition of different kinds of coal is very great, as has been shown in the previous table. The amount of carbon in coal ranges from 30 to 93 per cent., the best steam-coal having a high percentage. The amount of ash left after combustion varies from $1\frac{1}{2}$ to 26 per cent.

The highest temperature reached in the combustion of average coal is given by Mr. D. K. Clarke as 5027 degrees Fah., when the temperature of the external air is 62 degrees. This would represent the actual temperature in the fire-box of a locomotive. The temperature of the gases at the base of the chimney after passing through the tubes has been ascertained by experiment to be about 600 degrees when the temperature of the external air has been 55 degrees. Mr. F. Kolm gives the total heat of the combustion of 1 lb. of coal as follows—

Units[1] of heat developed, 11,947, the percentage distribution being as follows—

7,400 units = 62·2 per cent., in the formation of steam.
2,172 ,, = 18·3 per cent., loss by heat of gases in smoke-box.
2,375 ,, = 19·5 per cent., waste.

11,947   100·0

---

[1] The thermal *unit* is the heat required to raise 1 lb. of water by 1 degree Fahrenheit.

In October 1887, a series of very interesting experiments was made with a Great Eastern locomotive in regard to the combustion of coal, and the following are some of the figures that were arrived at upon a trip made from Stratford to Lynn on October 19—

DISTANCE RUN, 95 MILES.

Total coal used, including ashes and clinker, in lbs., 1701.

Percentage of ash and clinker in total coal used: Ash, 3·8; clinker, 1·7.

Percentage of moisture in fuel, ·5.

Total weight of pure and dry coal used per hour, 327 lbs.

Total coal used, including ash and clinker, per hour, 348 lbs.

Weight of ash and clinker: Ash, 64·5 ; clinker, 21·5.

Stoking : Thickness of fire in inches, 4 to 5.

    ,,   Number of times stoked per hour, 5.

Temperature of external air in degrees, Fah., 48·5.

    ,,   ,,   furnace gases at base of chimney, 570·0.

Chimney draught, inches of vacuum, 1·07.

PRINCIPAL RESULTS.

Combustion—

    Lbs. of coal per square foot of grate surface, per hour, 28·1.

    Lbs. of coal per square foot of heating surface, per hour, ·406.

Evaporation—

    Lbs. of water evaporated per lb. of coal from feed temperature, 10·34.

In locomotive practice, the amount of water evaporated or turned into steam varies from 6 to 10 lbs. for every lb. of coal burnt, according to the class of coal used. This, however, depends upon the correct regulation of the air admitted to the fire-box and the skill used in firing. In testing the performance of an engine, one simple calculation is invariably made. All that has to be done to arrive at the result is to correctly measure the coal used and the feed-water supplied to the boiler, and divide the number of lbs. of coal burned by the number of lbs. of water evaporated.

By thus noting these two factors, it can easily be ascertained whether the steam generated is in a fair proportion to the amount of fuel burned.

Another equally simple observation enables the locomotive superintendent to determine whether the engine is performing a fair amount of work in proportion to the steam generated and fuel burned. This is the amount of fuel burned per mile run, which is in practice worked out in pounds.

These results vary greatly, and depend upon the weight, composition, and speed of the trains, the gradients on the line, the class and state of repair of the engine, the weather, and numerous other considerations.

It does not therefore always follow that because the engines working passenger trains on one line of railway are averaging 28 lbs. as against 33 lbs. per mile burned by another company's locomotives on passenger work, the former's must of necessity be the best and most economical. Indeed, the conditions under which they work may differ in so many respects that a comparative statement of this kind is worth very little.

It is only by testing engines upon exactly the same work, and under precisely the same conditions, that accurate comparative statements can be arrived at. As a matter of fact, locomotives of the present day burn a much greater quantity of fuel than they did twenty or thirty years ago ; not because of any fault in their construction, but because the fire-boxes and boilers have had to be enlarged to keep pace with the increasing power of the engine, necessary to meet the increased weight and speed of trains.

Some of the most modern engines show rather a high consumption in the monthly sheets, but it must be remembered that in most cases they are actually saving fuel, because they work trains that less recent types of engines could not take without an assistant engine.

The following figures represent about a fair average consumption on different classes of work—

	LBS. PER MILE. SUMMER.		LBS. PER MILE. WINTER.
Express passenger, heavy trains ...	33	...	37
,, ,, light ,, ...	25	...	30
Slow passenger trains ...	35	...	38
Express goods trains ...	41	...	46
Slow goods trains, when a lot ⎱ of shunting has to be done ⎰ ...	60	...	71
Heavy mineral trains ...	58	...	62
Shunting engines, (estimated ⎱ at five miles an hour) ... ⎰	32	...	40

It has been stated that, assuming trains of equal weight, a difference in speed does not affect the consumption of coal per mile, although the consumption per hour increases in proportion to the speed. This, however, is not borne out by the results of the following experiments made on the London and North-Western Railway—

On April 17, 1887, a train was run from Crewe to Wolverton. These are particulars of the trial—

	TONS	CWT.	QRS.
Weight of engine and tender	65	0	0
Weight of train, exclusive of engine and tender	259	3	3
Total weight moved ...	324	3	3

Distance run, 105 miles.

Average speed, including starting from Crewe and stopping at Wolverton, 24 miles per hour.

Consumption of coal, 21·3 lbs. per mile.

Evaporation of water, 9·77 lbs. for each lb. of coal burned.

On June 5, 1887, a similar trial was made between the same points at a speed of 45 miles an hour—

	TONS	CWT.	QRS.
Weight of engine and tender	65	0	0
Weight of train exclusive of engine and tender	264	12	3
Total weight moved ...	329	12	3

Distance run, 105 miles.

Average speed, including starting from Crewe and stopping at Wolverton, 45·6 miles per hour.

Consumption of coal, 57·6 lbs. per mile.

Evaporation of water, 7·6 lbs. for each lb. of coal burned.

These figures, which are the result of a carefully-made experiment, prove beyond doubt the greatly increased cost entailed by running heavy trains at high speeds.

Another experiment was tried with a shuttle train working a local service between Birmingham and Harborne, a distance of 4¼ miles, with three intermediate stops in each direction. It was proposed to decrease the time between the terminal points from 18 to 15 minutes, and it was proved that the reduction in the running time increased the consumption of coal about 20 per cent.

A new departure has lately been made in locomotive fuel by the introduction of petroleum to take the place of coal. This has been tried on the Great Eastern Railway with great success.

The following is a description of the apparatus which is fitted to the Great Eastern engine " Petrolea," shown on p. 245.

The liquid fuel is carried on the tender in a tank, the capacity of which is 500 gallons. It is led by pipes to two injectors or burners placed in holes provided for them in the fire-box plates, immediately below the foot-plate, and some 14 inches above the fire-bars, on which a fire of small coal is maintained. Each injector has two separate steam supplies; one used for inducing and atomizing the liquid fuel by a centre cone or jet, and the other for supplying atmospheric air to the atomized fuel by means of small jets, arranged round a ring blower, placed near the nozzle of the injector. This blower not only ensures perfect combustion, but also atomizes and distributes the oil to such an extent that no fire-brick is necessary to receive and break up the spray, as in other systems. This secures very distinct advantages—the fire-box being as available for a solid fuel fire after the addition of the apparatus as before.

The fuel at present in use on the Great Eastern Railway consists of coal gas tar, oil gas tar, and various tar oils, and one ton of these in practice will approximately equal two tons of steam coal in heating effect.

The actual consumption of fuels on engines of the class referred to is as follows—

(1) Liquid fuel and coal combined—

Oil	...	...	12·2 lbs. per mile.
Coal	...	...	11·0 ,,
			23·2 ,,

as against

(2) Coal only ... 34·0 ,,

lighting up, etc., included in both cases.

From practical experience, liquid fuel appears to have much to recommend it. The ease with which a constant steam pressure can be maintained; the facilities for controlling the fire to exact requirements; its cleanliness and the reduction in the wear and tear of the fire-box and tubes, are all points in its favour. At the same time, objections might be urged against a system requiring liquid fuel alone. For instance, the difficulty in lighting up and raising steam may be mentioned; also the sudden reduction in temperature in the fire-box when the fuel is shut off. But with a combined system, such as that in use on the Great Eastern Railway, none of these difficulties arise.

CHAPTER XIX.

ENGINE-DRIVERS AND THEIR DUTIES.

PERSONS interested in locomotive engine-driving cannot do better than read Mr. Michael Reynolds' book, in which the subject is dealt with in a very interesting and comprehensive manner.

To become a "first-class" engine-man requires a vast amount of experience and training. The period of training is longer than the ordinary term of apprenticeship considered necessary to render a man an expert craftsman in any other particular trade which he may take up as a means of earning his livelihood, and to follow the career of an engine-driver from the time he enters the railway service until he is promoted to the position of an express passenger train-driver, would take more space than can be allotted to this branch of locomotive work. In most trades the skill of the workman is equally valuable wherever he may be employed, but unfortunately this is not altogether the case with the engine-driver, whose knowledge is essentially limited to his particular line. A very important part of his training is to "learn the road," that is, to gain a knowledge of the gradients and signals on every part of the line over which he has to run. He must be able to read off at sight the meaning of every signal, and to pick out those he must obey from the gigantic array that present themselves to his gaze, when he approaches a complicated junction or busy station.

It takes a driver years to thoroughly learn all the signals over a large railway system, and the knowledge when acquired is only of use upon the line on which he is trained.

The larger railways are divided into districts with a staff of drivers attached to each. Thus, on the London and North-Western Railway the men working local trains about Birmingham, Wolverhampton, and Walsall are thoroughly acquainted with the complicated junctions and signals in that part of the country, but do not know the main line. In the same way the Crewe drivers, who know the road over 300 miles from London to Carlisle, could not work trains on the branch lines. On the London and North-Western Railway alone there are 17,000 signals lighted every night, and the driver working from Crewe to London and back, for his day's work, is controlled by no less than 570 signals, to say nothing of those coming under his observation which do not affect the working of his train.

In the early days of railways, engine-drivers were usually men who had previously been employed as mechanics, in many instances assisting in the building of the machines of which they afterwards took charge. However, it soon became evident that these were two entirely different branches of locomotive work, and that a good mechanic did not necessarily make a good engine-man.

A separate department therefore sprang into existence, which was called the "Running Department," and it is through the various grades in this department that men rise step by step until the highest rank, viz., that of an express passenger train driver, is attained.

The youth who enters the railway service with the aspiration of ultimately becoming an engine-driver, first commences work as a cleaner, and has to pass through the following stages before he reaches the top rung of the ladder—

Cleaner.—Cleaning shunting engines, goods engines, and passenger engines.

Extra Fireman.—Viz., a cleaner who is passed to act as a fireman when a man has to be drawn from the cleaning staff for special work.

Fireman.—Firing on shunting engines, on local good trains, on express good trains, on local passenger trains, on express passenger trains.

Extra Driver.—Viz., a fireman passed to act as a driver when required for special work.

Driver.—On shunting engine, on local goods train, on express goods trains, on local passenger trains, on express passenger trains.

In some cases main line express goods drivers rank before those of local passenger trains, and are paid at a higher rate.

Promotion goes by seniority, combined with merit. A cleaner who takes a pride in the thoroughness of his work and the appearance of the engine with the cleaning of which he is entrusted, should be singled out for promotion before one whose only idea is to do the minumum amount of work that will enable his engine to be passed by the foreman.

The cleaner who eventually succeeds as an engine-driver is always trying to *learn* something; while he is employed in the running-sheds he has constant opportunities of seeing the fitters at work on different parts of the mechanism of the engines, and, if he is bright and intelligent, he will make use of such opportunities to get knowledge that will be useful to him hereafter.

Many engine-drivers have been degraded from their positions simply from a lack of mechanical knowledge, which they should have acquired even before they were made firemen, much less engine-drivers. These are the people who go wrong on the road when there is a break-down, and it is necessary to uncouple an engine and work with one side only, or when some slight temporary repair would enable the engine to work forward to the next loco-motive station. It is then that an indolent man finds him-self altogether at sea, and having caused an unnecessary delay, his incompetency is established, and he is put back to a lower grade in the service, where self-reliance and capability are not likely to be called into requisition.

The man who keeps his eyes open and intelligently observes what is going on around him, whether he be cleaner, fireman, or driver, is the one who will surely work his way to the front; while his fellow-servant, who has not made the most of his opportunities, is still compelled to remain in the lower grades of the service.

To the uninitiated the life of an engine-driver appears to be a pleasant and perhaps an easy one. It cannot be denied that even to many who gain their living by the occupation it has a fascination that never wanes, and when once a man has attained the position of an express passenger train driver, his lot is one that well may be envied by the majority of the artisan class. His rate of pay is high, his hours are short, and his work neither monotonous nor arduous.

But, on the other hand, it has cost him many years of real hard work to gain this position ; and, although the life may have its picturesque side, it must be remembered that the responsibilities are great, and that the driver is called upon to take his turn on night duty, and to be out in all weathers, at all seasons of the year. It is no light matter to be responsible for the safe conduct of an express pas-senger train through the country in the dead of night, at the rate of fifty or sixty miles an hour, past busy stations and mazy junctions.

We will not attempt to follow the different gradations of service in the Running Department, but will try to gain some idea of the duties of an engine-driver during his day's work.

Every engine-man is supplied weekly with printed notices giving particulars of extra trains arranged, signal alterations, repairs to the permanent way, and all special arrangements of every kind and description affecting the part of the line over which he has to work.

A careful driver will take these notices home with him and look them over; so that, when he goes on duty, he has all the instructions fixed in his mind, and can give his whole attention to his engine. When there are important alterations in the signals or roads at any station, it is the practice on the London and North-Western Railway to supply every driver with a diagram giving full details of all such alterations. This is an excellent system, and keeps the men well advised of everything of the kind that is going on. The driver, however, must not be satisfied with the information to be gleaned from these printed notices, but whenever he books on duty his first care must be to study the special notice board hung up in the shed, upon which he will find posted all special instructions which are issued from time to time. Many of these instructions refer to the Locomotive Department only, and are not included in the traffic superintendents' weekly notices. A water-pipe has burst somewhere, and there is no water to be obtained at that station, the driver must therefore make a special stop to fill his tank elsewhere. It is autumn, and a gale of wind followed by a sharp shower has caused a plentiful fall of leaves from the trees. What has this to do with the engine-driver, it may be asked? There is a notice calling attention to the fact that the falling leaves will make the rails very slippery, and drivers must exercise additional care in descending the incline between Camden Town and Euston Station, which is overshadowed by trees. It is, of course, the driver's duty to observe such things for himself, but the district locomotive superintendents are ever on the watch for all these little pitfalls which may lead their men into trouble. Complaints have been made that trains are running through some particular junction too fast, and drivers are cautioned to moderate the speed. Some irate householder has written to the general manager, complaining of the noise or smoke made by engines standing at some signal in the vicinity of his residence, and the locomotive superintendent threatens dire penalties to the offender who again transgresses in this respect.

These are the kind of notices the driver finds displayed upon the special notice board.

But we are going to follow him through his day's work, and we have somewhat anticipated. His first duty is to "book on," that is, to give his name in at the "check office" at the gate where the time of his coming to work is recorded, together with his train and the number of his engine. The keys of his tool-boxes are kept at this office, and must be obtained by the driver or fireman, whichever books on duty first.

Having booked on duty and examined the notice board, the driver proceeds to his engine, which he finds ready placed in a convenient position for moving off the shed. Arrived there his first duty is to examine the gauge glass, and ascertain what water there is in the boiler. He should then try the test taps (which are provided in case the gauge glass breaks or fails), and satisfy himself that they are in working order. Having seen that the water in the boiler is all right, he next examines the steam-gauge and notes what pressure is recorded. The engine has been lighted up some two to three hours previous to his arrival, and is beginning to make steam, and it is important to note the pressure in order that he can so regulate matters that the boiler will gradually generate steam at such a rate as to be just at blowing-off point, when it is time to back on to his train. He should then look in the fire-box and note the condition of the fire, which the fireman should by this time be engaged in making up—a process described a little farther on. After satisfying himself as to the state of affairs with regard to the amount of water in the boiler, the pressure of steam, and the condition of the fire, the driver's next duty is to make a thorough examination of his engine. There is not one thing in locomotive engine-driving which contributes more to the success or failure in the career of an engine-driver than the capability he possesses for making a thoroughly minute and intelligent inspection of his engine, before attaching to a train which he undertakes the responsibility of working.

There are men who will apparently make a complete examination of an engine before taking it off the shed, and who habitually spend a good deal of time in so doing, but who have been known to come to grief on the road, through some nut slackening back or pin working out—a mishap that might have been avoided if this particular nut or pin had received proper attention.

To make a really satisfactory and efficient examination, a man must not be content with spending a certain amount of time in making a general survey of the different parts of the machinery, but he must so train himself in habits of minute and careful observation as to be able to make his examination without overlooking the smallest and apparently least important detail. There are men who have been driving for years and have daily inspected their engines, as they thought thoroughly, and who may however have habitually overlooked some one small part, which has eventually led

to a bad failure on the road, from a want of proper supervision. *Everything* that could *possibly* go wrong should be
examined, no matter how improbable any mishap may be.

A case came under the writer's notice only recently, in
which a passenger train had to be stopped, the continuous
brake put out-of-gear, and the train worked to its destination
under control of the hand-brakes only, entirely owing to
the driver having omitted to examine a small valve on one
of the vacuum-pipes. This was a valve that has never
been known to go wrong before or since, but which, on this
occasion, caused a failure that might have been avoided by
a proper examination, thus saving the pocket of the driver,
who was fined for his carelessness.

More failures are brought about through nuts slackening
back and pins working out than from any other cause, and
every possible place where this might occur should have
special attention.

There is not space to give a detailed explanation of the
whole examination, but the following is a general survey
of the process : The engine must be placed over a pit, and if
possible during daylight, and unless the weather is bad, the
examination should be made outside the shed because of
the better light. The engine should be brought to a stand
with each driving-crank journal an equal distance below the
centre of the driving-axle. The hand-brake must then be
screwed hard on, the reversing lever or wheel placed in
mid-gear, and the cylinder taps opened.

The examination should be conducted systematically, the
same routine being observed on every occasion. By
following this plan a man trains himself to take every point
successively, and it comes natural to him to inspect everything in turn, whereas, if he dodges about from point to
point, he does not go to work on any properly regulated
system, and is always apt to overlook one thing or another.

The driver should commence his examination underneath the engine, beginning with the axle-boxes, the trimmings of which must be carefully inspected, to see that they are in good order and fit properly into the hole through which the oil has to syphon. It may be necessary to make new trimmings, but the driver will know pretty well what condition they are in by his last examination. Some axle-boxes are constructed to use tallow and oil, in which case the hollow part of the top of the axle-box is filled with melted tallow mixed with oil, and the top of the oil-hole is below the level of the mixture. A locomotive axle-box that uses oil only, and in which tallow cannot be used, has the oil-hole above the level of the oil, as the whole of the lubricant syphons through the trimming, which oil mixed with tallow is not sufficiently liquid to do.

The springs, spring pins, links, etc., so far as they can be seen from underneath, must be examined at the same time as the axle-boxes, and when this has been systematically done, attention should be given to the big ends, which are almost the most important things about the engine as regards the care and attention they require. To fail with a hot big end is unfortunately by no means a rare occurrence, but such a failure can nearly always be avoided if the brasses are properly fitted in the first instance, and subsequently attended to by the driver. They should be put up just loose enough on the journal to be moved by hand from side to side to the extent of the side play allowed. When it is necessary to drive the cotter down to tighten up the brasses, the set screws must be first slackened back, and it is advisable to make a mark on the cotter so that it can be seen exactly how far it is knocked down at each stroke.

Cotters should always be knocked down with a lead hammer in order to avoid damaging them. Great care must be taken not to tighten the brasses up too much, or the big end is likely to run hot. A careful driver will tighten the big end a little bit from time to time; a careless man often allows them to run till they get quite loose, and then, when they are tightened up, they have a tendency to bear unequally on the journals, which also causes them to run hot.

After tightening the cotters down if necessary, the set screws must be screwed firmly up against them to prevent their working back; and whether it is necessary to knock the cotter down or not, the set screws must always be tried over with the spanner.

Upon the care which is taken in adjusting the trimmings depends the amount of oil used by the big ends. When running, they should pass about four drops of oil per minute. If they use too little oil, the bearings are liable to run hot, and if too much, there is a continual waste going on.

The little ends must now be examined in a similar way if they are fitted with brasses and cotters; but if with steel bushes, as is the case with London and North-Western engines, they require very little attention.

The eccentrics come next, and particular attention should be given to the bolts, nuts, small safety cotters and set pins, which hold them in position. The bolts which hold the eccentric straps together must also be carefully tried over with the spanner; and the syphon cup and trimming on each eccentric must be carefully attended to, the trimming being the same as with a big end.

The different parts of the valve motion are held together by small pins, each of which should be most minutely examined, to see that it is tight in its place. More failures have perhaps been brought about by these small pins working out than from any other cause. The small cotters coupling up the valve spindles to the reversing-gear must be carefully tried, and the piston-rods and cross-heads examined. With

London and North-Western engines the end of the piston-rod passes through the cross-head, to which it is secured by a large nut, which must be carefully examined.

The glands must then be screwed up, great care being taken to keep them exactly square with the rods upon which they work, and the nuts on the gland studs must be securely locked.   These gland nuts should also be examined during the trip whenever opportunity offers.

If an engine is fitted with a feed-pump for supplying the boiler, or air-pump for working the vacuum brake, every detail of these must also be very carefully looked over.

For examining the motion of an engine, it is necessary that it should be in mid-gear, as in this position the driver can get at every part of it.

Having examined all the machinery, including the cylinder tap gearing, the driver should look into the ash-pan, and if there are any ashes in it, should instruct his fireman to rake them out.   He should also inspect the fire-bars, and satisfy himself that they are in proper position in the carriers. Other people are responsible for doing this work before the driver comes to the engine, but he should make a point of satisfying himself that it has been properly done ; as, if either of these points has been neglected, he may get into trouble through the engine not steaming properly.

This completes his survey underneath the engine.   The smoke-box door should now be opened, and he should satisfy himself that all the ashes have been properly cleaned out, and that there is no leak at any of the tubes.

After shutting the smoke-box door, he should thoroughly examine the joint, and satisfy himself that it is air-tight, and that the handle is in working order and properly secures the door.   Everything outside the engine that can possibly become disconnected should now be examined, such as springs, spring-links, feed-pipes, sand-pipes, brake gear, etc.

A look should be also given to the bolts securing the horn-blocks to the frames. Although it is a very unusual occurrence, these have been known to work loose, and sometimes two or three nuts have been allowed to work off without the driver finding it out.

A particular examination should be made of the brake gear, which consists of levers, pull-rods, brake-blocks, and screw, held together by various bolts and pins, all of which require individual attention. Part of this inspection must be made from underneath, and part from outside. If the engine is fitted with a steam, vacuum, or Westinghouse brake, the cylinder gear must be carefully overhauled; and, in the case of the two latter brakes, all the pipes should be examined, especially at the joints, which the driver should satisfy himself are all air-tight.

In the vacuum brake, the vacuum should be raised by the ejector, and when the proper amount of vacuum has been created, the needle should stand fast after the ejector is shut off. If there is any leakage the needle at once commences to go back, when the ejector is shut off, and in that case an endeavour must be made to locate the leakage.

With the hand-brake, the brake screw and the nut into which it works must be examined, and if it requires taking up, a fitter's attention must be called to the matter.

As the driver proceeds with his examination, he should at the same time oil all the parts requiring it with the exception of little ends, slide-bars, and glands, which should be left till the last moment in order to avoid the waste of oil which would go on while the engine is standing.

The tender axle-boxes and bearings, as well as the screw-shackle and draw-bar, must also receive attention before the driver concludes his part of the work on the steam shed and the engine goes out.

Some drivers leave all the oiling to their firemen, but

this is not the proper thing to do, although the work may be divided with advantage, the fireman oiling the tender, coupling-rods, and horn-blocks, and other parts which can be oiled from the outside, whilst the driver takes the parts underneath which have to be oiled at the time the examination is made, and to which he should in all cases see himself.

The fireman is allowed the same marginal time before the train starts as the driver. He also has his appointed duties, and it is for him to decide whether he will perform them in a perfunctory manner, giving to them the exact number of minutes allotted by the company, or whether he will come to the shed a little in advance of his booked time and make all his preparations with comfort to himself and satisfaction to his driver.

Cases have been known of men arriving at the shed as they considered a little too soon, and instead of proceeding to their engine and getting on with the work, remaining outside smoking and idling until the exact moment when they were obliged to go on duty.

Such men are not likely to make good drivers or be a credit to the company in whose service they are employed. The man who takes a real interest in his work is not particular to half-an-hour as to how long before train time he comes, so long as he gives himself plenty of time to do his work thoroughly and well. He knows how much he has to do before train time, the class of work upon which the engine is going to run, and whether there are any special jobs which require time to be satisfactorily attended to. In many cases there will be an aggregate of several hours of leisure during the day between the trips the engine runs. He is paid for these hours, and therefore should not grudge a little extra time to ensure a good start with the first trip—time that will undoubtedly bear good fruit before the day's work is over. A good fireman will make a point of arriving at the engine before the driver, and his first care should be to make the same examination of steam and water as has been explained among the driver's duties. He should then unlock the tools, and, if the engine is supplied with Welsh coal, at once commence to make up the fire, on the foundation of burning coal which has been put in some time before his arrival. With ordinary coal a large fire is not put on before train time, and the engine is run with a comparatively low fire; but with Welsh steam coal, which is by far the best for locomotive purposes, the making up of the fire in the shed is a most important duty. This kind of coal does not give out much heat until well burned through, and the most economical method is to make up a good thick fire, leaving just sufficient time for it to be well burned through by the time the train is due to start away. Hard coal cannot be treated in this way, as it burns away far more quickly and begins to generate steam at once, and is therefore only put on just before starting.

Firing with Welsh coal is a more scientific operation, and requires observance and skill both in making up the fire before starting and in manipulating it on the road.

The fire is made up as follows : First the damper is opened to give a free circulation of air through the fire-box. The largest lumps of coal should be picked out—it does not matter how big they are, provided they will go through the fire-hole door—and put on by hand round the sides of the fire-box. The space all round the fire-box should be completely covered with lumps placed side by side against each other. The middle part of the fire-bars should then be covered with smaller lumps evenly distributed over its surface. There is now a layer of coal completely covering the whole of the grate surface, and this is the foundation upon which the fire is built up. More large lumps should then be dropped underneath the fire-hole and in the back corners of the box.   The shovel may now be used to complete making up the fire with smaller lumps, and when finished the back part of the fire should be almost up to the door and gradually slope down so as to be the thinnest underneath the brick arch in the front of the fire-box. There must be no holes in the fire, but the bars must be well covered all over to avoid cold air being drawn through into the fire-box without first coming in contact with the bottom part of the fire.

Having built up the fire in this way, it will gradually burn through in a period of time, so calculated as to allow it to get hold of every lump by the time when the train has to start.

A fire of "blind" (or Welsh) coal not properly burned through will not develop the required heat when subjected to the blast ; and once start away with a defective fire of this kind of coal, troubles will begin before many miles of ground are covered, and there will be a struggle to maintain steam for the rest of the journey, even though the driver may in some cases be able to get on, without coming to a standstill to " blow the fire up " and get up steam, an episode that has frequently happened from this cause.

During the time the fireman has been making up the fire, the driver has arrived at the engine, and gives him instructions what stores to get out before starting.   For a run from Rugby to London and back, the stores required for a compound engine would be about

1 lb. tallow,

3 quarts rape oil,

3 pints cylinder oil ;

but if an axle is running badly, an extra quantity would be used.

Having obtained these, he cleans up the " front " of the

engine—that is, the back fire-box plate and all the brass work upon it, fills the sand-boxes, and does such part of the oiling as the driver entrusts to him.

Having completed all this work, the engine is, if necessary, taken to the turn-table to be turned, and to the water column to have its tank filled. The driver then " whistles up," and the engine is run off the shed to stand in some convenient place till the arrival of its train, or, if starting from a terminal station, to back on to the train, and start "right away " when time is up.

CHAPTER XX.

DUTIES OF DRIVERS AND FIREMEN WHEN WORKING A TRAIN.

AFTER an engine is backed on to a train, there are certain duties to be performed by the driver and fireman before starting.

When engines are changed at an intermediate station, and there are only a few minutes to do these duties, the oiling of the little ends, slide-bars, and glands should be done just before the train arrives. When starting from a terminal station, the driver should take care to be attached to the train in time to do this part of the oiling the last thing before starting away.

With a train fitted with the automatic vacuum brake, the following work has to be done between the time of backing on and starting away :—

The fireman's duties are—

1. To hook the engine-shackle on to the carriage draw-bar hook, and screw it up tightly.
2. To couple up the vacuum pipes.
3. To attach the communication cord.
4. To take the tail lamp from the rear of the tender, and place it on the front buffer plank.

The driver's duties are—

1. To deliver up his "ticket" to the guard, who will during the journey record upon it all particulars of the running of the train.

2. To ascertain from the guard the number of vehicles upon the train, and the brake power under his control.

3. To raise the vacuum by opening the ejector, and keeping it open until the vacuum gauge shows the required amount to be maintained while running.

4. To re-create the vacuum after it has been destroyed by opening the emergency valve in the rear van to test the continuity of the vacuum pipes.

5. To pull back the communication cord, and close the whistle after the cord has been pulled, from the rear of the train, to test its continuity.

If the driver does not raise sufficient vacuum in the train-pipe, a white flag is held out of the rear van, and he must again open the ejector and continue to "blow up" until the flag is waved—an indication that the proper figure is registered by the rear van vacuum gauge.

When time is up and the station business completed, the guard gives a "right away" signal by exhibiting a green flag (by day) or green lamp (by night). This signal is only an indication to the engine-driver that so far as the station business is concerned he has permission to start the train. Before he does so he must, however, be careful to look at the starting-signal, and see that it is "off," and the line ahead clear for him to proceed.

When he has satisfied himself on these points, he must carefully open the regulator. If it is suddenly thrown wide open there is a severe strain on the pistons and valve gear, and the result frequently is that the wheels spin round on the rails without moving the engine.

The ease or otherwise with which a driver starts his train

depends greatly upon the state of the rails. The adhesion per ton of load on the driving-wheels varies from 200 lbs., when the rails are slippery, to 600 lbs., when they are dry. In starting the driver has to take into consideration the state of the rails, the load of the train, and the gradient upon which the engine and train are standing.

As already explained, every engine carries a supply of dry sand, stored in boxes fitted with outlet valves worked from the foot-plate. When the rails are slippery the sand is allowed to stream on to them, and thus promote adhesion. It is the fireman's duty to manipulate the sanding gear, and he must exercise care in the discharge of this duty, which is a very important one; for, in frosty weather, for instance, when the rails are covered with rime, it is almost as useless to attempt to start a train with a single engine without opening the sand-valves as without opening the regulator.

If an engine is slipping badly, and the sand-valves are opened while steam is on, the wheels pass directly from a slippery rail upon which they are spinning round on to a well-sanded rail, and they thus receive a sudden check which causes a great strain on the machinery—in fact axles have been known to break from this cause.

Another matter to be watched carefully in starting is the tendency that a boiler full of water has to prime when the regulator is opened. This is especially the case if the inside surfaces of the boiler-plates are at all greasy or dirty. Unless care is exercised in opening the regulator, water is apt to pass with the steam from the boiler into the cylinders, and be thrown out from the blast-pipe.

When once the train is well on the move, and the engine begins to *feel* the load, the regulator may be more fully opened and the engine allowed to run for a short distance with the reversing lever or wheel right over in full gear.

few beats with the engine in full throw help to clear the tubes of any small cinder or ashes that may be left in them, and the strong blast gives a good start to the fire. After running a short distance with the lever in this position, the driver should "pull the engine back" a little at a time as the speed increases.

As has been already stated, the terms "pull back" or "notch-up" mean to place the reversing-wheel, lever, or whatever kind of apparatus is used for this purpose, in the position for working the steam expansively. When the engine is in "full throw" the lever is right over, and the steam is admitted to the cylinder during the greater part of the stroke of the piston. As the engine is "pulled back" the period of "cut-off" is shortened, until eventually "mid-gear" is reached.

The way in which the reversing-gear is manipulated must depend upon the gradient and the load of the train; but it may be laid down as a general rule that the notching-up should be done gradually as the speed increases, *without shutting the regulator.*

It is a very bad plan to work up to a certain speed in full gear, and then to shut the regulator and pull the engine up almost into middle gear. Unfortunately this is a system adopted by a good many careless drivers, especially those who work local trains which only run a short distance between the stops. It saves trouble but involves a waste of fuel and great strain upon the working parts of the engine.

The driver should carefully study the working of his engine when starting away with a train, especially if he has a heavy load behind him and is going to make a long run without a stop. It is while the engine is working slowly and heavily in full gear that he can most readily detect when there is anything not quite as it should be, such as pistons blowing, big ends knocking, and other similar defects.

The driver must stand on his engine in such a position that he can see best straight ahead. His side of the foot-plate is that always upon which the reversing-gear is placed ; but this varies from right to left on the different lines. The reversing-screw on the London and North-Western Railway engines is always on the left side. The driver's position is therefore on the left of the foot-plate, and in this position he is, with a few exceptions, on the same side as the platform and the starting-signal, which is a great advantage. The regulator is in a convenient position for his right hand, the reversing-wheel for his left, and the window in the cab is just in front of him. He can therefore manipulate the regulator and reversing-gear without taking his attention off the signals.

Having followed so far the starting away of an engine with a passenger train, let it be supposed that the engine is working an express from Rugby to London and back. The train has travelled some 200 yards, and a speed of from fifteen to twenty miles an hour attained. The engine has been partly notched-up, but is still emitting sonorous puffs, the steam as yet only being cut off at about half stroke, because the engine must continue to work hard until a higher speed is attained. As long as it is running in full gear, or only partially notched-up, a great quantity of steam is being used for working the engine ; also the fire has not yet developed the fierce heat which the blast will shortly produce, and consequently the pressure drops back a little, because the steam used exceeds that which the fire at this stage is capable of producing. Having started away with a full boiler, the driver can however afford to lose a little steam at first, because he need not put on the injector until the water-level is considerably reduced.

By the time the train has travelled about half-a-mile or so, if everything is right, the blast has so acted upon the fire that the whole mass has burst into flame ; and in a short time the fire develops sufficient heat to generate steam faster than the engine is using it, and the needle of the steam-pressure-gauge, which has perhaps gone back 5 or 10 lbs., gradually begins to rise, until it again reaches "blowing-off point." By this time the water-line will show about half-way up the gauge-glass, whereas before starting it was out of sight in the top stand.

As soon as the engine shows signs of blowing-off, then is the time for the fireman to commence firing. The fact that the pressure-gauge needle has crept round to this point indicates to him that his fire is in good order, and has properly burned through before starting. He may therefore put on his first instalment of fuel without fear of throwing it upon other coal not yet burned through. To heap coal upon a fire in this latter condition is a most fatal thing to do. If the engine does not begin to make steam at once, it will not mend matters to commence putting coal on. In such case the fireman should *wait* until he sees the pressure-gauge needle moving in the right direction, and in the meantime keep the feed off as long as is consistent with safety.

The great secret of good firing is to fire *a little at a time and often*. This is especially the case with "blind" coal. To throw on a dozen to twenty shovelfuls at once has much the same effect as starting away with a made-up fire not properly burned through. The fireman should almost instinctively know the exact condition of his fire throughout the trip, and by this knowledge he will regulate the amount of coal he puts on each time he fires.

The *maximum* number of shovelfuls put on at one time should be about eight, applied as follows—

No. 1. In the left back corner of the fire-box.
,, 2. In the right back corner of the fire-box.
,, 3. In the left front corner of the fire-box.
,, 4. In the right front corner of the fire-box.
,, 5. In the front of the box under the centre of the brick arch.
,, 6. In the middle of the right side.
,, 7. In the middle of the left side.
,, 8. Underneath the fire-hole door.

This is about the usual routine each time the engine is fired, but sometimes the fire gets a little too thick in one place, and the firing must then be regulated accordingly. For instance, if it gets too thick in front under the brick arch, the three shovels directed to that part of the box may be omitted on the next occasion of firing.

While running, the fire must be kept of the same structure and thickness as when made up in the shed before starting, viz., right up to the door at the back, and thin in the front. It is, however, most essential that the bars in the front of the box be *always* well covered, so as to avoid drawing air, and care must be taken to shoot each shovelful into its place in the front. An unskilful fireman, instead of properly directing it into the front corners, will sometimes shoot the coal against the brick arch ; the coal then falls into the centre of the fire-box, and gets clogged up against the brick arch, stopping up the passage down the front of the fire-box, and impeding the circulation of air through the fire. In such case, the front of the fire next the tube-plate burns away, and the bars become uncovered, and draw cold air direct on to the tube-plate.

The fireman, by putting on the first lot of coal, has in doing so caused the steam pressure to drop a few pounds, partly through the admission of cold air into the fire-box, and partly through the heat of the fire being checked by the fresh coal thrown upon it.

In a few seconds, as the fire gets hold of the fresh coal,

the needle again reaches blowing-off point, and it is now time to put the feed on. The injector is therefore set to work by the fireman, and commences to supply the boiler with water. When the injector is once put on, if the train be a heavy one, it should not be necessary to again shut it off until the next stop. The water-regulating wheel must be screwed down and adjusted until the supply to the boiler is just equal to the water evaporated by the working of the engine.

A skilful fireman will manage this, and if everything goes right he will not have to shut the injector all the way from Rugby to Willesden, and during the whole run the water in the boiler will not vary half-an-inch, nor the steam pressure more than a pound or two per square inch. The steam should be always just at blowing-off point, without the pressure being sufficiently high to cause the safety-valve to lift, and allow a quantity of steam to pass from the boiler to the atmosphere without any work being got out of it.

Upon the skill and care of the fireman to a great extent depends the amount of coal consumed by the engine. If a driver finds his mate is not possessed of the necessary skill, it should be his duty to train and instruct him until he is satisfied with the manner in which the work is performed.

The train has now got well under weigh, and has travelled some five or six miles, during which distance the driver has gradually "notched" the engine up. The speed has considerably increased, but the line is on a gently rising gradient for the seven miles from Rugby to Welton, and a great speed is not attained between these points, and the engine must not be pulled back too far.

Having passed Welton, the gradient is descending, the engine is notched up to its maximum, and the speed increases to fifty or sixty miles an hour.

The engine has now settled down to its work. The glass

gauge shows the water in the boiler at its full working height, the steam gauge records the maximum pressure without blowing off, the vacuum gauge twenty inches of vacuum, and the sight-feed lubricator is working and passing about four or five drops of oil per minute into the steam-chest to lubricate the valves and pistons.

London and North-Western engines are fitted with air-pumps for causing the vacuum in the train-pipe, and at this speed the driver will be able to see whether the pump is maintaining the proper vacuum.

The fireman fires up at regular intervals, his attention being called to the necessity for doing so by the fact that the safety-valve shows signs of blowing-off. When the door is opened and coal put on, the pressure is slightly reduced, and the steam does not begin to blow off again until it is time to put on more coal.

The damper must be so adjusted as to bring about the regular routine of firing every time the engine begins to blow off; if opened too wide, the engine steams too freely, and begins to blow off before it is time to fire ; if not open wide enough, the time to fire arrives before blowing-off point is reached, and the engine will gradually go back in steam.

When the engine is steaming properly it should never be necessary to touch the fire with the fire-irons, and a good fireman with a good driver and a good engine will never need to use them at all when running. Sometimes when the fire begins to go wrong, a gentle stirring up with the pricker may put things right again, and there are circum-stances when this is necessary, but they should be excep-tional, for the more the fire is knocked about by the fire-irons, the greater the consumption of coal.

There are no heavy gradients between Rugby and Bletchley, and having once got up express speed, and put the reversing-wheel and regulator in their proper position, it should not be necessary to alter them between these points.

The driver's attention should be concentrated upon keeping a strict look-out ahead, occasionally glancing at the gauges to see that everything is right, and swinging the door for the fireman when coal is put on.

Between Castlethorpe and Wolverton are the first water-troughs, and the moment the engine gets on to them the scoop must be let down by the fireman, and, as soon as the tank is full, the driver must assist in shooting back the scoop-handle. During the night great watchfulness must be observed not to miss the water-troughs, but the sound made in travelling over them is sufficient to call the driver's attention to his whereabouts.

The fireman must, when not engaged in firing or breaking coal in the tender, assist his driver to keep watch ahead, and should always make a point of being on the look-out when passing through stations or junctions, where extra care is required in sighting the signals.

After passing Bletchley the line is more or less on a rising gradient as far as Tring, the last four miles from Cheddington being a pretty stiff gradient. Here it is necessary to give the engine a little more lever, that is to say, to work in fuller gear. Having passed Tring, the ruling gradient is downwards all the way to Willesden, except between Bushey and Pinner, where there is a piece of level road and another water-trough, from which the water-tank must be again replenished as before.

During the last fifteen or twenty miles the fire is gradually worked down, little or no coal being put on after passing Watford—$17\frac{1}{2}$ miles from London. To work the fire down, a rake is used to gradually push forwards the thick part of the fire in the back of the fire-box a little bit at a time as the thin part of the fire in the front burns away. By the time the train arrives at Euston, there should be a level thin fire covering the fire-bars.

Before the stop at Willesden is made, special preparations are made by the driver. The speed from Watford is very high, greater as a rule than any other part of the up journey. After passing this station there is an excellent piece of road, slightly down-hill, and if there is a minute or two to be made up, the driver need not be afraid of spoiling his fire and knocking his engine "out of time" by "punishing" it— that is, running at a high speed with the engine nearly in full gear. He is close to a stop, and can get up steam again while standing, besides which he has only another five miles from Willesden to complete the journey. This hard running makes an extra powerful blast, and the consequence is that the fire, which is being run down, develops a very fierce heat, which is not checked by the addition of fresh coal.

If the driver were to shut off steam while working under these conditions, the steam would continue to be generated very rapidly, and finding no outlet through the cylinders, would blow off furiously at the safety-valve, causing a great nuisance while standing at the station, besides wasting fuel by the generation of steam to no purpose.

To avoid this, before the time arrives for shutting off steam, the damper is lowered, the fire-hole door opened, and the injector shut off. The two former operations reduce the heat in the fire-box, and the latter lowers the water in the boiler. By thus lowering the pressure, there is, when the regulator is shut, a margin for the accumulation of steam before it reaches blowing-off point, and its further generation can be checked by putting on the injector and filling up the boiler.

The last station to pass before reaching Willesden is Sudbury, soon after passing which the regulator should be shut, and the steam jet put slightly on to clear away the smoke and sulphur from the fire.

After closing the regulator the vacuum brake should be partially applied, in order that the driver may satisfy himself that it is in good working order, and properly checks the speed of the train. Finding this to be the case, he should again release the brake, and allow the train to run forward. This partial application of the brake will check the speed, and the regulator being shut, the train will gradually slow down as it approaches the station. The second application must be made on nearing the platform, and the brake must be so regulated as to bring the train to a stand exactly at the proper place. Of course the manipulation of the brake, and the decision as to how far from the station it ought to be applied, must depend upon the speed and weight of the train and the state of the rails; but in any case the speed should be so far reduced on the first application as to render it unnecessary to apply the brake to its fullest extent in making the final stop. The driver thus has a reserve of power to make use of if necessary when entering the station. As the train comes to a stand the ejector should be opened and the vacuum re-created, so that at the moment of stopping the brake is in the act of being released. This causes the train to stop without any unpleasant jar to the passengers; whereas, when a driver runs sharply up to a station and then turns the vacuum and steam brakes fully on, keeping them so till the train comes to a stand, he brings up with a sudden jerk. This is specially the case with a heavy main line train with long buffers between the carriages.

After leaving Willesden the train passes through a thickly-signalled piece of line to Euston. For the last mile and a quarter the line is on a steep falling gradient, and special care must be observed in approaching the station. A terminal platform cannot be over-shot with the same immunity from accident as a roadside station, and disastrous consequences must ensue unless the train is brought to a stand at the proper place, and accordingly a terminal station at the foot of a descending gradient must be approached with extra precaution. In order to ensure this being done, engine-drivers are instructed to use their hand-brakes only approaching Euston Station, so that the speed must be checked a considerable distance outside, and if by any chance the speed is a little too fast, there is always the continuous brake to use in case of emergency. Its use in this case proves that a man has not had his train under sufficient control, and the fact of its being necessary to apply it gets the driver into trouble.

For ordinary stops, where the vacuum brake is used, the guards do not apply their hand-brakes, but they should render assistance in descending the Euston incline.

After arrival at Euston, the driver obtains his ticket from the guard, and the fireman detaches the engine, which is then taken on to the turn-table and turned with the head towards Rugby. Adjoining the table are different engine-pit roads, on to one of which the engine is run.

The driver's next care is to go underneath and again examine his engine. This examination need not be of such a comprehensive character as the one he made on the shed previous to starting, but all those parts which are most likely to become disconnected should be carefully looked at, and all the bearing surfaces and axles should be felt to see that they have not been running hot. Should this be found to be the case with any of them, the trimmings should be taken out, the oil-holes cleaned out, and the part re-trimmed if necessary. By receiving proper attention in this respect, an axle or journal, which may just be beginning to go wrong, may be cured of any further tendency to do so.

When standing at Euston or elsewhere, between the time

of arrival with one train and departure with another, the driver often has a very much better chance of doing little odd jobs to his engine than before starting away with the first trip; because, with engines making long runs without stopping, there is frequently ample leisure for him to take as much time as he likes for such work. The fire, which has been run down as explained, must be again made up ready for the return trip, and the engine must be oiled.

The fireman also has an opportunity of thoroughly cleaning the brass work on the foot-plate, which he may not have had time to finish to his satisfaction before.

Of course, the time given to these various details must depend upon the marginal time allowed. If a long run has been made, it is advisable to clean the fire. To do this the fire-bars must be knocked with a rod from underneath to loosen the clinker on them, and the clinker must be taken out through the fire-hole door with a small shovel supplied for the purpose.

With a run from Rugby to London and back, it should not be necessary to thoroughly clean the fire at Euston, but the bars should in all cases be knocked so as to loosen and break any clinker that may have formed upon them. The fire must then be made up again as before, in readiness for the return journey.

A room is provided in which the men can rest and have their meals when they have done all the necessary work to their engine.

The engine must not under any circumstances be left by the driver and fireman, except when in mid-gear with the hand-brake screwed on and the cylinder taps open. If the driver finds on arrival that there are any repairs which require the attention of a fitter, he must take his engine up to the steam-shed at Camden Town and have the work done there. When train time approaches, the same preparations are made as before starting from Rugby, and the engine is backed on to the train which stands ready at the platform. Immediately after leaving Euston, the heavy gradient to Camden Town has to be faced. This gradient is in some places as steep as 1 in 70.

When the London and North-Western Railway was first opened, it was not considered feasible to work trains with locomotives on such a steep incline ; in fact, the locomotives of that period were not strong enough to do so, and no engines ran beyond Camden Station, which was the terminus as far as they were concerned. The trains were worked between Euston and Camden by winding-gear. There were powerful engines driving windlasses at Camden, and the trains were wound up from Euston by ropes, and let down in the same way. Indeed, up till quite recently one engine was not thought capable of working any trains up the Euston incline, and a "bank engine" ran up behind every train.

This engine stood in a convenient siding and ran out after the trains, catching them up, and propelling them as far as Camden. The Board of Trade Regulations now discountenance assisting trains from behind in this manner, and trains are worked up the incline entirely by the engines drawing them.

When the bank engine was discontinued, a trial was made of the most suitable engines for drawing trains from Euston to Willesden, with the idea that it would be advisable to construct special engines for this purpose, and work the main line engines up to Willesden only. The result of the experiments, however, proved that a 6 ft. compound engine was capable of drawing a train of twenty-five coaches from Euston to Willesden in ten minutes. The standard time for express passenger trains between these points is nine minutes, but as trains are limited to twenty vehicles, it was rightly considered that engines of this class were perfectly capable of starting the main line trains from Euston, and working them up the incline without loss of time. But when it is necessary to assist trains from Euston to Willesden, which is frequently the case when they are worked by less powerful engines than those to which allusion has been made, the assistant engine is attached in front of the train engine, and runs to Willesden.

An ordinary coupled engine is capable of working twelve or thirteen vehicles up the incline, and the driver knows that he must have his engine in the best possible trim to take the train up the bank. The fire must be in thoroughly good order before starting, and the sand gear working properly. Indeed, this steep incline, coming at the commencement of the journey, tries the engine as much as anything can, because of the very severe strain upon its powers, with a fresh fire that has not yet been stimulated by the action of the blast. With a train of the weight mentioned, the engine must probably travel most of the way from Euston to Camden with the reversing lever almost in full gear, and a large quantity of steam is used in consequence. Still, this heavy working causes a very strong blast, and therefore by the time the train gets half-way up the incline, the fire is so acted upon as to develop a great heat, and if the coal is properly burned through, sufficient steam is generated to carry the train up to the summit of the incline without eventual loss of pressure.

There have been a considerable number of cases of trains " sticking " on the incline through starting away with the fire not in good condition. The driver should therefore be thoroughly satisfied that everything is right in this respect before attempting to take a heavy load out of Euston without a pilot engine.

The run down from London is always a little more

troublesome than the up journey, because there is a continuous rising gradient nearly all the way to Tring, a distance of 30 miles ; on the other hand, the stop at Willesden gives the driver a chance to make a good start again in case he has run short of steam through " punishing " his engine when working up the incline.

The usual time taken in running from Euston to Tring, a distance of 30 miles, with an express train, is about 48 minutes, and, as many of the trains are timed at an average speed of 50 miles an hour from London to Rugby, some good running has to be made after passing Tring.

If the engine is going to finish its trip at Rugby, care must be taken to run the fire down as low as possible before arriving at the end of the journey.

When an engine is run with a big fire of blind coal, firing must be discontinued some 20 or 30 miles before the point at which the trip ends.   The thick part of the fire at the back of the box must be gradually pushed forward by the fire-irons until there is a thin fire of equal depth all over the bars.   If properly managed, the lower the fire gets the fiercer the heat developed, and it may be run down until not more than five or six inches deep on the bars.

If the fire gets down as low as this a few miles before the end of the trip, and steam cannot be kept up without putting on more coal, a few shovelfuls of small coals should be put on as required, being lightly scattered over the whole surface of the bars, so that when the engine arrives at its destination the grate is just covered by the fire.   When the fire gets very low and is composed only of incandescent cinders, the pressure will drop, but so long as the gauge shows 60 lbs. at the time of closing the regulator, the heat in the fire-box will go on generating steam after the regulator is shut, so that probably on arrival at the station there is sufficient pressure to make a shunt or two if necessary, and then take the engine on to the shed.

A great deal of experience and skill is required in judging exactly how to run the fire down so as to maintain sufficient steam to the last, and yet avoid waste by taking the engine on to the shed with an unnecessary amount of fire in the fire-box.

Upon the manner in which the driver manages his fire in this respect depends to a great extent the position his engine occupies upon the monthly consumption sheets.

Upon detaching from the train, the driver obtains his ticket from the guard, and takes his engine into the loco-motive yard, where he places it over a pit near the coaling stage, gives it over to the care of the turner, and gives instructions as to the amount of coal to be put on the tender for the next trip.

The turner is a man employed at large locomotive stations for turning and marshalling the engines in the shed, and taking them to and from the coaling stage.

Before leaving the engine, the driver should look round all the axle-boxes and journals, and see that none of them have run hot. He should look in the fire-box and see that none of the tubes are leaking. He must also test the pistons and steam-pipe joints by placing the engine in the position with the cranks in front of the axle, each crank being equi-distant from the cylinder. The hand-brake should be screwed hard on, and the cylinder taps opened. The regulator must then be opened, and the driver will be able to detect whether the pistons are blowing through. He must also open the smoke-box door and see that the steam-pipes are not leaking.

While the driver is making this examination, the fireman should clean his lamps and lock up the tools. Both men then proceed to the engine-shed; the driver makes out his tickets, which record particulars of the run he has made and the stores obtained.   He must also insert in the "repairs book" particulars of any repairs required to his engine, and make out reports of any special circumstances that have arisen in connection with the working of his train.   He is then at liberty to leave the shed, having delivered up the keys and "booked off" at the check-office.

Having now taken the reader over the ground set forth on the title-page of his work, the author leaves him, he hopes, with some clear notions as to the practical side of a subject of vast national importance.   We have seen how, in a wonderfully short period of time, the application of steam has been developed from a theoretical idea to an almost ideal practice, a development bringing with it a complete revolution of society and commerce.   In the age in which we live the public accepts too much as a matter of course the wonders of science, by which we are gradually eliminating the factors of time and space from our lives. Hence it has been the author's aim to bring into a popular but not inaccurate work, some account of the industry, perseverance, and intellect that have been consumed in making it a matter of course for any one of his readers to travel one mile in one minute for one penny ; and although the purpose of this book has only been to deal with one branch of railway work, it should be remembered that it is only by strict discipline, anxious care, and the observance of the most minute precautions that the employés and officials of all departments of a great railway system co-operate to ensure the safety of their passengers, under circumstances that seem all but beyond control. When one reflects on all that may depend on the safe arrival at or near the stated time of any of our countless express trains, it becomes apparent that there can be few subjects of greater interest to every thinking being than the history and working of the locomotive.

INDEX.